Strategies to Promote Inclusive Practice

How can we develop a more inclusive education system?

Strategies to Promote Inclusive Practice considers the development of policies to promote inclusive education for pupils with special educational needs from the perspective of individual pupils, schools and local education authorities. It provides a critical commentary on co-ordinated approaches to inclusion.

The book draws upon the experience and expertise of teachers, policy makers, and researchers, and identifies the factors that need to be considered in the development of an inclusive education system. The authors explore the link between the current debate on inclusion and policies that ensure access to learning for all pupils, and good classroom practice. They provide examples of successful approaches that have enabled schools to meet the needs of a wide range of pupils.

Strategies to Promote Inclusive Practice will be of interest to practitioners, policy makers and researchers who wish to develop practical approaches to the teaching of pupils with special educational needs. It is a companion text to *Promoting Inclusive Practice* edited by Christina Tilstone, Lani Florian and Richard Rose (RoutledgeFalmer, 1998), which was the joint winner of the 1999 TES/ NASEN Academic Book Award.

Richard Rose is Head of the Centre for Special Needs Education and Research at the University College Northampton. **Christina Tilstone**, formally Senior Lecturer in Special Education at the University of Birmingham, is also the co-author of *Child Development and Teaching Pupils with Special Educational Needs* (RoutledgeFalmer, 2002).

Strategies to Promote Inclusive Practice

Edited by Christina Tilstone and Richard Rose

RoutledgeFalmer
Taylor & Francis Group

LONDON AND NEW YORK

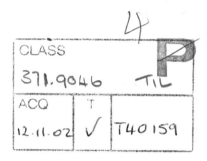
First published 2003 by RoutledgeFalmer
11 New Fetter Lane, London EC4P 4EE

Simultaneously published in the USA and Canada
by RoutledgeFalmer
29 West 35th Street, New York, NY 10001

RoutledgeFalmer is an imprint of the Taylor & Francis Group

Typeset in Garamond by M Rules
Printed and bound in Great Britain by MPG Books Ltd, Bodmin

British Library Cataloguing in Publication Data
A catalogue record for this book is available from the British
Library

Library of Congress Cataloging in Publication Data
A catalog record for this book has been requested

ISBN 0–415–25484–1 (hbk)
ISBN 0–415–25485–X (pbk)

Contents

   of practice   97
   CHRISTOPHER ROBERTSON

PART II
Policies into practice through two core subjects   117

8. Raising standards in mathematics   119
   JILL PORTER

9. Policies for promoting literacy: including pupils with severe   134
   and profound and multiple learning difficulties
   RICHARD BYERS AND LINDA FERGUSON

PART III
**Policies and strategies: a consideration of the wider
context**   151

10. Policies to support inclusion in the early years   153
    ROB ASHDOWN

11. Education for an inclusive adult life: policy for the
    16–19 phase   164
    CAROLINE BROOMHEAD

12. The role of LEAs in promoting inclusion   174
    SUE FAGG

13. 'The tide has turned': a case study of one inner city LEA
    moving towards inclusion'   187
    JIM WOLGER

14. The role of the educational psychologist in the inclusion
    process   203
    SUE SANDERSON

15. Professional development of staff: steps towards
    developing policies   215
    CHRISTINA TILSTONE

    Author index   226
    Subject index   232

Notes on contributors

Rob Ashdown is head teacher at St Luke's School, Scunthorpe, an all-age day special school for pupils with severe learning difficulties. He is headteacher designate for a new primary special school for children with moderate, severe and profound and multiple learning difficulties that will open in 2003 as part of local plans for special education reorganisation. He is line manager for the local education authority's support service for pupils with autism and three services for children at the Foundation Stage who have developmental difficulties.

After training to teach business studies, **Caroline Broomhead** taught in secondary and further education and developed a particular interest in integration and inclusion before moving into special education. She is now head teacher of High Birch School, Rochdale, a Beacon Special School for pupils with moderate, severe or complex learning difficulties. Caroline was a regional tutor on the University of Birmingham Distance Education Course from 1993. She is actively committed to promoting and supporting the professional development of those working in education, recognising its key role and importance in improving the quality of education for pupils with special educational needs. She has recently been appointed an HMI

Richard Byers is a tutor in the Faculty of Education at the University of Cambridge. He previously worked as a teacher in mainstream and special education and as an education consultant working on special needs issues. Richard has edited several books in the area of special education, many of which have focused upon providing effective curriculum access. His work has been published in many journals and he is the editor of the *British Journal of Special Education*.

Ted Cole is a senior research fellow at the University of Birmingham. Since 1995 he has been the lead researcher on a number of national and local research projects on emotional and behavioural difficulties and disaffection, funded by the Department for Education and Employment, the Department of Health,

Nuffield Foundation and the Department of Education and Skills. He has published widely on inclusion, EBD and related issues.

Trudy Duffield is deputy head teacher at St. George's School, Peterborough, and has several years experience of working in special schools. Trudy has a long commitment to supporting families who have young people with special needs and to encouraging mother tongue teaching in special schools.

Sue Fagg is head of Outreach Services with Lancashire Education Department. Her current responsibilities include the provision of education services for excluded pupils with a view to early return to mainstream or specialist provision. Sue was previously head teacher of Piper Hill School in Manchester and was joint author of *Entitlement for All in Practice*.

Linda Ferguson works at Clayton School in Peterborough where she teaches pupils with severe, profound and multiple learning difficulties. She is a communications therapist as well as being a teacher and recently completed a Masters of Education degree. A summery of her MEd thesis was published as a chapter in Hart and Dadds *Doing Practitioner Research Differently*. While continuing to teach, Linda now lectures on a part-time basis in the programme of Continuing Professional Development courses run by the University of Cambridge in the Faculty of Education.

Ann Fergusson is lecturer in special education at the Centre for Special Needs Education and Research, University College Northampton. She has worked as deputy head teacher in a special school and on projects for the National Curriculum Council and Qualifications and Curriculum Authority. Ann has published widely in the field of special education and is currently working in the area of citizenship for pupils with special educational needs.

Lani Florian is a tutor in the Faculty of Education at the University of Cambridge. She has conducted research on several aspects of inclusive education and has published extensively in this area. She was joint editor with Christina Tilstone and Richard Rose of *Promoting Inclusive Practice*. Lani has a wide range of experience in both schools and higher education in the UK and USA. She was Legislative Assistant to the US Senate Sub-committee on the Handicapped during the 99th congress where she had staff responsibility for the development of PL 99 – 457, the federal law which established the US early intervention programme for infants and toddlers with disabilities and their families.

Liz Gerschel is an independent inspector, trainer and education consultant. She has worked, and written, on equality in education for many years, has taught in the UK and Jamaica and was a senior adviser for equal opportunities and special educational needs in inner London. She works with LEAs, school staff and governors on approaches to inclusive practice which encompass 'race', gender, and social-cultural group equalities as well as disabilities and learning and behavioural difficulties.

Marie Howley is senior lecturer in special education at the Centre for Special Needs Education and Research, University College Northampton. Her particular interest is in the education of pupils with autistic spectrum disorders, an area in which she has published a number of papers and chapters. Marie's research interests include investigations into the use of Social Stories to increase social understanding, and multi agency work to support pupils with autism.

Sue Kime has had wide experience of teaching in primary schools in both the UK and overseas. Immediately prior to taking up her current post as senior lecturer at the Centre for Special Needs Education and Research, University College Northampton, she was working as an advisory teacher for Northants LEA. Sue's research interests are focused around the area of reading and dyslexia, including recent work on the efficacy of additional literacy support.

Penny Lacey is a senior lecturer in education at the University of Birmingham and co-ordinator of an interdisciplinary course for staff working with children or adults with profound and multiple learning difficulties. She has published widely on collaboration between professionals and on multidisciplinary teamwork.

Jill Porter taught pupils with moderate, severe and profound learning difficulties before entering higher education where she has been involved in both initial and in-service teacher training in special educational needs. She is currently senior lecturer at the School of Education, University of Birmingham where she is Director of Studies for Research degrees,. Her own research includes curriculum development, self-assessment and challenging behaviour, but her particular interests are in the development of early counting skills in pupils with learning difficulties.

Christopher Robertson is a lecturer in inclusive and special education at the University of Birmingham. He has had extensive experience in teaching pupils with physical disabilities, severe learning difficulties, and profound and multiple learning difficulties. His research interests are in curriculum theory, philosophy of education and the development of inclusive practice, both in the UK and in low-income countries. He has co-authored books on special educational needs, and published articles and chapters on teacher education, autonomy, quality of life, teacher stress, and the social theory of disability.

Richard Rose is head of the Centre for, and professor in, Special Needs

Education and Research, University College Northampton. His previous posts have included teaching in schools in four LEAs, headship of a special school and local authority inspector. Richard has been co-author and editor of several books on special education and has published in a wide range of journals. His current research interests are in the areas of inclusive education in primary schools, and pupils with severe learning difficulties as personal target setters.

Sue Sanderson trained with primary-aged and taught children with severe learning difficulties before embarking on her career as an educational psychologist. She currently works in Cumbria as an EP and has particular interests in autism and therapeutic work. She contributes to the EP training course at Newcastle University and acts as a regional tutor for Distance Education Courses (Autism, Learning Difficulties, Challenging Behaviour) at the University of Birmingham. She has contributed to course materials on the latter course.

Christina Tilstone was, until her retirement, senior lecturer in special education at the University of Birmingham where she was responsible for the co-ordination of the Distance Education Course in Learning Difficulties. She has taught abroad and in mainstream and special schools and has published widely on teaching children with severe difficulties in learning and on their inclusion into mainstream schools. She is Chair of the Editorial Board of NASEN journals on special needs and her research interests are in curriculum design and development for pupils with learning difficulties.

Jim Wolger is head teacher of Rosemary School in Islington. Prior to entering a career in education he served as a police officer with the Metropolitan Police. Having taught in mainstream schools, Jim trained as a craft specialist before taking up posts in special schools. He has recently been involved in working closely with education officers in Islington in the development of new special needs provision.

Foreword

Lani Florian

When the previous publication, *Promoting Inclusive Practice*, went to press the new Government had just issued the landmark 1997 Green Paper 'Excellence for All Children – Meeting Special Educational Needs'. Since that time the Government has been actively promoting an agenda of inclusion and participation for pupils with special educational needs in mainstream education. This agenda of inclusion has not been limited to school placement but extends to the curriculum. Inclusion is an important aspect of the call for high standards for all learners.

The level of government activism in developing national SEN policy has been extraordinary. Following the Green Paper, the Government issued a 'Programme for Action' in 1998. In 1999 the Disability Rights Task Force issued a report calling for the right to a place in a mainstream school for all children, including those with statements of special educational needs. From January 2002 new anti-discrimination legislation, the Special Educational Needs and Disability Act 2001 (SENDA), marks another step on delivering this promise.

There can be no doubt we have entered a new era in providing for children with special educational needs. In 1970 the [Handicapped Children] Education Act transferred responsibility for so-called ineducable children from local health to education authorities and in so doing firmly established the principle of education for all. The 1981 Education Act established the principle that mainstream education was the preferred option for delivering that provision. Today SENDA makes it *unlawful* to discriminate against pupils on the basis of their disability and thereby makes real the right to education in mainstream schools for all pupils who desire it. This marks what Phillippa Russell, Director of the Council for Disabled Children and a member of the Disability Rights Commission, has called a major sea change in provision. No longer is the question shall we include? but rather how might we include all who choose a mainstream school place?

New statutory guidance from the Government (DfES, 2001) sets out the principles of an inclusive education service as follows:

- Inclusion is a process by which schools, local education authorities and others develop their cultures, policies and practices to include pupils.
- With the right training, strategies and support nearly all children with special educational needs can be successfully included in mainstream education.
- An inclusive education service offers excellence and choice and incorporates the views of parents and children.
- The interests of children must be safeguarded.
- Schools, local education authorities and others should actively seek to remove barriers to learning and participation.
- All children should have access to an appropriate education that affords them the opportunity to achieve their personal potential.
- Mainstream education will not always be right for every child all of the time. Equally, just because mainstream education may not be right at a particular stage it does not prevent the child from being included successfully at a later stage.

From September 2002 schools' and local education authorities' ability to refuse a mainstream place for a child with special educational needs will be severely restricted. They will be able to refuse a mainstream school place to a child if it would be incompatible with the efficient education of others; however, 'reasonable steps' must be taken to prevent that incompatibility. The statutory guidance gives many specific case examples of reasonable steps but rightly notes that they will depend on the circumstance of an individual case (p.15). By focusing on policies to promote inclusive practice, the editors of this book have much to offer in helping to elaborate the concept of reasonable steps.

The idea of inclusion as a process by which schools develop their cultures, policies and practices to enable them to include all pupils is a main theme of the book. Like *Promoting Inclusive Practice* it values the expertise developed by colleagues in mainstream and special schools, and emphasises the importance of the relationship between them. Richard Rose and Christina Tilstone set the tone of the book in the introductory chapter which highlights the important role effective policies can play in supporting the process of inclusion. Each contributor then considers an aspect of policy in depth.

A strength of the book is its breadth of coverage. Policy is considered from a range of perspectives from multiagency collaboration and a consideration of the role of therapies in supporting inclusion to pupil involvement and achievement. But the editors do not stop there. Also included is an examination of the role of the educational psychologist as a resource to promote the learning of all pupils as well as an exploration of the complex issues of gender and including pupils with special educational needs for whom English is a second language.

Three chapters examine the role of the LEA in promoting inclusion. Sue Fagg and Jim Wolger focus on how LEA developments on inclusion and school commitment to the process can lead to more effective practices in including learners with special educational needs. Jim Wolger presents a case study of how a privatised LEA manages the tension between the often conflicting government policies of high standards and inclusion. Sue Fagg considers the present and future challenges facing LEAs.

Jill Porter shows how policy is related to pupil learning and achievement through an in-depth exploration of mathematics teaching. She has much to say about the importance of understanding children's learning difficulties and helpfully includes a series of 'policy audit questions' teachers can ask to help them examine the extent to which their school's current policy promotes or inhibits true inclusion of pupils in the subject areas. Marie Howley and Sue Kime use case studies to identify key issues in the management of individual learning within the context of whole class teaching, an important but under-researched topic. Notably, they show how strategies identified for individuals can be of benefit for others.

Not content to focus on the school years, the book includes chapters on early years and post-16 provision, two important areas often overlooked by an emphasis on the school years. Rob Ashdown provides a very accessible summary of current initiatives in early years provision. This chapter is important, not only for early years providers, but for primary school teachers in mainstream and special schools because it contextualises the sort of provision young children with disabilities and special educational needs will be transitioning from when they start the school years. Likewise, secondary school teachers should have an understanding of post-16 provision because it enables them to support the post-school transitions all young people make as they prepare for adult life.

The emphasis of this book is on inclusion and learning difficulties although many of the chapters are relevant to supporting the inclusion of a wide range of special educational needs, for example, Ted Cole's chapter on positive behaviour management. It is refreshing to see generic case examples developed using prototypes that are usually overlooked. Ann Fergusson and Trudy Duffield write about multiculturalism and pupils with profound and complex learning difficulties. They show how staff in a special school can apply research conducted in mainstream settings and develop policy that is sensitive to the multicultural heritage of their pupils. Inclusion is a process but it is a complex, multi-faceted and layered process as this book makes clear.

The book is timely. The inclusion agenda is developing rapidly and government policies need to be translated into practice. The contributors to this book are a mix of academics and practitioners. Together they possess a wide knowledge of inclusion. They have produced a book that will be of use to educationalists everywhere wanting to make the ideals represented in government policy a meaningful reality in schools.

REFERENCES

DfES (2001) *Inclusive Schooling: Children with Special Educational Needs* (DfES/0774/2001), Nottingham: DfES Publications.

Acknowledgements

We are grateful to the many colleagues who have supported us throughout our work on this book. Our regular contacts with teachers, pupils and parents have always provided us with the incentive to embark upon projects such as this, and, in particular, the regional tutors on the University of Birmingham's Distance Education Course for Teachers of Children with Learning Difficulties inspired the book's genesis. Our thanks are also due to colleagues at the Centre for Special Needs Education and Research at University College Northampton and to Natasha Mycawka for administrative assistance. Staff at Taylor & Francis have been patient and supportive and we are especially grateful to Alison Foyle and to Jude Exley for their invaluable help and advice.

We also are, as ever, indebted to Philip Tilstone and Sara Rose without whose unstinting commitment, affection and understanding we could never have completed this work.

Introduction

Christina Tilstone and Richard Rose

Since we edited *Promoting Inclusive Practice* with Lani Florian in 1998, developments in the complex processes of inclusion, through cautious explorations of practice, have led to a greater understanding of the complexities and challenges of inclusion by staff in schools. All schools are having to examine what 'inclusive practices' means within the context of the visions and values of the school community. They also need to develop strategies to prepare their pupils for what the Government terms 'an inclusive society'. The recently published Department for Education and Skills Guidance Document: Inclusive Schooling (2001), reiterates a commitment to place inclusive education at the heart of a policy addressing the UK Government's agenda of social inclusion. The principles upon which this document is framed are further strengthened through the new Special Educational Needs Code of Practice (DfES, 2001) and the Special Educational Needs and Disability Act (DfES, 2001).

In *Promoting Inclusive Practice* (which won the National Association of Special Educational Needs and the *Times Educational Supplement* award for the best book in the field of special educational needs in 1999) we took as a starting point a definition of inclusion which embraces the aims of education for all pupils and young people with special educational needs and disabilities, in whatever context their education is taking place. A definition, which implies their increasing participation and active involvement in all aspects of their education, was first used by Inclusion International (an organisation which includes people with disabilities) in 1996 which stated:

> Inclusion refers to the opportunity for persons with a disability to participate fully in all the educational, employment, consumer, recreational, community and domestic activities that typify everyday society.

In the book, we challenged schools to develop their own definitions of inclusion which reflected the beliefs, working practices and values of both staff and pupils. Many have done so, and have produced statements which go beyond the definition above and which, in many cases, focus on the diverse learning characteristics of pupils with special educational needs. The definitions imply that mainstream and special schools need to work together in order to respond most effectively to diversity. This sequel to the first book, therefore, does not advocate the closure of all special schools but stresses the importance of the development of a process that recognises the individuality of children and provides positive learning experiences that will help them, however complex their needs, to become valued and active members of an 'inclusive society'.

Inevitably schools are at different points in the move towards inclusive practices and many have developed their own policies to aid the process. In our work with a range of staff it is apparent that such policies are often general in nature and do not reflect upon, or steer, the day-to-day practices of teaching and learning. *Policies to Promote Inclusive Practices* represents a genuine attempt to help the development of inclusive strategies through policies which *do* reflect upon practice.

The chapters are diverse: some give guidance on the drawing up of policies; others on policy development; and others provide case studies of the implementation of policies for individuals or groups of pupils. The structures of the chapters are also varied and readers will find that the articulation of the processes of inclusion are, on the one hand, embedded within the ideas presented or, on the other, explicitly expressed throughout a chapter or detailed in specific sections of it. All are written by practitioners and professionals who are grappling with the challenges of bridging the gap between the rhetoric and the reality of inclusion on a daily basis.

Many of the authors who contributed to *Promoting Inclusive Practice* are part of the tutorial team of the Distance Education Course in Learning Difficulties at the University of Birmingham. They are joined by colleagues who provide, or contribute to, similar campus-based courses at University College, Northampton. All are committed to the view of inclusion put forward by Inclusion International and to the idea that people who experience difficulties in learning, however complex, or who have a disability of any sort, are entitled to the same opportunities in life as anyone else. The collective experiences of this unique team are extensive and each member offers distinctive perspectives on the promotion of inclusive policies and strategies that are relevant to the education of a wide range of pupils with special educational needs (including those whose needs are multiple and complex).

THE ORGANISATION OF THE BOOK

Part I
Responding to diversity: the development of policies and strategies

In her foreword, Lani Florian has highlighted many of the strengths of individual chapters, and it is not our intention to repeat the points made. In a book which contains a large number of contributions, however, it is the editor's job not only to provide a coherent 'map' of the ideas presented, but also to enable the reader to explore the terrain in any logical way. In other words, we feel it important to explain why certain chapters have been brought together, but at the same time we recognise that the routes that individual readers will wish to take through the book will depend upon their interests and their professional responses.

Our first concern was to place *practice* at the forefront, and all the chapters have a direct bearing on the teaching and learning of pupils with special educational needs. The first section, however, is aimed at helping professionals to draw up policies and to select strategies designed to meet many of the diverse learning characteristics of these pupils. Richard Rose sets the scene by calling for greater clarity in the relationship between theoretical perspectives of inclusion and the practicalities of implementing inclusive policies at school and classroom level. He suggests that the need to develop a more inclusive education system has been generally accepted and that the priority must now be to provide teachers with the means of establishing teaching approaches to make inclusion a reality.

The next chapter by Marie Howley and Sue Kime is concerned with specialist teaching approaches for individual pupils, and other chapters, by Ann Fergusson and Trudy Duffield and by Liz Gerschel, consider issues often neglected in the SEN field: those of ethnicity, gender and race. The last three chapters in this section, by Ted Cole, Penny Lacey and Christopher Robertson, explore the establishment of policies in areas which challenge the resources and management systems of schools: managing behaviour, collaborative work with a range of professionals and meeting therapy needs.

Part II
Policies into practice through two core subjects

The second part of the book takes two subject areas around which there are particular tensions and dilemmas for teachers of pupils with learning difficulties: Maths (Jill Porter) and English, with a specific focus on literacy (Richard Byers and Linda Fergusson). Both of these subjects are central to the Government's agenda of raising standards, and the Department for Education and Employment, now the Department of Education and Skills, has presented further challenges to staff by outlining specific approaches to their teaching through the introduction of the National Strategies for Numeracy and Literacy. The placement of this section indicates the importance that we attach to the subjects, but also signals that we do not wish them to overshadow other important aspects of the curriculum.

Part III
Policies and strategies: a consideration of the wider context

Internal policies are highlighted in the first and penultimate chapters of this section (both written by heads of schools). Rob Ashdown considers strategies for inclusive early years settings, and Caroline Broomhead focuses upon policies for the 16 to 19 phase of education. Policies cannot, however, be drawn up in isolation from the wider context and Sue Fagg discusses the tensions that LEAs face in an attempt to put into practice strategies for inclusion. Her views are taken further by Jim Wolger, in his detailed case study of a school and an LEA which are working together to achieve an inclusive environment; and then by Sue Sanderson who discusses the role that educational psychologists can play in supporting schools and LEAs in the process of inclusion. Christina Tilstone brings this section, and the book, to a close by highlighting the professional development needs of staff as they attempt to establish inclusive strategies that enable their pupils with special educational needs to become an active part of an inclusive society.

Finally, this book is intended to add to the ongoing debates on inclusive practices. Throughout, it is recognised that inclusive education is a complex *process* and, as such, there is no 'end'. It is hoped that the ideas and examples given, increase our abilities to respond with greater creativity, sensitivity and confidence to exciting challenges.

REFERENCES

Department for Education and Skills (2001) *Inclusive Schooling.* London: DfES.
Department for Education and Skills (2001) *Special Educational Needs: Code of Practice.* London: DfES.
Department for Education and Skills (2001) *The Special Educational Needs and Disability Act.* London: The Stationery Office.

Part I

Responding to diversity

The development of policies and strategies

Chapter 1

Ideology, reality and pragmatics

Towards an informed policy for inclusion

Richard Rose

In this chapter Richard Rose considers the current debate on the development of inclusive education. In particular he reviews the ways in which the theoretical and philosophical arguments for inclusion have been developed and how the balance is now shifting towards a greater consideration of how ideals may be translated into policy and ultimately inform school practice.

> There are many features of the Utopian Republic which I should like – though I hardly expect – to see adopted in Europe.
>
> Thomas More (1516) *Utopia* (Book Two)

During the latter half of the twentieth century great strides were made in the UK to provide a more equitable and comprehensive system of education which addressed the needs of all pupils. Milestones, such as the Education (Handicapped Children) Act (1970), which brought a small but significant number of pupils into the education system for the first time, and the Warnock Report (1978), which attempted to provide a blueprint for future educational provision for pupils with special educational needs, whilst never fully realising their ambitious agenda, brought special needs issues to the forefront of education consideration. The desire to provide a fairer society that would enable each individual to play a full part has been a driving force behind many of the developments in special education. At the heart of the recent debate has been the means by which schools may become more inclusive and effective in enabling all pupils to receive a balanced education which recognises individuality whilst overcoming segregation. The attainment of a more inclusive society, whilst not solely the responsibility of teachers in schools, is most likely to be achieved only when we have developed a more equitable education system. Florian (1998) has emphasised the necessity to adopt a definition of inclusion which enables us to clarify our meaning and to ensure that we work together towards a common goal. In a previous book (Tilstone, Florian and

Rose, 1998) we adopted the definition of inclusion put forward by Inclusion International:

> Inclusion refers to the opportunities for persons with a disability to participate fully in all of the educational, employment, consumer, recreational, community and domestic activities that typify everyday society.

This definition provides a guiding principle which has been adopted throughout the book and places inclusion as an educational concept within the wider context of society. In so doing it emphasises not only the importance of addressing inclusion within schools, but also of working in collaboration with colleagues outside education who have an equally important role to play in making fundamental changes to the ways in which we move towards a fairer society for all.

Mittler, who has invested more time in exploring the means by which we can improve the lives of pupils who have been disadvantaged by the education system than most, in a recent book recognised that the complexities surrounding the provision of an appropriate curriculum for all pupils has inevitably resulted in progress towards inclusion being slower than many would wish. He suggests that generations of researchers and scholars have explored the issue of inclusion and the means by which it can best be achieved, but have been unable to provide either practitioners or policy makers with a clear message.

> This is not the fault of the researchers but is a reflection of the immense complexity of the subject and the impossibility of unravelling its many strands in ways that make sense to those who have to make decisions.
>
> Mittler, 2000, p.vii

He suggests that there is no doubting the commitment of the UK Government towards providing a more equitable education system. Recent government policies such as those put forward in the Green Paper, *Excellence for All Children* (1997) and *Meeting Special Educational Needs: A Programme of Action* (1998) have defined an intention to support all schools in developing policies and procedures for more inclusive practices. However, even within these documents there are contradictions and confusions which suggest that an adequate definition of inclusion, such as that proposed above, has not been embraced by everyone.

The complexities of inclusion as recognised by Mittler and Florian may well be a significant factor in the difficulties which both central government and local education authorities (LEAs) have experienced in providing adequate policies. The lack of clear guidance has led to considerable confusion on the part of teachers and has been a significant causal factor in the reluctance of some schools to move towards greater inclusion. Whilst many LEAs have issued statements regarding their intentions to move towards greater inclusion, progress has been slow. Debates continue on the means by which inclusion may be achieved. Whilst there are now a number of examples of successful inclusive practice, which have enabled pupils formerly educated in special schools to take their place in the mainstream (Sebba and Sachdev, 1997; Powers, 2001), concerns remain about the ability of all schools to adapt to meet the requirements of a population of widening needs (Kidd and Hornby, 1993; Hornby, 1999). Similar concerns are expressed about specific groups of pupils such as those described as having emotional and behavioural difficulties, who are widely regarded by teachers as presenting a challenge for which most feel inadequately prepared (O'Brien, 2001).

Whilst it is easy to express frustration with the seemingly slow progress in developing inclusive policies which actually impact upon practice, it is important that the debate surrounding how this may best be achieved is continued. There have been times in recent years when some writers and researchers, who have contributed to the inclusion debate, have appeared to become entrenched in their own viewpoint and have been unable to engage in a dialogue which may ultimately move policy forward and promote effective practice. Those who have written about inclusion from a human rights perspective (Young, 1990; Barton, 1999) have undoubtedly assisted policy makers in moving forwards towards establishing clearer statements of intent and have enabled teachers to undertake a more critical view of existing classroom practices although they have at times alienated some teachers who have given many years to the education of pupils with special needs. The problem has come about through a failure to recognise the commitment which many teachers have made to work with pupils who have over time been rejected by others. Similarly, those teachers who have taken an insular standpoint, and who fail to acknowledge the need to find a way of ensuring that all pupils have greater opportunities to fully engage in the education system alongside their peers, are in danger of hindering progress towards a more equitable education system providing improved access to learning for all. It is unlikely that genuine progress towards inclusion will be made until a more constructive form of dialogue is achieved. Those who advocate a move towards fully inclusive schooling need to acknowledge the genuine apprehensions which many teachers currently express regarding their ability to provide effectively for all children within their classrooms. Teachers and researchers must work together to examine the conditions which need to be created to support inclusion and to enable schools to put these into place for the benefit of all pupils. Policies, which consider inadequately the pragmatics of classroom implementation, are quite possibly destined to fail. Recent inclusion literature (Ainscow, 1999; Loxley and Thomas, 2001) has discussed a number of ideological issues and has resulted in a variety of ways in which progress can be made towards a more inclusive schooling system. In order to move forward it is essential that policies are implemented which are founded upon a sound, shared philosophy and that this is supported by a pragmatic analysis of what works in an inclusive classroom.

Farrell (2001), in a provocative review of special education over a twenty year period, suggests that arguments for inclusion based entirely upon a human rights perspective, which fail to question the ability of schools to provide a 'good education' fully meeting the needs of the individual pupil, are 'logically and conceptually naïve'. He further suggests that the placement of some pupils, described as having special educational needs, into mainstream schools, and here he particularly considers those with extremes of disruptive behaviour, may pose a threat to the rights of their mainstream peers to receive a good education.

Many of the arguments put forward by Farrell equate to those of the teachers and head teachers, whose opinions are discussed by Croll and Moses (1998, 2000). These researchers suggest that those who have written about inclusion from a largely humanistic perspective are advocating a 'Utopian' model of thinking about a complex issue. Referring to the work of Giddens (1994) they suggest that such thinking may be too idealistic within the current educational climate. An education system which has been driven by market forces, i.e. open competition based upon league tables and examination performance, may be seen to be at odds with a policy which intends to welcome pupils considered by many teachers as 'challenging' into schools. They propose that it may be necessary to adopt an approach which aspires to creating an inclusive system but recognises current concerns and begins to address them as a precursor to achieving the ultimate goal of full inclusion. This approach, described by Giddens as 'Utopian realism', would certainly find greater favour with the teachers in Croll and Moses' sample. However, Thomas and Tarr (1999) maintain that the argument which suggests there is a fundamental tension between the principles of inclusion and the evidence to suggest that in practice this will present difficulties for schools, as put forward by Croll and Moses and others (Hornby, 1999; Wilson, 1999, 2000), may be a false one. They suggest that the adoption of policies which are based upon principles generally accepted to be right often bring challenges and difficulties. The fact that these principles are perceived as right should be a driving force to establish their position, whilst accepting a need to examine the means by which undesired effects resulting from their implementation can be eliminated. Thomas and Tarr put forward a strong moral case for inclusion based upon the principle that if an action is deemed right it should be taken. Indeed, Thomas and his colleagues (Thomas and Loxley, 2001) would suggest that the evidence in support of retaining segregated provision is limited and that any theoretical basis for the retention of special education is at best tenuous. It is, they would argue, difficult to defend the *status quo* in a system which claims to value inclusion and has placed it so high on the political agenda. Deficit models continue to dominate the ways in which we categorise pupils and result in those labelled as 'special' being regarded as a source of difficulty. If we are to move towards a more inclusive form of schooling it will be necessary to reform schools as a whole, including the curriculum, the means of assessment and the ways in which we value the performance of pupils.

Thomas and Loxley (2001) further develop this argument by suggesting that evidence to support a notion that segregated schooling, or indeed special education in general, has been effective is at best tenuous. The development of special education, they assert, has been founded upon the methods and findings of psychology which has often placed an emphasis upon deficit models and has led to the perception of pupils as problematic and not suited to the mainstream of education. This in turn has resulted in an inordinate consideration of individual learning difficulties as opposed to the development of an educational system capable of embracing the needs of all pupils. In calling for a deconstruction of special education, Thomas and Loxley (2001) recognise that many of the structures which have been put into place through the legislation of the past twenty years, far from supporting the development of inclusion, have erected further barriers in the path of progress.

The endeavours of teachers to ensure that pupils with special educational needs receive their educational entitlement should never be underestimated. Far too often their efforts have had to be made against a background of ill-conceived and poorly introduced procedures which have resulted from ideologically driven legislation. A drive to raise standards and develop a more effective education system and the introduction of procedures to monitor and review the efficacy of teaching is to be welcomed. However, the processes which have been introduced to effect changes in the curriculum, to raise achievement in literacy and numeracy and for the inspection of schools have far too often failed to consider the needs of the whole school population, and have in some instances militated against the furthering of inclusion. Whilst much of the legislation of recent years has paid lip service to inclusion, several writers (Rouse and Agbenu, 1998; Hill, 2001) have claimed that an examination of the original intentions of policy after its implementation is not the same as reviewing its impact upon the education of the whole school population. Rouse and Agbenu cite the introduction of National Curriculum assessment procedures as one example of a policy which, far from being inclusive, resulted in teachers having to make considerable modifications to the materials provided. As they comment, this was seen as permissible through a system of 'special arrangements' but there is 'considerable uncertainty about how valid and reliable the results of these adapted tests are' (p.83).

Similar concerns are expressed by Wearmouth and Soler (2001) over the National Literacy Strategy. This they suggest is based upon an 'ill-defined' definition of literacy and a lack of advice on how 'good practice' may be achieved or identified. Furthermore, they identify contradictions between the rationale of the National Literacy Strategy and the General Statement of Inclusion to be found within the National Curriculum. Wearmouth and Soler (2001) state that the emphasis within the National Literacy Strategy upon teaching to a level designed specifically for a chronological age group, 'as if pupils with difficulties should be expected to catch up with their peers', is in total opposition to the emphasis upon well-differentiated planning and diverse teaching approaches advocated within the General Statement of Inclusion. Here, it is suggested, is an example of poorly conceptualised and contradictory policy, which is likely to alienate teachers and cause difficulties for pupils with special educational needs.

Critics of national education policy appear to be divided between two camps: those who believe that there is a fundamental lack of understanding on the part of policy makers, and others who perceive some level of political conspiracy.

> Within the culture of 'self-help' that has arisen within the Right and with the introduction of the National Curriculum in the United Kingdom, a language has built up around entitlements, rights to education for all, rights to a curriculum suitably differentiated to meet individual needs, and the introduction of standards and quality control in the educational process. Yet within a declared egalitarian approach, activities are taking place that in fact restrict rather than enhance children's opportunities. Since the introduction of the National Curriculum and the free-market approach to education we have seen a marginalization of children who in terms of an older vocabulary would have been described as having 'special educational needs'.
>
> John, 1995, pp.115–16

Booth, Ainscow and Dyson (1997, 1998), whilst not subscribing to conspiracy theories, do believe that increased competition within the education system has come about at the very time when the inclusion agenda was beginning to have an impact. An increased reliance upon league tables, which celebrate academic success whilst indicating those schools which have not achieved such heights, has done little for the self-esteem of teachers or for those pupils deemed to be falling short of 'end of key stage expectation'. Other writers (Byers, 1999; Rose and Howley, 2001) have urged teachers to give careful consideration to their interpretation of national strategies and to avoid either tokenistic approaches to participation or the development of contrived means of engaging with inappropriate procedures.

It is certainly true to say that the successful inclusion of pupils with special educational needs within the framework of initiatives such as the National Curriculum and national strategies for literacy and numeracy has been achieved by teachers who have shown a determination that all pupils should play a full part in all aspects of education. Initiatives in curriculum development (Byers and Rose, 1996; Byers, 1999; Aird, 2001; Carpenter, Ashdown and Bovair, 2001) have often been developed in individual schools and adopted by teachers across the country. Similarly, approaches which provide curriculum access for those pupils who often give the greatest of challenges to teachers have been devised and have enabled pupils to play a full part alongside their peers (Pietrowski and Reason, 2000; Howley, 2001; Wilson, 2001). Recently, experienced teachers of pupils with special educational needs have been brought together to produce new general guidelines for planning, teaching and assessing the curriculum for pupils with learning difficulties. These documents, which are built upon good practice developed in special and mainstream schools across the country, provide support for teachers in their efforts to plan for an increasingly diverse school population. In addition to providing advice on access to all subjects of the National Curriculum, the guidelines also provide performance descriptors to support teachers in assessment and the measurement of attainment. The documents constitute a major step forward, not only because of their recognition of exactly the type of support which teachers need, but also because they were approved and supported in their development by both the Department for Education and Employment (DfEE) and the Qualifications and Curriculum Authority (QCA). However, at a time when government policy is promoting greater inclusive practice, it is at best unfortunate that such guidance needs to be provided as an addendum to the earlier published National Curriculum modifications, thus signalling that special educational needs is still considered to be a separate entity.

If inclusion is to become a reality for those pupils who currently receive their education in segregated provision, policies will need to be developed that bridge the gulf between philosophies which embrace the ideal of a more equitable society, and procedures which currently inhibit the successful management of pupils with special educational needs in the classroom. The differences of opinion which have developed between those advocates of full inclusion, who have largely written from a moral or humanistic perspective, and others who continue to perceive major obstacles in the path of developing inclusive schools must be continued as an essential part of the process of change. It may well be that in the present climate our ability to achieve an ultimate goal of full inclusion remains at a distance, but as Berlin (1996) reminds us:

> The passionate advocacy of unattainable ideals may, even if it is Utopian, break open barriers of blind tradition and transform the values of human beings.
>
> Berlin, 1996, p.53

Berlin also suggests that whilst we need vision before we can effect change in the societies in which we live, simply to go on stating the vision without examining and putting in place the conditions necessary to achieve this is likely to lead to frustration and adverse reaction. The need to move towards more inclusive education is well established, it is now beholden upon policy makers to assist in the development of systems which will make this a reality. This will be achieved only through a renewal of efforts to undertake critical examination of how pupils with special educational needs learn and by ensuring that classrooms change in ways which enable this to happen.

Lewis and Norwich (2001) have opened an important debate which recognises the possibility that there may be distinct pedagogies affording advantages to pupils with special educational needs. Whilst suggesting that, as yet, there is little evidence to support a specific pedagogical distinction for pupils labelled as having SEN, they accept that these might exist and that further research is necessary to examine this notion. Within their paper, they explore the ideas put forward by Skrtic (1999) who suggests that all pupils have unique learning needs which should be addressed on the basis of careful assessment and through detailed planning. They also consider that it may be that whilst there is no distinctive difference in terms of the teaching approaches and principles to be deployed in teaching pupils with special educational needs, it may be necessary to establish a continuum of teaching related to issues of intensity or the explicit nature of the teaching approaches used.

The research conducted by Lewis and Norwich (2001) is highly significant and may well signal a way forward in assisting teachers to develop more inclusive classroom management skills. They suggest that at present pupils who have a variety of learning difficulties are not well catered for in many classrooms. It is possible that, whilst there is little evidence to support the need for different teaching approaches for most pupils with special educational needs, there is a requirement to enable pupils to gain new skills, knowledge and understanding and to retain this through an additional emphasis upon those approaches already in place. Lewis and Norwich specifically list seven approaches as examples of ways in which pupils with special educational needs may be more effectively supported:

1. More practice to achieve mastery
2. More examples to learn concepts
3. More experience of transfer
4. More explicit teaching of learning strategies and reinforcement of them
5. More frequent and more specific assessment of learning
6. More time to solve problems
7. More careful checking for preparedness for the next stage of learning
   Lewis and Norwich, 2001, p.5

The work being undertaken by Lewis and Norwich is significant in the debate about furthering inclusion. It is important in addressing the conditions necessary to create inclusive classrooms to examine the fundamental issues of teaching and learning which should be at the heart of all change within education processes. In recent years prominence in the inclusion debate has been given to a relationship between school effectiveness researchers and policy makers. However, whilst the emphasis upon technocratic and managerial approaches to school development has established consistent systems in terms of the curriculum, its planning, development and evaluation, this has often failed to recognise diversity and has in some instances marginalised populations within schools (Gray, Goldstein and

Jesson, 1996; Carpenter and Ashdown, 2001). Imposed systems, such as the National Curriculum and strategies for literacy and numeracy, have been important in emphasising the requirements of breadth and balance and have renewed discussion about teaching methodologies. However, the determination of policy makers to bring new systems into place quickly has far too often resulted in teachers having to redesign these in order to ensure that pupils with special educational needs can gain their rightful access to a broad, balanced and relevant curriculum.

A concentration upon pedagogy and a return to examining the fundamentals of teaching and learning may yet prove to be a critical factor in achieving a more inclusive education system. Such an approach will require further efforts on the part of researchers who must continue to question and investigate those procedures which may enable all pupils to become more effective learners. It will also be dependent upon a new generation of policy makers who are prepared to take full cognisance of research findings, to consider carefully the implications of their policies for *all* pupils and *all* teachers. It also demands that policy makers should listen to those teachers who spend each day in the classroom attempting to do their best for all the pupils in their care.

Although many will regard the progress which has been made towards inclusion as having been much slower than is desirable, few would deny that the endeavours of teachers and researchers to gain a greater understanding of those pupils labelled as having special educational needs have been considerable. The immediate challenge for all who work within the education system must be to develop policies which promote those practices which are most likely to enable all pupils to become effective learners. These will demand a continuum of provision which accepts that not all pupils learn in the same way and which, while celebrating diversity, recognises those innovative practices that enable pupils to participate fully in a curriculum which addresses their needs. In too many instances efforts to develop a policy for inclusive schooling has been divorced from an analysis of those practices which lay claim to being effective in enabling pupils with special needs to learn. Such claims must never be taken for granted, but it is essential that those teachers who are committed to finding effective teaching practices for all pupils have their voice heard. At various points in this chapter the notion of a Utopian education system in which the needs of all pupils would be addressed within mainstream schools has been considered. Readers familiar with More's work, which still has a resonance almost five hundred years after it was written, will know of his conclusion that there can never be a single Utopia so long as man has freedom of opinion and personal choice. Bertrand Russell, writing in his seminal work *A History of Western Philosophy* concludes that:

> Diversity is essential to happiness and in Utopia there is hardly any. This is a defect of all planned social systems, actual as well as imaginary.
>
> Russell, 1957, p.543

REFERENCES

Aird, R. (2001) *The Education and Care of Children with Severe, Profound and Multiple Learning Difficulties*. London: David Fulton.

Barton, L. (1999) 'Market ideologies, education and the challenge for inclusion', in H. Daniels and P. Garner (eds.) *World Yearbook of Inclusive Education*. London: Kogan Page.

Berlin, I. (1996) 'Political judgement', in I. Berlin *The Sense of Reality*. London: Chatto and Windus.

Booth, T., Ainscow, M. and Dyson, A. (1997) 'Understanding inclusion and exclusion in the English competitive education system', *International Journal of Inclusive Education*, 1 (4) 337–55.

Booth, T., Ainscow, M. and Dyson, A. (1998) 'England: Inclusion and exclusion in a competitive system', in T. Booth and M. Ainscow (eds.) *From Them to Us*. London: Routledge.

Byers, R. (1999) 'The National Literacy Strategy and pupils with special educational needs', *British Journal of Special Education*, 26 (1) 8–11.

Byers, R. (1999) 'Experience and achievement: initiatives in curriculum development for pupils with severe and profound and multiple learning difficulties', *British Journal of Special Education*, 26 (4) 184–8.

Byers, R. and Rose, R. (1996) *Planning the Curriculum for Pupils with Special Educational Needs*. London: David Fulton.

Carpenter, B., Ashdown, R. and Bovair, K. (2001) (2nd edition) *Enabling Access*. London: David Fulton.

Carpenter, B. and Ashdown, R. (2001) 'Enabling access', in B. Carpenter, R. Ashdown and K. Bovair (Eds.) *Enabling Access* (2nd edition). London: David Fulton.

Croll, P. and Moses, D. (1998) 'Pragmatism, ideology and educational change: the case of special educational needs', *British Journal of Educational Studies*, 46 (1) 11–25.

Croll, P. and Moses, D. (2000) 'Ideologies and Utopias: education professionals' views of inclusion', *European Journal of Special Needs Education*, 15 (1) 1–12.

DES (1970) *The Education (Handicapped Children) Act*. London: HMSO.

DES (1978) *Report of the Committee of Enquiry into the Education of Handicapped Children and Young People* (The Warnock Report). London: HMSO.

DfEE (1997) *Excellence for All Children*. London: The Stationery Office.

DfEE (1998) *Meeting Special Educational Needs: A Programme of Action*. London: Department for Education and Employment.

Farrell, P. (2001) 'Special education in the last twenty years: have things really got better?', *British Journal of Special Education* 28 (1) 3–9.

Florian, L. (1998) 'Inclusive practice: what, why and how?', in C. Tilstone, L. Florian and R. Rose (eds.) *Promoting Inclusive Practice*. London: Routledge.

Giddens, A. (1994) *Beyond Left and Right: The Future of Radical Politics*. Cambridge: Polity Press.

Gray, J., Goldstein, H. and Jesson, D. (1996) 'Changes and improvements in school effectiveness trends over five years', *Research Papers in Education*, 11 (1) 35–51.

Hill, D. (2001) 'The National Curriculum, the hidden curriculum and equality', in D. Hill and M. Cole (eds.) *Schooling and Equality: Fact, Concept and Policy*. London: Kogan Page.

Hornby, G. (1999) 'Inclusion or delusion: can one size fit all?', *Support for Learning*, 14 (4) 152–7.

Howley, M. (2001) 'An investigation into the impact of social stories on the behaviour and social understanding of four pupils with autistic spectrum disorder', in

R. Rose and I. Grosvenor (eds.) *Doing Research in Special Education*. London: David Fulton.

John, M. (1995) 'Children's rights in a free market culture', in S. Stephens (ed.) *Children and the Politics of Culture*. New Jersey: Princeton University Press.

Kidd, R. and Hornby, G. (1993) 'Transfer from special to mainstream', *British Journal of Special Education*, 20 (1) 17–19.

Lewis, A. and Norwich, B. (2001) 'A critical review of systematic evidence concerning distinctive pedagogies for pupils with difficulties in learning', *Journal of Research in Special Education*, 1 (1) online @ www.nasen.uk.com/ejournal/.

Loxley, A. and Thomas, G. (2001) 'Neo-conservatives, neo-liberals, the new left and inclusion: stirring the pot', *Cambridge Journal of Education*. 31 (3) 291–301.

Mittler, P. (2000) *Working Towards Inclusive Education*. London: David Fulton.

More, T. (1516) *Utopia* (Translated by Paul Turner). London: Penguin.

O'Brien, T. (2001) 'Learning from the hard cases', in T. O'Brien (ed.) *Enabling Inclusion: Blue Skies . . . Dark Clouds?* Norwich: The Stationery Office.

Pietrowski, J. and Reason, R. (2000) 'The National Literacy Strategy and dyslexia: a comparison of teaching methods and materials', *Support for Learning*, 15 (2) 51–7.

Powers, S. (2001) 'Investigating good practice in supporting deaf pupils in mainstream schools', *Educational Review*, 53 (2) 181–9.

QCA/DfEE (2001) *General Guidelines: Planning, Teaching and Assessing the Curriculum for Pupils with Learning Difficulties*. London: Qualifications and Curriculum Authority.

Rose, R. and Howley, M. (2001) 'Entitlement or denial: the curriculum and its influence upon curriculum processes', in T. O'Brien (ed.) *Enabling Inclusion: Blue Skies . . . Dark Clouds*. Norwich: The Stationery Office.

Rouse, M. and Agbenu, R. (1998) 'Assessment and special educational needs: teachers' dilemmas', *British Journal of Special Education*, 25 (2) 81–7.

Russell, B. (1957) (6th edition) *History of Western Philosophy*. London: George Allen and Unwin.

Sebba, J. and Sachdev, D. (1997) *What Works in Inclusive Education?* London: Barnardos.

Skrtic, T.M. (1999) 'Learning disabilities as organisational pathologies', in R.J. Sternberg and L. Spear-Swirling (eds.) *Perspectives on Learning Disabilities*. Yale: Perseus Books Group, Westview Press.

Thomas, G. and Loxley, A. (2001) *Deconstructing Special Education and Constructing Inclusion*. Buckingham: Open University Press.

Thomas, G. and Tarr, J. (1999) 'Ideology and inclusion: a reply to Croll and Moses', *British Journal of Educational Studies*, 14 (1) 17–27.

Wearmouth, J. and Soler, J. (2001) 'How inclusive is the literacy hour?', *British Journal of Special Education*, 28 (3) 113–19.

Wilson, J. (1999) 'Some conceptual difficulties about inclusion', *Support for Learning*, 14 (3) 110–13.

Wilson, J. (2000) 'Doing justice to inclusion', *European Journal of Special Needs Education*, 15 (3) 297–304.

Wilson, J. (2001) 'Conductive education and the National Curriculum: an integrated approach', *Support for Learning*, 16 (4) 168–73.

Young, I.M. (1990) *Justice and the Politics of Difference*. Princeton, N.J.: Princeton University Press.

Chapter 2

Policies and practice for the management of individual learning needs

Marie Howley and Sue Kime

The setting of appropriate learning objectives for pupils with special educational needs, and addressing them in a whole class teaching context, is a major challenge to teachers. This chapter considers the importance of providing a structured approach to the management of individual learning needs and ways in which school staff might adopt policies to enable all pupils not only to be included, but to have their entitlement to a balanced curriculum addressed.

As there is an ever-increasing focus on inclusion (DfEE, 1997), teachers are faced with the challenge of managing the learning needs of individual pupils, whilst at the same time meeting the needs of all the pupils in a class. The National Curriculum (DfEE/QCA, 1999a; 1999b) reinforces earlier statements made (National Curriculum Council, 1990) about the need for schools to develop an 'entitlement curriculum' and identifies three principles for inclusion:

- setting suitable learning challenges;
- responding to pupils' diverse learning needs;
- overcoming potential barriers to learning and assessment for individuals and groups of pupils.

The National Programmes of Study have assisted teachers in identifying what pupils should be taught, making clear statements such as 'teachers should teach the knowledge, skills and understanding in ways that suit their pupils' abilities', and places an emphasis on meeting and managing individual needs within inclusive classroom contexts.

Norwich (1996) proposes three types of educational need: common needs, arising from characteristics shared by all; exceptional needs, arising from characteristics shared by some; individual needs, arising from characteristics different from all others. All pupils have educational needs that may be described in one or more of these three ways and teachers are required to take into account this range of needs to provide effective teaching and learning opportunities. It should be recognised, however, that the individual and exceptional needs of some pupils require specialised teaching approaches and strategies in order to enable them to make progress and to be included successfully in mainstream classrooms. Nevertheless, if such specialised approaches are to be incorporated successfully within the general classroom context, it is critical that the management of individual learning needs is considered in relation to whole class and whole-school contexts.

CASE STUDIES

The individual needs of two pupils, from different primary schools, will be considered in this chapter, together with the approaches adopted by the schools to meet their needs. The strategies used by the class teachers to manage individual learning within inclusive classroom contexts are discussed, leading to the formulation of some key principles which can inform whole-school policies.

Ben

Ben arrived at primary school towards the end of Year 2. He had an engaging smile, was quietly spoken (although not very articulate), was taller than the majority of his peers and heavily built. His personal file showed that he was at Stage 2 of the Code of Practice (DfEE, 1994) and all his records indicated that he had behavioural difficulties, which had led to the production of a behaviour monitoring/modification programme.

Individual needs

Although Ben was fairly quiet for the first few weeks in his new school, his class teacher noted some minor disturbances in the playground and a reluctance to tackle new work in the classroom. As the second half of the summer term drew to a close, the incidents in the playground grew more frequent and he also began to display frustration in the classroom, often refusing to start or to continue with set work.

Behaviour

At the start of Year 3, his behaviour became more of a concern and he displayed real anger and a loss of self-control, both in the playground and in the classroom. He was aggressive in the former and often hit other children, although when he was calm he was a very reasonable, likeable boy. He enjoyed PE and was good at large apparatus work. The school's special needs co-ordinator (SENCo) decided to implement a learning assessment as well as continuing with an analysis of his behaviour and the maintenance of a programme to address his needs.

Reading and writing

The initial learning assessment indicated that Ben might be dyslexic, and his mother revealed that she had always found reading and writing difficult and she believed that her father had also had literacy difficulties (Hornsby, 1997; Ott, 1997). Ben's reading and spelling scores were low in comparison to other pupils of his age and, although his understanding of basic mathematics was good, he made errors in the written assessment. His receptive vocabulary and his visual memory were good but both his auditory memory and his working memory were weak, and consequently his self-esteem was very low. Both of the latter were making it difficult for him to process information presented orally; he had difficulties with understanding when literacy and numeracy activities were explained verbally; and he could not follow a sequence of instructions. The conclusions drawn from the learning assessment and behaviour analysis were that Ben's frustration and anger were related to his inability to cope with work in the classroom. The ABC analysis of his behaviour had shown that the days on which there was a high proportion of creative and physical activity were those on which he was more likely to display appropriate behaviour in both the classroom and the playground.

Priority areas of learning

Ben's difficulties in school were related to areas of strengths and weaknesses which were specific to him and which would require an individual learning programme that would lead to a rise in his self-esteem, the development of basic skills and the modification of his behaviour. In order to support Ben it was considered that four main areas needed to be addressed: Ben's self-esteem, liaison with his parents, the classroom environment and unstructured times in the school day.

Strategies and individual approaches to Ben's learning

Ben's overall programme needed to be both structured and cumulative and to have small, achievable targets for literacy and numeracy. It was decided that intervention had to include one-to-one support from an adult, in order to help him to cope with his frustrations and to build his self-esteem, and small group teaching for basic skills. Ben's classroom programme required differentiated materials that also looked age-appropriate and had a visual format wherever possible. His assignments needed to be differentiated by outcome and, consequently, the approach needed to be practical or visual. Instructions would be given one at a time or supplemented by visual prompts. All teaching would aim to be multi-sensory; recognising that his visual input channel was good and that his auditory channel was weak and needed support.

Ben's Individual Education Programme (IEP) was planned for periods of half a term, with a focus on basic skills and behaviour management. The basic skills teaching was carried out in a small group by the SENCo, who was not class-based and was responsible for all the support teaching at that time. Ben worked with two other boys, one from a parallel class and one from the year above, both of whom needed similar basic skills work. Specialist advice was sought for a programme to raise Ben's self-esteem, and this was provided by the authority's support service through five one-to-one sessions from a specialist teacher who also gave advice about supporting Ben during unstructured times. Lunchtimes had been particularly difficult for him and although a programme was already in place, whereby some children were allowed to take 'time out', it was not as effective as the staff had hoped and often resulted in children being taken to class teachers during the lunch break. The programme was adapted for Ben and one lunchtime supervisor was identified as someone he could relate to and to whom he should go if he felt he was having a problem. He was also given permission to leave the playground to find the SENCo at times when he felt his anger was getting the better of him, which gave him the opportunity to calm down and, sometimes, to talk through his problems. In order to be effective, this strategy required that a second member of staff acted as backup if the SENCo was away, through illness or on a course, and consequently Ben still had someone to go to who would respond to him in a similar manner. This strategy was not immediately successful because initially Ben did not leave the playground until after he had been involved in an incident, but he gradually learned to remove himself before there was any physical contact; a significant step forward.

Sarah

Sarah's parents reported concerns about her development from an early age, mainly due to her lack of social interest and her delayed communication skills. She was closely monitored by the health visitor and her GP and was eventually assessed at a child development centre where, at the age of four, she was diagnosed as having autism. During her Reception year at the local primary school, she was formally assessed and was issued with a statement of special educational needs. She continued to attend her local primary school where she was fully included in a Year 1 class with full-time support from a learning support assistant.

Individual needs

Sarah's individual needs were identified in relation to the triad of impairment associated with autistic spectrum disorder (ASD), namely difficulties with communication, social interaction and imagination leading to inflexible behaviour and thinking (Wing and Gould, 1979). In addition, she experienced sensory disturbances and had difficulties with organisational skills and sequencing. She had a number of strengths and interests, and liked to use the computer.

Communication

By the time Sarah entered Year 1, she had made significant progress in the area of communication, and her expressive language appeared, on the surface, to be quite good. Her expressive ability masked her problems with comprehension; she also had difficulties following multi-step directions; interpreted language very literally; and did not understand non-verbal communications such as gesture and facial expressions. She frequently interrupted the teacher and her peers by calling out answers or making comments. When she became confused, she would echo phrases that she had just heard; when asked a question, for example, she would echo the question back if she had not understood it.

Social interaction

Sarah was fairly isolated during Reception and in Year 1; she had little interest in her peers unless they engaged with her in her favourite activities, such as talking about dinosaurs, and she was frequently on the periphery of social activities, especially at play times. Sometimes, she would become aggressive, hitting out at her peers if they sat too close to her or if they took their turn on the computer.

Imagination, flexibility of behaviour and thinking

Sarah had limited play skills, most of which took the form of learned routines; she would, for example, play with the dolls' house and put the dolls to bed in the same way and using the same language on every occasion. As she was not able to co-operate with her peers, sharing and turn-taking were difficult. On occasions she would play in parallel; at other times she was not able to tolerate other children near her and would hit out or spit at them. She became upset when school routines were altered and had a number of interests that would dominate her thinking; in particular dinosaurs and the computer.

Organisational skills and sequencing abilities

As a result of poor organisational skills, Sarah often failed to complete tasks, not because she did not understand them, but because she spent too long organising herself. If faced with choices, she would take a long time to make any decision. She frequently did not start tasks, as she spent too long finding materials and resources and became upset if tasks were left unfinished. She was unable to plan the necessary steps to complete activities and would frequently become muddled half way through a task. She also became confused and distressed if the routine of the day was altered. In class, she relied mainly on her learning support assistant and was felt to be dependent upon her to an extent that discouraged her from interacting with others.

Strengths and interests

Sarah was very knowledgeable about dinosaurs and had a good rote memory for facts. Her ITC skills were more advanced than her peers and she had a particular interest in using encyclopaedias to find out factual information. She loved to use both the class CD-ROM encyclopaedia and reference books from the library. She was able to read factual information and, although she had difficulties understanding fiction, she could follow written information to complete tasks independently.

As a result of her specific needs, it was agreed at Sarah's annual review that a range of strategies should be implemented in order to manage her learning effectively. It was acknowledged that while she had a number of individual needs, these could be met in her current class if specific approaches and strategies were implemented. Such interventions, however, would only be successful for her in the context of the needs of the class and thus she needed to be considered in relation to all pupils.

Priority areas of learning

Sarah had a number of targets identified in her individual educational plan (IEP) which focused on the areas identified above, examples of which, during Year 1, were to:

- become more independent in terms of organisation, sequencing and completion of activities;
- raise her hand to answer questions and offer information (rather than interrupt);
- play in parallel with two peers, sharing materials;
- develop alternative strategies for coping with the proximity of peers.

Sarah's annual review was attended by her parents, her class teacher, the head teacher, the special educational needs co-ordinator (SENCo), the school's educational psychologist and a teacher from a specialist autism provision in another school. A number of specialist strategies and approaches were suggested to implement the programme in a way that would be possible in a mainstream classroom. Sarah was provided with numerous opportunities within the curriculum to work towards her targets. Like all other pupils in the class, she was involved in monitoring and recording her own progress in each target area; her recording system was linked to her interest in dinosaurs as an additional motivator. In order to achieve a consistent approach for her, the teacher and LSA liaised closely with her parents who were introducing similar approaches at home with the additional support of a specialist, 'autism family support worker'. The approaches were monitored by the SENCo, the educational psychologist, the specialist teacher, the class teacher, her parents and Sarah herself.

Strategies and individual approaches to Sarah's learning

The educational psychologist identified a range of specialised teaching approaches that would address Sarah's individual learning needs. It was agreed that elements of visual structure, consistent with the TEACCH approach (Treatment and Education of Autistic and related Communication handicapped Children, Schopler, Mesibov and Hearsey, 1995) should be introduced for Sarah, but in a way that would be practical in the context of the needs of the class. It was intended that visual structures would be used to address Sarah's learning needs in relation to her communication, social interaction, inflexibility and difficulties with organisation, sequencing and adult dependence. In addition, the use of Social Stories (Gray, 1998; Gray and Garand, 1993) would be introduced to develop Sarah's understanding of social proximity and to introduce strategies for coping. Again it was felt that this would be more successful if used in a whole class context in addition to meeting Sarah's individual needs.

Visual structure

When considering the preferred learning styles of individuals with autistic spectrum disorders, it is widely agreed that the use of visual support and visual teaching are effective intervention strategies for many individuals with ASD (Schopler, Mesibov and Hearsey, 1995). Their use is further supported by personal accounts of individuals with autism such as Temple Grandin (1995), who says:

> I think in pictures. Words are like a second language to me. I translate both spoken and written words into full-color movies, complete with sound, which runs like a VCR tape in my head. When somebody speaks to me, his words are instantly translated into pictures.
>
> Grandin, 1995, p.19

Sarah, too, showed well-developed visual skills and was already able to follow simple written directions. Thus the use of visual structure as described in the structured teaching approach of TEACCH (Schopler, Mesibov and Hearsey, 1995) was felt to be appropriate to meet some of her individual needs, some of which were:

- a written schedule was introduced enabling Sarah to understand and keep track of the day's activities; a visual 'work system' with labelled tasks and numbered instructions was also introduced to help Sarah with organisational and sequencing difficulties;
- visual cue cards with a 'hands up' symbol reminded Sarah to raise her hand rather than interrupt;
- picture/written cues were used to give instructions for sharing materials and shared areas of working space (showing where to sit and work in relation to others);
- Social Stories were written to address Sarah's lack of understanding of why people sit near to each other and how to react.

The challenge was how to implement such specialised approaches within the context of a mainstream classroom in such a way to be effective both for Sarah, her peers and the class teacher.

Using specialised teaching approaches in inclusive classroom contexts: meeting individual needs

When viewed in isolation, specialist support programmes for individual pupils would stretch the resources of even the most well-organised school. In many cases they would highlight the pupil's difficulties for his/her peers and possibly make him/her the target for unkind, peer-group remarks They might also lead to negative feelings on the part of the staff teaching him/her because of the requirement for additional preparation and recording work in an already full planning schedule. It is unlikely that such programmes would be implemented in full with the necessary adult support, given that several other pupils in the class may have learning difficulties requiring equally individual programmes. How could Ben and Sarah be included and have their needs met without diverting resources from other pupils? For both pupils to be successful in their learning, it was essential that their individual learning needs were addressed within the context of the needs of the whole class and the individual needs of all pupils. The case studies illustrated here indicate a number of key issues if teachers are to be empowered to manage individual learning needs within an inclusive framework.

The SENCos in both Ben's and Sarah's schools felt that individual support issues had a number of implications within the whole class context. Support issues identified related to the management of IEPs, the organisation and implementation of specialist strategies, the raising of pupil awareness, training for teaching and non-teaching staff, and communication with parents. Inevitably, such issues lead to a consideration of the management of individual and whole-school learning needs, and the overall school policy.

The management of IEPs

Tod, Castle and Blamires (1998) suggest that 'the IEP is central to the development of inclusive practices' (p.9) and identify a number of characteristics of effective IEPs. The ones that are particularly relevant to this discussion (p.26) are that:

- targets should be linked to the whole curriculum;
- IEPs should allow for the efficient use of resources;
- IEPs should be manageable.

The case studies described illustrate how the ways in which IEPs are implemented are fundamental to teachers being able to manage individual learning in inclusive class contexts.

Linking IEPs to the curriculum

IEPs for Ben and Sarah were planned for each half term, and the priorities for both of them were wide-ranging and combined SMART (Specific, Measurable, Achievable, Relevant and Time-related) and non-SMART targets. While Ben's programme focused on reading, writing and self-esteem, Sarah's generally focused on areas of personal and social development in order to address her specific difficulties in communication, social interaction and inflexibility. As they both needed help to generalise their skills and understanding, it was felt that some of their individual targets could be incorporated into a range of curriculum activities. In this way, Ben and Sarah could continue to work within the curriculum, alongside their peers, while at the same time having opportunities to address their individual learning needs. Thus the curriculum can be viewed as a vehicle for enabling pupils to make progress in specific areas of need (Rose, 1998). Sarah's target ('to develop independent working'), and the issues of raising her hand to answer questions, sharing materials and working in proximity with peers, could be addressed in a number of curriculum subjects. Byers (1998) suggests that for some pupils there needs to be a focus on personal and social development, at the same time ensuring that balance and breadth are maintained across the whole curriculum. The areas of personal and social education were by necessity prioritised for Sarah, with the National Curriculum providing a means of developing social and personal understanding (Rose, 1998).

Incorporating specialised strategies into general classroom practice

Clearly the issue of efficient use of resources and the need for IEPs to be manageable are critical for any school. Ben's and Sarah's individual needs had considerable implications in the classroom and neither the SENCos and their class teachers wanted the pupils to be singled out, nor did they want the support to increase the class teachers' workload at the expense of any child. It was agreed that many of the support strategies that Ben and Sarah needed would also benefit other children and would also allow for more efficient use of resources and prove to be helpful in managing individual needs in an inclusive classroom context.

Ben

The numeracy and literacy areas were rearranged, and alphabet and number strips were attached to the tables as a visual reminder that any of the children could use. High frequency and subject specific words were on strips on the wall and the strips were also available in pockets to use for near point copying. Practical materials for mathematics were readily available and would be used by the class teacher as part of the acceptable, regular multi-sensory teaching input. Visual instructions for using equipment such as the computer and tape recorder were provided as picture books and, when instructions were given verbally or written on the board, sheets of pictorial/written instructions were provided on the tables for anyone to use. Where possible, children were given a choice of recording methods for work across the curriculum and a quiet work area was set up to allow any child to work away from the main group.

Sarah

A number of strategies identified for Sarah were incorporated into general classroom use and were of particular benefit for other pupils. The introduction of a class timetable, presented visually, had positive effects for several pupils and meant that everyone in the class was better informed about each day's activities. The teacher combined a written timetable with symbolic representations for subject areas in order that all pupils could access relevant information. In addition, two independent 'office' centres (work systems) were established in the classroom to develop pupils' independence in their learning and, while Sarah was allocated time slots to utilise the 'office', other pupils could also be allotted time or could use the office space on a rota basis. This proved beneficial for those pupils who found it difficult to concentrate or who had poor organisational skills. The visual cues used to help Sarah to complete tasks independently were also useful for other pupils. The 'office' systems were managed by the LSA, and work that Sarah and other pupils completed independently was monitored by the LSA and the teacher. The systems were used effectively during literacy, in particular, but also at other times during the day.

As with Ben, the use of visual materials was helpful for Sarah in a number of ways and cues reminded her of class rules such as raising your hand to answer questions, as well as defining areas for working, sharing materials and improving understanding. The teacher found that other pupils benefited from these cues and was delighted, for example, at the number of pupils who also began raising their hands to contribute to class discussion, rather than calling out. This positive impact has been reported by other teachers (DfEE, 2000) and is seen to be a useful strategy that can benefit several pupils, enabling individual strategies to be implemented for the benefit of many where appropriate.

The use of Social Stories was helpful in developing Sarah's social understanding of a number of situations: in particular, in her understanding of proximity and appropriate behaviour when working alongside others. A class story was also written to remind all pupils of the rules, as the teacher felt that Sarah was not the only pupil who had difficulties in this area. Again, the impact was perceived as positive for several pupils and the approach continued to be developed for Sarah's own requirements, for other individuals and to address whole class issues such as bullying, within the personal, social and health (PSHE) curriculum.

Raising pupil awareness

The issues of raising pupils' awareness of differences (and that everyone would not necessarily be treated the same, because some children needed more support than others at times) were similar both for Ben and Sarah and for all pupils in school. In class this issue was tackled through the individual class Circle Time (Bliss and Robinson, 1995; Curry and Broomfield, 1994; Moseley, 1996), which was already in place throughout both schools. In addition, Sarah's teacher introduced the Social Story approach to develop social understanding of issues relating to Sarah and also to the whole class as part of both the PSHE curriculum and half-termly planning.

All the pupils in Sarah's class were aware of their individual targets, which were regularly monitored and reviewed by them and their parents. The use of individual target setting was incorporated across the class and across the school, and pupils' individual achievements in target areas were celebrated at individual, class and whole-school level.

Parental involvement

Tod, Castle and Blamires (1998) suggest that IEPs should foster collaborative support systems that include parent partnerships (p.8) and both studies illustrate this principle. Ben's parents were invited to discuss his individual education plan and, although they did not attend that meeting, his mother did attend the evaluation of his IEP at the end of the first half term. As it was difficult for either of Ben's parents to attend regular meetings, a home-school liaison book was introduced, which was used by the class teacher to highlight the positive aspects of Ben's work and behaviour. A deliberate strategy was also put into place of making a point of talking to Ben's mother when she collected his younger sister in order to ensure that she was aware of Ben's achievements and progress. In Ben's case, the class teacher and LSA were proactive in keeping Ben's parents informed in ways that were acceptable to them and to ensure that they were aware of positive developments in Ben's progress.

Sarah's parents were described as 'very needy' and her mother, in particular, was very keen to be informed of her achievements and difficulties. As Sarah related little of what happened at school to her parents, they were anxious to find out if there had been any problems each day and also to reinforce specific concepts with Sarah at home in order to help her to generalise what she had learned at school. They attended all meetings and followed advice from a number of professionals on ways of helping Sarah at home. A home-school book system was used for several other pupils with special educational needs in the class, and a similar liaison book was introduced to keep Sarah's parents informed of daily events and Sarah herself was encouraged to contribute to it; this was a particularly useful strategy as the information could be referred to in order to prompt Sarah to recall each day's activities. Sarah's mother would also provide information about events at home in order that Sarah's teacher and her LSA could ask her, for example, about her weekend. Finally, as Sarah's mother needed ongoing reassurance, it was agreed that she could chat with Sarah's LSA at the end of each day.

WHOLE-SCHOOL ISSUES

School ethos, attitudes and policies

The individual needs identified for Ben and Sarah were not the only specific ones identified among pupils within their schools and, if Norwich's (1996) notion of 'individual needs' is accepted, it becomes clear that a whole-school approach is necessary. If specialised teaching strategies are to be implemented, Ben and Sarah require support at a whole-school level. A supportive school ethos was described by Sarah's teacher as 'vital to the success of her inclusion' and also for her and the LSA to feel equally supported. A school's approach to valuing individuals and celebrating differences will inevitably impact upon their attitude to meeting individual learning needs. Both case studies illustrate the importance of developing whole-school approaches to the management of individual learning for all pupils.

A single-class issue, which was deliberately turned into a whole-school one, was the need for appropriate differentiated materials for Ben and for other older children, and this was discussed at a staff meeting. The decision was made to produce materials, linked to National Curriculum topics, which would be a resource for future use. This task could not be completed in the first year, but it was felt to be of sufficient importance for many children in the school to warrant some staff meeting/training time on a termly basis. A topic would be planned, initially for Ben's age group, and materials prepared by those with the necessary skills, regardless of which Key Stage they taught in. The long-term plan was to produce materials for the main topics throughout the school and this obviously had time and teamwork implications.

The introduction of multi-sensory teaching was also tackled as a whole-school issue. Ben's class teacher was very receptive to the idea and a number of other teachers expressed an interest. It was felt that the shift of emphasis in teaching style would help many children throughout the school and could form part of the arrangements on many children's IEPs. Likewise visual approaches for Ben and Sarah were incorporated into whole-school practice for the benefit of many pupils, and assemblies in Sarah's school, for example, were presented with additional visual resources and cues, for all to benefit.

In Sarah's case it was essential that consistent approaches were established to facilitate the generalisation of her needs and to ensure effective management strategies to improve her social behaviour. The school had developed a number of systems of co-operation and support (Todd, Castle and Blamires, 1998) that included teaching and non-teaching staff, and peers and parents. Sarah's school had a well-established practice of celebrating individual achievements through the use of individual target setting, class incentive schemes and cele-bratory assemblies. This meant that Sarah's achievements could be celebrated within an existing framework that actively encouraged and celebrated indi-viduality, thus Sarah's initial incentive scheme and recording of achievements centred on dinosaurs!

Individual and whole-school training

Although Ben's school's special needs policy included a behaviour policy, it did not necessarily meet the needs of the current situation. All the staff, both teaching and non-teaching, needed to be made aware of the outcomes of Ben's difficulties and a short training session was led by the SENCo which focused on specific learning difficulties, showing the overlap between Dyslexia, Dyspraxia and Attention Deficit Hyperactivity Disorder (ADHD). This slightly wider view was taken because it was felt that there were a number of children in the school with minor difficulties who would be helped by a whole-school policy relating to problems with following instruction. It was stressed that the consequences of not following instructions were likely to be the same regardless of whether the difficulties were caused by auditory memory problems, manipulative difficulties or inattention. Staff were encour-aged to accept that these pupils might not always be able to control their behaviour and that they were likely to have good days and bad days. This short training session was not successful with all the staff, but it initiated a process which the senior management planned to develop.

A comprehensive plan for meeting training needs was prepared by the SENCo in Sarah's school and, consequently, Sarah's teacher and LSA attended an in-service course on autistic spectrum disorder and the use of the TEACCH approach, which had previously been attended by the SENCo. Information gained was then disseminated through staff meetings and meetings with lunchtime supervisors. A specialist teacher of children with autistic spectrum disorders from a neighbouring special school, acted as an adviser on the implementation of visual structures for Sarah and provided whole-school input during a training day. The SENCo, class teacher and LSA also visited the specialist provision to observe and discuss strategies with the teacher. In addition, a specialist speech and language therapist worked with Sarah's teacher on developing Social Stories and addressed a number of staff meetings to raise awareness of the approach. The dissemination of teaching strategies led to the adoption of aspects of various approaches across the school for other pupils that were used by teaching and non-teaching staff; the lunchtime supervisors were also provided with support and the strategies were used at lunchtimes.

The role of learning support assistants

The role of learning support assistants with individual pupils has traditionally been embedded in the need for them to work on a one-to-one basis (Rose, 2000), although, as he suggests, their role may be more effective if they are allocated to teachers rather than to specific pupils. In Sarah's case, the LSA's role became focused on enabling Sarah to become more independent, thus reducing the need for intensive one-to-one support. The LSA became involved in the preparation of resources to support Sarah, through the design of the 'office' system, the labelling of resources, the writing of Social Stories, and visual cues at appropriate times during lessons. The emphasis on one-to-one support was reduced and the LSA was encouraged to work with *groups* of pupils where appropriate, thus many other pupils benefited from extra help.

Regular communication and collaborative practices

As with many pupils with identified special educational needs, a considerable number of professionals were involved with the education of Ben and Sarah. For specialised strategies to be effective, it is crucial that regular communication is established between all those involved (see Chapter 6 by Penny Lacey). Sarah, in particular, required a consistency of approach and, consequently, communication between professionals and parents was critical. In addition, the school benefited from links with the local special school, which had specialist expertise in the education of pupils with autistic spectrum disorder. Rose and Howley (2001) identify a number of steps to be taken if special and mainstream schools are to work in partnership; Sarah's school had taken one small, but important, step towards this aim. Similarly, Howley, Preece and Arnold

(2001) advocate a 'multi-disciplinary approach' to the use of specialist strategies such as those used for Sarah. They are critical if Sarah's needs are to be met consistently, and consequently meetings on Sarah's progress and needs were attended by relevant professionals from statutory agencies, including health, social services and the family support worker involved with Sarah's family.

In Ben's case the school's SENCo had attended a number of training initiatives that enabled whole-school issues to be addressed, without the need for specialist advisers. It was acknowledged, however, that in the long-term specialist input would benefit the whole school and, therefore, additional input from specialist advisers would be needed.

Regular communication, however, is seriously impeded by the lack of time for regular liaison; frequently Sarah's teacher's only spare time was during her breaks. If regular communication is to be established between multi-disciplinary professionals, mainstream and special schools, and parents, it is crucial that the importance of such collaboration is recognised and time allowed for effective communication to become part of good practice.

CONCLUSION

The management of individual learning poses a necessary challenge to teachers working in inclusive schools. The case studies illustrate how the individual learning needs of two pupils were managed within inclusive class and school contexts and leads to the formulation of policies and principles that we suggest underpin the successful management of individual learning of all pupils:

- specialised teaching strategies will be more successful, and of benefit to many pupils, if they are adapted for use within a class context, at the same time addressing the individual needs of specific pupils;
- the innovative implementation and management of IEPs (that are manageable, make sufficient use of resources and link to the whole curriculum) are central to the effective management of individual learning in inclusive school and classroom contexts;
- the recognition of the learning needs of all pupils should form part of the inclusive classroom and school ethos to enable pupils to develop an awareness, an understanding and an appreciation of individual differences;
- the role of learning support assistants should be redefined to enable pupils to develop independence and to utilise the LSA's skills in a flexible way in order to respond to individual and whole class needs;
- the establishment of regular opportunities for the development of collaborative partnerships, between multi-disciplinary professionals, mainstream and special schools, and parents, are essential to successful management of individual learning. They should be supported where possible by opportunities for appropriate collaborative training.

REFERENCES

Bliss, T. and Robinson, G. (1995) *Developing Circle Time.* Bristol: Lucky Duck Publications.

Byers, R. (1998) 'Personal and social development for pupils with learning difficulties', in C. Tilstone, L. Florian and R. Rose (eds.) *Promoting Inclusive Practice.* London: Routledge.

Curry, M. and Broomfield, C. (1994) *Personal and Social Education for Primary Schools through Circle Time.* Tamworth: NASEN Enterprises Ltd.

DfEE (1994) *Code of Practice on the Identification and Assessment of Special Educational Needs.* London: HMSO.

DfEE (1997) *Excellence for All Children: Meeting Special Educational Needs.* London: HMSO.

DfEE (1999a) *The National Curriculum: Handbook for Primary Teachers in England.* London: HMSO.

DfEE (1999b) *The National Curriculum: Handbook for Secondary Teachers in England.* London: HMSO.

DfEE (2000) *The National Literacy Strategy: Supporting Pupils with Special Educational Needs in the Literacy Hour.* London: DfEE Publications.

Gray, C. (1998) 'Social stories and comic strip conversations with students with Asperger Syndrome and High Functioning Autism', in E. Schopler, G. Mesibov and L. Kunce (eds.) *Asperger Syndrome or High Functioning Autism?* New York: Plenum Press.

Gray, C. and Garand, J. (1993) 'Social Stories: improving responses of individuals with autism with accurate social information', *Focus on Autistic Behaviour,* 8 1–10.

Hornsby, B. (1997) *Overcoming Dyslexia: A Straightforward Guide for Families and Teachers.* London: Vermilion.

Howley, M., Preece, D. and Arnold, T. (2001) 'Multidisciplinary use of "Structured Teaching" to promote consistency of approach for children with Autistic Spectrum Disorder', *Educational and Child Psychology,* 18 (2) 41–52.

Moseley, J. (1996) *Quality Circle Time in the Primary School.* Wisbech: LDA.

National Curriculum Council (1990) *Curriculum Guidance 3: The Whole Curriculum.* London: NCC.

Norwich, B. (1996) 'Special needs education for all: connective specialisation and ideological impurity', *British Journal of Special Education,* 23 (3) 100–3.

Ott, P. (1997) *How to Detect and Manage Dyslexia: A Reference and Resource Manual.* Oxford: Heinemann.

Rose, R. (1998) 'The curriculum: a vehicle for inclusion or a lever for exclusion?', in C. Tilstone, L. Florian and R. Rose (eds.) *Promoting Inclusive Practice.* London: Routledge.

Rose, R. (2000) 'Using classroom support in a primary school: a single school case study', *British Journal of Special Education,* 27 (4) 191–6.

Rose, R. and Howley, M. (2001) 'Entitlement or denial? The curriculum and its influences upon inclusion processes', in T. O'Brien (ed.) *Enabling Inclusion: Blue Skies … Dark Clouds?* London: The Stationery Office.

Schopler, E., Mesibov, G. and Hearsey, K. (1995). 'Structured teaching in the TEACCH system', in E. Schopler and G. Mesibov (eds.) *Learning and Cognition in Autism.* New York: Plenum Press.

Tod, J., Castle, F. and Blamires, M. (1998) *Individual Education Plans: Implementing Effective Practice.* London: David Fulton.

Wing, L. and Gould, J. (1979). 'Severe impairments of social interaction and associated abnormalities in children: epidemiology and classification', *Journal of Autism and Childhood Schizophrenia,* 9 11–29.

Chapter 3

Multicultural inclusion for pupils with severe or profound and multiple learning difficulties

Ann Fergusson and Trudy Duffield

Pupils with special educational needs have in many instances been denied opportunities to participate fully in all aspects of school life. When such pupils encounter further difficulties because of the inability of a school to address cultural or linguistic needs this can lead to increased disadvantage in providing an effective learning environment. This chapter explores the challenges faced by some of these pupils and their teachers, and considers how schools may develop strategies to overcome discriminatory practice.

The current state of inclusive practice in our schools relies on the awareness and sensitivity of staff at one level and, at another, the knowledge, understanding and responsiveness of the school and its staff in developing a commitment to meet the diverse needs of its population, both as an entirety and as individuals. For some pupils it may be necessary for staff to consider those discriminatory factors in order to ensure that inclusion becomes a reality.

Wolf (1999), in a review of services provided by Sense (a national organisation which addresses the needs of those with multi-sensory impairments), describes the common needs of its deafblind, adult users, when considering ethnically sensitive services. She writes of the necessity of taking into account people's race, religion and culture, as well as their needs and abilities. She sees an awareness of, and access to, other cultures, as essential to providing services which address individual needs and reflect the diversity of users. Without this awareness, she suggests that what we offer will be: 'not only impoverishing but can lead to "double discrimination" – on the grounds of race as well as disability' (p.14). This chapter will explore this issue in more detail.

The focus will be upon the situation of pupils with severe or profound and multiple learning difficulties (SLD/PMLD) who do not have English as their mother tongue. It is written in the belief that such pupils may have their learning difficulties compounded if they are not offered support in their home language in a learning environment that respects their culture and backgrounds.

The chapter will further seek to identify some principles for developing policies and practices to ensure that we provide equitable educational opportunities for all of our pupils. These issues are drawn both from the literature and the ongoing developing practice of a special school for pupils with severe and profound learning difficulties which has been the focus of a case study conducted by the authors (Fergusson and Duffield, 2001).

PROPORTIONAL REPRESENTATION: THE SLD PERSPECTIVE

Within mainstream education, many positive developments have been, and continue to be, made in more effectively supporting and raising the achievement of pupils from minority ethnic groups. Similarly, there is within this area a wealth of valuable research and literature for practitioners to draw upon. Indeed, the issue of raising the attainment of minority ethnic pupils is recognised and addressed to some degree for practitioners in the field, beginning at Initial Teacher Training Level.

However, the literature on pupils with severe and profound and multiple learning difficulties who come from minority ethnic groups is severely limited and offers little for practitioners, in the way of research or sources of guidance, to develop their practice in meeting the needs of this very specific group or in establishing partnerships with their parents (Diniz, 1999). Policy and practice appear to be influenced arbitrarily either at an LEA level or by individual schools, a situation which identifies this need as a priority. Consequently, policy and practice, may:

- be wide ranging;
- reflect the geographical settlement of minority ethnic populations;
- have greater or lesser developed services;
- reflect the size of the LEA or the scale of the pupil representation;
- be better developed for some ethnic groups than for others;
- reflect the interests, experience and expertise of individuals within a school or LEA to develop and share practice.

Not only is policy and practice disparate within the field of pupils with SLD and English as an additional language (EAL), but school staff from minority ethnic groups are often disproportionately under represented. In some instances, it appears that representatives of these communities tend to be staff in support roles with poor representation within the teaching staff (Fergusson and Duffield, 2001). These factors impact greatly on many aspects of effectively meeting the needs of this pupil population.

When questioning how this position has arisen, particularly in view of the strides made for EAL pupils in mainstream education, it is apparent that there may be many contributory factors. The field of special education is still relatively young and focused initially on the development of practice for the needs of the majority and minority pupil groups (those with PMLD, multi-sensory impairments [MSI] or on the autistic spectrum) have more recently been given a higher profile. It may be that the needs of pupils with learning difficulties and EAL, at this stage, have still not been fully identified and in some instances may be marginalised within specialist schools. There is much in the way of both theory and practice, however, that can be valuably learnt from developments by colleagues working in both mainstream and SLD/PMLD schools.

Areas of impact

Assessment

Well-managed assessment must be considered when working with pupils who have special educational needs. Accurate baselines are essential for planning, teaching and providing appropriate and effective support. The difficulties of the accurate assessment of pupils within the SLD/PMLD population have been well documented (Aird, 2001; Ouvry and Saunders, 2001). These difficulties can be exacerbated when pupils do not have English as their home language. Problems exist in finding suitable assessment tools for pupils with learning difficulties and EAL, and Cline (1998) raised the issue of norm-referenced tests which, he suggests, may often be culturally biased. Schedules appropriate to assessing the levels of communication in pupils with SLD/PMLD often address non-verbal responses but not necessarily the difference in competence between home language and English (Fergusson and Duffield, 2001).

Much of the work focused on encouraging the development of early communication skills in pupils with PMLD stems from models of child development that build on mother–child interaction (Coupe-O'Kane and Goldbart, 1998; Nind and Hewett, 1994). These models, however, have not been reviewed for parenting styles that may differ from those commonly deployed by white Europeans. Fergusson and Duffield (2001) noted that parents of pupils from Pakistani origins appeared to have a different, more tactile, interaction style with their sons and daughters. This factor needs further examination, but could impact dramatically on early communication development, both at a policy and a practice level.

Interpreting communication

Communication is the key to the effectiveness of any educational or social intervention. In the previous section, the possibility that styles of interaction may well differ between ethnic groups in establishing early communication was alluded to. Diverse styles may present confusing messages, at a non-verbal level; this may be compounded by the use of a language that is not their mother tongue, and consequently pupils may be at a distinct disadvantage.

Bilingual support in a home language is documented as being advantageous, particularly when new concepts are being learned (Cummins, 1984). For teachers of pupils with SLD and PMLD, mother-tongue support, which is not always available in school, presents a major challenge and may place the pupil from an ethnic minority at a disadvantage. Hall (1995) discusses how many EAL pupils learning about something new, often 'think in their home language'. We do not know whether or not pupils with learning difficulties work in this way, and we do not always enable them to do so by providing opportunities for bilingual support. The importance of 'thinking skills', as a key skill in learning, is again highlighted in the context of pupils with learning difficulties in recent curriculum support materials (QCA, 2001).

Other strategies offering meaning to pupils are those now considered to be good practice in the context of working with pupils with severe and profound and multiple learning difficulties. The use of a multi-modal or 'total communication' approach to augment, or to offer alternatives to, speech has increasingly become standard practice, but may have a multiple value for EAL pupils and school staff who do not share a home language as it provides a shared system of communication.

Increasingly pupils are being admitted to school from diverse origins, each with its own language, culture and heritage, which can enhance the learning environment. LEAs may be right to recognise that it is not reasonable to expect schools to have bilingual assistants in languages other than local, community languages (Peterborough City Council, 1999), but for pupils with EAL and learning difficulties, they need to ensure that the learning environment is meaningful. The accepted practice of using symbols or 'objects of reference' for pupils as a shared means of communication may well provide the necessary bridge for those without home-language support.

Another 'good SLD practice' strategy is that of ensuring meaningful contexts for learning, which corresponds well with the 'good EAL practice' model described by Cummins (1984). It offers an axis where the vertical continuum has 'cognitively demanding' at the top and 'less demanding' at the bottom; the horizontal continuum includes 'context embedded' at one end and 'context-free' at the other. He suggests that good practice for supporting EAL pupils most effectively always places activities in a meaningful context and makes increasing demands on the learner in terms of cognition. Although this may be true of the learner with SLD and PMLD in many instances, cognitive demands may be fewer if the focus is on independence or the generalising of skills to new contexts.

Curriculum focus

Diniz (1999) questioned the extent to which 'knowledge about biculturalism and bilingualism has permeated curriculum practice for pupils with complex learning and communication difficulties' (p.216). Certainly, Fergusson and Duffield (2001) claimed that this was not the case in the school being studied at the introduction of the National Curriculum or shortly afterwards and they document how a culturally sensitive curriculum evolved as the school's practice developed to meet the needs of a bilingual group. Revisions to curriculum documentation include statements on effective principles of inclusion (DfEE/QCA, 1999a; 1999b) and, although EAL is not a special educational need, when considered in relation to early concept developments for pupils with SLD and PMLD, it may present a 'potential barrier to learning' which this guidance suggests we should 'overcome'.

In addition to the obvious subject links to RE, Geography and History, via religious and cultural origins and heritage, Citizenship is a subject that is foregrounded in the debate and it offers great potential for supporting the inclusion movement (Lawson and Fergusson, 2001). Its very focus on recognising and respecting differences between individuals and groups, on learning that there are different ways of viewing things and for different reasons (sometimes connected to our diverse linguistic, cultural or religious backgrounds or lifestyles) seeks to develop a more sensitive and inclusive society.

In discussions about pupils with SLD and PMLD learning Modern Foreign Languages (MFL), Robertson (2000) describes how they experience similar stages of language acquisition to a bilingual pupil learning an indigenous language. She suggests that the challenges of learning a second language are similar to those encountered with a first language for where English is not the home language, even pupils with complex needs, who experience difficulties in processing language, are taught in the unfamiliar language of English. They consequently become bilingual at the 'primitive level' of their language development and respond to different languages at home and school. They demonstrate that it is possible to respond to a new language when the need arises despite their complex needs.

Although not recognised as a modern foreign language, the home language of EAL peers can take on a similar role. In the case study school reviewed later (Fergusson and Duffield, 2001) pupils whose home language *was* English were observed to count and greet peers in Panjabi, as a result of the enriched language and meaningful context that the environment offered to support EAL pupils and not as a result of direct teaching.

Cline (1998) suggests that bilingualism can be educationally enriching and have a positive effect on intellectual performance, but stresses that it is essential that the context empowers their achievement; this is certainly true of the example previously noted. He also cites Grosjean (1985) when developing the complexity of bilingualism; bilinguals use their languages together and separately, different languages for different contexts, purposes and people. Such processes have an impact on the framework for the assessment of EAL pupils, although it should be borne in mind that it is easy to misjudge, make assumptions or ignore their skills. They may lack the ability to adjust their use of language to the needs of the listener or the maturity to 'code-switch', but they may have awareness or skills at the 'listening level'. He goes on to suggest that such pupils may be at a more sophisticated level as bilinguals, than children whose competence in a second or an indigenous language is seen as poor when monolingual norms are employed.

LEARNING FROM PRACTICE: HOW PRACTICE CAN INFLUENCE POLICY

So far we have examined issues that are, by and large, policy-led, either at a central or a local level. Research has identified (Fergusson and Duffield, 2001) that ongoing and developing practice can often impact upon policy. Some strategies, commonly deployed in mainstream schools, need a different approach within the SLD and PMLD sphere. Generally, in mainstream, the aim is to enable EAL pupils to become fluent English users as quickly as possible and certainly within the first two years in school. One approach is by 'immersing' EAL pupils in the English language and discouraging withdrawal or bilingual support unless they are having specific difficulties. Developing practice within SLD and PMLD settings has highlighted the need for a very different practice, largely driven by pupil needs. In order to meet the specific needs of an SLD/PMLD population, current good practice within the field needs to be examined in order to identify where it can influence policy-making.

The review of a case study school highlights some interesting issues and potential strategies for overcoming some of the difficulties of meeting the complex needs of a group of pupils who have SLD, PMLD and EAL.

The case study school

The number of children at St George's School in Peterborough (a day school for pupils with severe and profound and multiple learning difficulties) who have a mother tongue other than English has been consistently 40%, as opposed to the 17% in mainstream within the LEA. The majority of their families speak Mirpuri Panjabi, Urdu or Panjabi and have a Pakistani heritage, although other languages and heritages are represented in the school. It has always been concerned with implementing national and local policies on equal opportunities and, more recently, inclusion, in ways that are meaningful to the wider school community including pupils, parents, staff and governors.

In 1991, the head teacher appointed a bilingual assistant to support

Pakistani pupils and their families (it is worth noting that Section 11 funding had not supported the school previously as the total number of pupils was small compared with the total numbers of pupils within the mainstream). For the first time, the school had the opportunity to promote equality for all pupils and to endorse the United Nations Convention on the Rights of the Child, ratified by the UK Government in 1991 (United Nations, 1989), that all children are entitled to participation, provision, play and protection. More specifically, Article 23 states:

> The right, if disabled, to special care, education and training to help enjoy a full and decent life in conditions which ensure dignity, which promote self-reliance and which maximise the opportunities for participation and integration into society.

And Article 30 urges:

> The right of a member of a minority community or indigenous people, to enjoy her/his own culture, to practise her/his own religion and use her/his own language.

The appointment of a bilingual assistant helped the school to further the aims of the Peterborough City Council Equal Opportunities Policy, based on five core values that provide a framework for service delivery:

1. Equality – recognition that everyone is of equal value and should be respected according to individual needs and abilities.
2. Equity – to be fair, reasonable and just in all school activities.
3. Empowerment – to help individuals take responsibility so that they can participate in and influence the decision-making process.
4. Accessibility – equal access for all in employment and service delivery.
5. Quality – obtaining the highest standards in service delivery.

In order to discover what would be the most effective strategies to meet the needs of minority pupils in the spirit of equality and inclusion, the following fieldwork was undertaken:

Meetings were arranged at the homes of each family and some small-scale research was undertaken, through interviews, to discover what value each family attached to their mother tongue when used at school for their children. Some important themes emerged, with families expressing the clear belief that their children had knowledge of their home language despite their high level of disability. Furthermore, families said that even when they had competence in English they would prefer to discuss the needs of their children in their home language because of the emotional aspects associated with caring for a disabled child. For example, Azra said of caring for her brother Ghulum:

You see, although I went to school in England and my English is good, when it comes to talking about Ghulum and what he needs there are no words to express how I feel in English, only Panjabi.

All the families articulated the difficulties they had with written English and Urdu reports on their children. Many of the mothers were not literate in either language and all family members needed mother tongue explanations of the educational language used. A valuable benefit for the school staff was a clearer understanding of how the Pakistani community had grown up in Peterborough in the early 1970s; the close links between each family as they had all come from the same region within Pakistan; and the impact that their children's disability had on each family within the community.

After the initial discussions with the families the following approaches were considered and agreed between staff and governors:

Staff development

A series of in-service training sessions was arranged for staff to be delivered by family members from the Pakistani community within school and supported by the bilingual assistant. The sessions covered a range of themes related to family beliefs, heritage and child-care practices, and gave staff the opportunity to ask direct questions. They avoided the possibility of stereotyping the Pakistani Muslim community within Peterborough, by the staff, and were based on individual understanding about Muslim communities elsewhere in Britain. Again, family members reinforced their belief that their children had abilities and strengths in their home language, which were not necessarily apparent in their school life. This period in the school's development was useful in helping the school community to avoid unlawful racial discrimination and, more importantly, to avoid other forms of racial discrimination that are not covered by law. It also helped school staff to develop their abilities to treat all children and their families equally. More recently, the children of asylum seekers, with other mother tongues, have moved in and it is pleasing that the school was viewed by members of the LEA educational psychology staff as having the strengths to 'include' them.

Including parents

The school's management reviewed the organisation of the termly record of achievement evening (parent consultation meeting) supported by individual 'Record of Achievement' folders for each child. The bilingual assistant accompanied all Panjabi speaking parents to each meeting and made an audiotape of the comments written in each folder, which the families could listen to prior to and after the meeting. Photographs were taken to illustrate each written comment and, if a family was unable to attend the evening, teachers' directed-time was reorganised to allow each family to be visited by the class teacher with the bilingual assistant, on a termly basis. A similar approach was adopted for annual review meetings and it is now common practice for the bilingual assistant to accompany families to health and social services meetings on request.

Staff appointments

The school's management team, including governors, reviewed the essential and desirable criteria when appointing staff. The Race Relations Act 1976 encouraged employers to take positive steps to ensure workers from ethnic minorities were represented on their staffs. For some teaching, learning support assistant and midday supervisor posts it was considered essential for staff to be Panjabi-speaking in order to provide role models for the children within the school. Whilst it has been possible to appoint members from Peterborough's Pakistani Muslim community to the learning support staff and midday supervisor team, it is disappointing that they have yet to appoint a suitably qualified Panjabi-speaking teacher. Consequently the bilingual assistant continues to play a pivotal role in joint planning with the existing teaching staff. The bilingual assistant also has a budget for providing appropriate multi-ethnic resources within school and advises the subject co-ordinators about resources that reflect the diversity of the school community.

Governor representation

The governing body has always included a member of Peterborough's Pakistani community as one of its members, thus ensuring that the important monitoring role of the governors is undertaken with reference to the principles of equality and inclusion for all family groups within the school community.

Assessment in mother tongue

The bilingual assistant and the deputy head worked with each individual family to collate a mother tongue language assessment for each child in order that comparisons could be made of their level of functioning in their home language and in English. In every case these assessments demonstrated that pupils were more effective communicators when supported by their mother tongue and it seemed apparent that their self-esteem was more developed when they were communicating in their home language. Recently the school has changed the assessment tool to one that more accurately reflects the needs of a school population of predominantly PMLD pupils (Latham and Miles, 2001). These assessments have been undertaken collaboratively with groups of parents (who know each other well now), school staff and the bilingual assistant. This work has enabled families to contribute directly to the development of policies and procedures for assessment, recording and reporting (Peterborough City Council, 1999).

Support in the mother tongue

Children whose mother tongue is Panjabi are represented in each class, and therefore decisions had to be made about the most effective ways of supporting them, within the constraints imposed by limited resources. The research evidence from mainstream school studies is contradictory on 'efficient resource utilisation'; some researchers favour the segregation of children with minority languages and some advocate an 'immersion' approach within mainstream classes. For pupils whose mother tongue development is damaged owing to a range of disabilities, the issues are even more complex (Fergusson and Duffield, 2001). At St George's School each pupil is supported for part of the week by a Panjabi speaker in the following ways:

- One-to-one support to help the teaching of IEP targets in the mother tongue.
- A weekly meeting of the Panjabi pupils to be taught in Panjabi to assist concept development. The work planned is often linked to the whole-school topic for the term and will be repeated in English at another time.
- A weekly meeting with a group of Panjabi-speaking parents who plan and deliver activities related to the interests of the local Pakistani community or with a religious theme.
- Panjabi-speaking midday supervisors to support feeding programmes. Lunchtime is considered to be a very important part of the teaching day at St George's and in reality provides the longest opportunity for one-to-one support for any pupil (1 hour). Communication aims are always written into individual feeding programmes and these can be accommodated even when pupils are gastro fed. The staff concerned have undertaken training provided by teaching staff and the bilingual assistant and understand the importance of the contribution their mother tongue can make at this time.
- Regular workshops for parents within the school day, involving their children, which have 'brought the curriculum to life' for the families and demonstrate recent educational initiatives through direct teaching (for example, literacy and numeracy strategies). Support for these sessions is high and is facilitated by the school providing transport to enable all parents to attend. The families report that this is an effective way of communicating, and consulting about, new educational initiatives affecting their children as it directly uses the community language and involves community workers (Panjabi-speaking staff, governors and the bilingual assistant).

Continuing professional development

It is recognised that all staff will continue to need training to ensure knowledge and understanding of the following equal opportunities and inclusion issues (Gerschel, 1998; CSIE, 2000):

- the law;
- facts about racism and other forms of discrimination;
- anti-discriminatory policies;
- working with the local community;
- developing concepts of inclusion within all school activities.

> Inclusion therefore involves a slightly different mind set or attitude towards the whole issue and the recognition of disabled children as individuals who have the right to become involved in all activities, not simply by allowing them to be there but by facilitating this involvement with the provision of appropriate resources, staff and equipment as a matter of course.
>
> *Childcare Quarterly*, 1999, p.6

MOVING FORWARD: SHARING IN DEVELOPING POLICY WITH PARENTS

New models of parent involvement

New models of parent involvement will inevitably be linked to the process of school evaluation and review. The purpose of all schools is to raise pupil attainment; LEA development planning (Peterborough City Council, 1999, for example) advocates frequent parental involvement as an effective way of monitoring pupil achievement. The DfEE *Programme for Action* (1998) promotes the notion that schools can, by enabling parents to play a more active role in their child's education, promote higher standards for pupils with special educational needs. For the pupils under discussion the need to involve parents (and to use their knowledge of their children as a means of interpreting their methods of communication and their behaviour) is even greater.

> At times of transition, a phased period of 'shared dialogue' is particularly important, to enable parents to discuss their feelings, alongside the needs of their children, during admission to school or a transfer between phases of education. Such discussions have the added benefit of providing meaningful information about pupils for school staff and, during this period, both parents and staff are able to clarify and articulate expectations of each other. This is not necessarily an easy process for

some parents as their experience of the education system may be limited or non-existent.

Shah, 1995

A meaningful learning environment

Practitioners working with pupils with learning difficulties are often aware of the great importance of linking the world of home and school. It is especially important that teachers draw on the home life and community experiences of SEN pupils with EAL when auditing resource provision. An awareness of the home life of individual pupils will lead to an understanding of subtle differences, which can then be acknowledged and reflected in classroom practices. This is essential to avoid the possibilities of stereotyping in community groups, and personalises and maximises the classroom experiences for each child; this insight is also beneficial where pupils belong to families who do not fit within what was previously perceived as being conventional models (for example, single-parent families, travellers or same-sex parents).

Appropriate resources drawn from the pupils' everyday experience are more authentic when sourced with the help of parents and are not necessarily reflected in the catalogues of educational suppliers. By looking at home environments, clues will be provided on what may interest and motivate pupils to promote more effective teaching and learning (CSIE, 2000). Schools need to ensure that their pupil population is reflected in their ethos, the learning environment and the resources utilised by, for example, regular 'cultural audits'. Bevan-Brown (1999; 2000) describes how governors (parents or people from the minority communities) could valuably fulfil this role.

Shared values, shared achievements: a more inclusive tomorrow

This chapter is based on the premise that, in order to become more effective in meeting the diverse needs of pupils, it is necessary to draw on good practice, to share experiences and expertise but, perhaps more crucially, to start from common values. If schools achieve shared status, they will be in a position to move forward and it may be helpful to revisit government guidance to schools in order to meet pupils' needs effectively in school settings that are educationally and individually inclusive. The revised National Curriculum puts forward clear aims for inclusion, which it is hoped that all schools will strive to achieve (DfEE, 1999a; 1999b). The guidance materials for supporting pupils with learning difficulties (QCA/DfEE, 2001) offer much for all schools at both general and specific levels to meet individual needs effectively by, for example, suggesting levels of potential progress for pupils at the earliest stages of learning and development. Guidance materials for PSHE and Citizenship (DfEE/QCA, 1999) clearly lay out the values which professionals should be sharing, and working from, with and for our pupils to promote inclusion, both as individuals and within a developing multicultural society.

> When the environment and ethos are accepting and inclusive, the range of human conditions is accepted as equally valuable and difficulties are minimised.
>
> Gerschel, 1998, p.64

REFERENCES

Aird, R. (2001) *The Education and Care of Children with Severe and Profound and Multiple Learning Difficulties*. London: David Fulton.

Bevan-Brown, J. (1999) *A Cultural Audit for Teachers: Looking out for Maori Learners with Special Needs*. New Zealand Centre for Educational Research and Australian Centre for Educational Research.

Bevan-Brown, J. (2000) 'Why are learners with special needs from ethnically diverse groups missing out on effective, culturally appropriate services and what can be done about it?' Paper given at the 5th International Special Education Congress, Manchester.

Cline, T. (1998) 'The assessment of special educational needs for bilingual children', *British Journal of Special Education*, 25 (4) 159–63.

Coupe-O'Kane, J. and Goldbart, J. (1998) *Communication Before Speech: Development and Assessment* (2nd edition). London: David Fulton.

CSIE (2000) *Index for Inclusion: Developing Learning and Participation in Schools*. Bristol: CSIE.

Cummins, J. (1984) *Bilingualism and Special Education: Issues in Assessment and Pedagogy*. Avon: Multilingual Matters.

DfEE (1998) *Meeting Special Educational Needs: a Programme for Action*. London: The Stationery Office.

DfEE/QCA (1999a) *The National Curriculum Handbook for Primary Teachers in England*. London: Department for Education and Employment.

DfEE/QCA (1999b) *The National Curriculum: Handbook for Secondary Teachers in England*. London: Department for Education and Employment.

Diniz, F.A. (1999) 'Race and special educational needs in the 1990s', *British Journal of Special Education*, 26 (4) 213–17.

Fergusson, A. and Duffield, T. (2001) Promoting cultural, religious and linguistic diversity in a special school', in R. Rose and I. Grosvenor (eds.) *Doing Research in Special Education*. London: David Fulton.

Gerschel, L. (1998) 'Equal opportunities and special educational needs: equity and inclusion', in C. Tilstone, L. Florian and R. Rose (eds.) *Promoting Inclusive Practice*. London: Routledge.

Grosjean, F. (1985) 'The bilingual as a competent but specific speaker-hearer', *Journal of Multi-lingual and Multi-cultural Development*. 6 (6) 467–77.

Hall, D. (1995) *Assessing the Needs of Bilingual Pupils: Living in Two Languages*. London: David Fulton.

Latham, C. and Miles, A. (2001) *Communication, Curriculum and Classsroom Practice*. London: David Fulton.

Lawson, H. and Fergusson, A. (2001) 'PSHE and Citizenship', in B. Carpenter, R. Ashdown and K. Bovair (eds.) *Enabling Access: Effective Teaching and Learning for Pupils with Learning Difficulties* (2nd edition). London: David Fulton.

Nind, M. and Hewett, D. (1994) *Access to Communication: Developing the Basics of Communication with People with Severe Learning Difficulties through Intensive Interaction.* London: David Fulton.

Ouvry, C. and Saunders, S. (2001) 'Pupils with profound and multiple learning difficulties', in B. Carpenter, R. Ashdown and K. Bovair. *Enabling Access: Effective Teaching and Learning for Pupils with Learning Difficulties* (2nd edition). London: David Fulton.

Peterborough City Council (1999) *Education Development Plan 1999–2002.* Peterborough CC.

QCA DfEE (2001) *Planning, Teaching and Assessing the Curriculum for Pupils with Learning Difficulties.* London: DfEE.

Robertson, J. (2000) 'Increasing access to modern foreign languages to pupils with special educational needs: a neuropsychological perspective', *Support for Learning*, 15 (2) 62–6.

Shah, R. (1995) *The Silent Minority: Children with Disabilities in Asian Families.* London: National Children's Bureau.

United Nations (1989) *Convention on the Rights of the Child.* New York: United Nations.

Wolf, F. (1999) 'Celebrating diversity', *Talking Sense*, 45 (2) 14–17

Chapter 4

Connecting the disconnected

Exploring issues of gender, 'race' and SEN within an inclusive context

Liz Gerschel

This chapter explores some of the links between gender, race and SEN; suggests where further research is required; and raises questions for practitioners to consider in the light of their own work. This approach supports what Corbett (2001a) calls a 'connective pedagogy' for inclusion, in which staff take a holistic view of the pupil within the wider school community. The components of this view include the ethnicity, gender, religion, language, sexuality, culture, housing and the leisure activities of the pupils and their parents.

WHAT ARE THE CURRENT ISSUES IN ETHNICITY, GENDER AND SPECIAL EDUCATIONAL NEEDS/DISABILITY?

Despite the recent focus on social and educational inclusion and on 'joined-up thinking' (DfEE, 1999), the discourses of SEN and of equal opportunities, in terms of race and gender, have remained distinctly discrete. Although the literature on learning difficulties and disability sometimes makes reference to 'social class', the gender or ethnicity ('race') of pupils is rarely mentioned. Similarly, research on ethnicity and gender issues rarely acknowledges special educational needs and disabilities. In a useful overview of race and special educational needs in the 1990s, Diniz (1999) identifies only four publications which report studies involving Asian children with SEN and three involving Black-Caribbean children. In most research, however, it is as if children with SEN or disabilities are white and genderless or 'degendered', to borrow a term from Arnot (Arnot, David and Weiner, 1999), and minority ethnic groups do not include children with SEN or disabilities. For the parents and children for whom ethnicity, gender, social class and SEN or disability interact, these factors cannot be separated.

Some examples of the current issues that link the fields of ethnicity and race, gender, SEN and disability are listed below. Although the list is not comprehensive and presents hypotheses without detailed exploration, areas where experience suggests that more research is needed are identified. An author's name is included where the published work could make a helpful starting point for reading.

The issues of ethnicity and SEN

- little acknowledgement of the impact of ethnic and cultural diversity on learning in some schools and in some professional services (Cline, 1998);
- little research on ethnicity ('race') and SEN (Diniz, 1999);
- institutionalised racism and the impact of the Macpherson report on the inclusion of minority ethnic group pupils (Ofsted, 2000a; Gillborn, 2001);
- the significant over-representation of African Caribbean pupils in the provision for emotional and behavioural difficulties (Cooper, Upton and Smith, 1991); changing populations in MLD schools (Male, 1996);
- the over-representation of Chinese and Asian pupils in the provision for SLD and PMLD; their under-representation in MLD and specific learning difficulties and when assessed as dyslexic (Diniz, 1999);
- the over-representation of Pakistani and Bangladeshi children in hearing loss and deafness (Ahmad, Oxley, McCann and Plackett, 1997);
- African Caribbean pupils identified as having 'general learning difficulties' rather than specific literacy difficulties and the consequent poorer provision (Daniels, Hey, Leonard and Smith, 1996);
- early high attainment followed by increasing underachievement among African Caribbean boys (Gillborn and Mirza, 2000);
- the gap between attainment at GCSE of African Caribbean and Pakistani pupils and that of white pupils is bigger than a decade ago (Gillborn and Mirza, 2000);
- a wider attainment gap as a consequence of ethnic origin, social class and gender (Gillborn and Mirza, 2000);
- the lack of research into the experiences of the parents of pupils with SEN from minority ethnic groups (Shah, 1995; Gross, 1996; Diniz, 1999; Warner, 1999);
- evidence that poverty and lower social class may impact more on minority ethnic groups and are related to increased SEN (Mittler, 1999; 2000);
- effects of teacher expectations based on ethnicity and class stereotypes on the identification, assessment and provision for pupils with SEN from minority ethnic groups (Epstein, Elwood, Hey and Maw, 1998; Wright, Weekes and McGlaughlin, 2000; Newham, 2001);
- confusions between language difficulties and learning difficulties for pupils with English as an additional language (EAL) (Troyna and Siraj-Blatchford, 1993).

The issues of gender and SEN

- gender imbalance: more boys than girls with SEN (2 boys, 1 girl in SEN generally; up to 12:1 in EBD) (Hill, 1994: Vardill, 1996);
- boys receive more teacher attention for inappropriate behaviour, and their emotional needs are recognised less than their behavioural needs (McNamara and Moreton, 1995);
- boys and girls are not treated with equity in identification, assessment and provision for SEN (Daniels, Hey, Leonard and Smith, 1999; Daniels, Creese, Hey, Leonard and Smith, 2001);
- boys get more and better provision for their identified needs (Daniels, Hey, Leonard and Smith, 1999);
- girls' emotional needs are often ignored or seen as health problems (McNamara and Moreton, 1995; Klein, 1999; Tierney and Dowd, 2000; Newham, 2001);
- the effects of the national emphasis on literacy on boys (Barrs and Pidgeon, 1998; QCA, 1998; Epstein, Elwood, Hey and Maw, 1998; Noble and Bradford, 2000);
- growing disaffection and underachievement amongst boys (Mac an Ghaill, 1994; Bleach, 1998; Holland, 1998; Klein, 1999);
- the increasing exclusion of boys; particularly the impact on those from Black Caribbean, white working class, and those with SEN (DfEE, 2000; Wright, Weekes and McGlaughlin, 2000; Osler, Watling, Busher, Cole and White, 2001);
- fewer opportunities for less able boys to find employment in unskilled or manual jobs (Holland, 1998);
- failure to acknowledge the needs of a minority of girls in some special schools (especially EBD);
- the need to address the sexuality of pupils with learning difficulties and disabilities; homosexuality is rarely addressed in special schools (Stewart and Ray, 2001);
- the issue of choice of, or consent to, sterilisation and contraception for girls with learning difficulties;
- the effects of teacher expectations (based on gender stereotypes) on the identification, assessment or provision for girls and boys with SEN (Green, 1993; Hill, 1994; Mac an Ghaill, 1994; Vardill, 1996; Wilson, 2000; Newham, 2001)

The issues of SEN, equality and equity

- increasing inclusion of pupils with learning difficulties and disabilities in mainstream education but inconsistencies in the quality of education received;
- a lack of data on the ethnicity and gender of pupils with statements, and

inadequate ethnic and gender monitoring of pupils with SEN at school, local and national level for placement, identification, assessment, provision and attainment (Male, 1996);

- a lack of data on children 'looked after' by local authorities in relation to ethnicity, gender and SEN (Brodie, 2000) and exclusion (Osler et al., 2001);
- little awareness in some schools of the minority ethnic group cultures of pupils with SEN, or the different needs of girls and boys with SEN (Daniels et al., 2001);
- a lack of clarity about what is 'underachievement' and what is SEN (Bleach, 1998);
- although the National Curriculum 2000 supports parallel inclusions, there is a need to develop connective pedagogy (Corbett, 2001a); the effects of league tables on pupils with SEN (Gillborn, 2001);
- although Ofsted reviews of NLS (National Literacy Strategy) and NNS (National Numeracy Strategy) in special schools do not mention ethnicity or gender, they acknowledge that NLS has been successful for many pupils with SEN but that those with PMLD are still not fully included (Ofsted, 2000b, 2001; Byers, 1999);
- the effects of policies and programmes for pupils which are 'gender and colour blind' (Mittler, 2000; Gillborn, 2001);
- QCA programmes offer access for pupils with learning difficulty but are 'gender and colour blind' (QCA, 2001);
- too little recognition of the rights of young people with SEN as sexual beings (Scott, 2001);
- a need for better sex education for pupils in special schools (Scott, 2001);
- little recognition of the links between pupils 'looked after' by local authorities, and SEN;
- 'summer-born' children have more identified SEN (Wilson, 2000); race, gender, SEN and setting (Ollerton, 2001)
- the links between poverty, health and social class and SEN (Dyson, 1997; Mittler, 2000);
- inconsistencies in SEN resource allocation associated with parental power and class (Gross, 1996);
- too little known about bullying within the field of special educational needs (Torrance, 2000);
- the increasing number of exclusions of pupils with statements of SEN (DfEE, 2000; Osler, 1997); the use of exclusion to access support for SEN (Osler et al., 2001);
- the higher rates of permanent exclusion from special schools (DfEE, 2000);
- the effects of the Disability Discrimination Act (1995) and the SEN and Disability Act (2001) on the education and the rights of pupils;
- the effect of the Human Rights Act on the rights of pupils with SEN;
- inequitable and sometimes ineffective distribution of resources to support

  pupils with SEN (Corbett, 2001b; Dyson, 2001; Gillborn, 2001);
- the effects of teacher expectations, based on gender, ethnicity or class stereotypes, on group organisation and settings (Wilson, 2000; Gillborn, 2001; Ollerton, 2001).

Some of these issues are long standing: Coard (1971) showed that disproportionately large numbers of pupils of African Caribbean origin were labelled ESN (educationally sub-normal) and sent to special schools. Two decades later, the labelling (now EBD) continues (DfEE, 2000; Wright, Weekes and McGlaughlin, 2000). Sewell (1997) and Mac an Ghaill (1994) see this as the result of a mismatch between pupil and school cultures. Exploring the reasons for exclusion, Osler, Watling, Busher, Cole and White (2001) suggest practical school and LEA action. The traditional remedy (pupils to 'adapt' to school culture) has failed and the increasing exclusion of some pupils is an indicator of the failure of the school to plan for the inclusion of all pupils and to adapt its teaching and learning culture accordingly (Mittler, 2000; Osler et al., 2001). The implementation of DfEE Circular 10/99 on social inclusion has created considerable concern in some schools but offers specific advice on reducing the number of exclusions by recognising the impact of social and cultural disadvantage on learning. Nevertheless, the majority of pupils excluded from school are boys (many from ethnic minority groups or lower social classes) and over one-third are registered as having special educational needs.

  There has long been a concern about the relationship between pupils who are learning English as an additional language (EAL) and who also have special educational needs. There has often been a lack of clarity in whether pupils are experiencing language or learning difficulties and how their needs are identified and met (Troyna and Siraj-Blatchford, 1993; Gerschel, 1998). There was a tendency in the 1970s and 1980s to identify pupils with language difficulties as having learning difficulties. A more recent problem, however, has been caused by the unwillingness of some schools to recognise that some pupils who speak English as an additional language also have special educational needs, which are consequently not being met.

  On the other hand, there has been considerably less attention to some issues linking SEN and gender. For example, a DfEE-funded study by the London Borough of Newham (2001) of girls' experiences of schooling draws attention to the lack of recognition given to girls' emotional difficulties; a neglected area compared to the attention given to the behavioural difficulties of boys. Although the sexuality and sexual orientation of pupils with learning difficulties and disabilities has been largely ignored in the literature, current approaches to sex education for pupils with special educational needs are being explored at Shepherd School in Nottingham, through the Standards Fund and innovative work in drama undertaken by 'Image in Action' (Scott, 2001; Stewart and Ray, 2001).

Underachievement or special educational needs?

Of particular significance to the media, is the underachievement of boys (see for example, Henry, 2001a, 2001b). Although girls have outperformed boys for many years in many areas of the curriculum, the publication of national test results (SATs, GCSEs and A-levels) highlights the differences and a body of literature is emerging which explores cause and effect (Ofsted, 1993; Mac an Ghaill, 1994; Pickering, 1997; QCA, 1998; Epstein, Elwood, Hey and Maw, 1998; Arnot, David and Weiner, 1999; Frater, 2000). Lively debate has focused on the extent to which the recent introduction of the National Literacy Strategy has exacerbated the difficulties boys experience with literacy and the solutions (Millard, 1997; Barrs and Pidgeon, 1998; Fisher, 2001; Rundell, 2001).

Gillborn and Mirza (2000) make it clear that the comparative attainment of boys and girls from different ethnic groups and social classes reflects a complex pattern, but that 'the gender gap is considerably smaller than the inequalities of attainment associated with ethnic origin and social class background' (p.23). They stress that neither social class nor gender differences:

> ... can account for persistent underlying ethnic inequalities: comparing like with like, African Caribbean, Pakistani and Bangladeshi pupils do not enjoy equal opportunities. (p.27)

To what extent are these ethnic and social factors considered in relation to planning and the teaching of pupils with special educational needs?

The current pattern of underachievement among boys applies across all abilities, most ethnic groups and all social classes, although it is difficult to say where 'underachievement' ends and 'special educational needs' begins. In some cases the demarcation is simply resource-driven and, as an example of the relationship between underachievement and SEN, Bleach (1998) cites the fact that the 'cut-off point' for providing support for special educational needs in a secondary school was placed at a maximum reading age of 8.5. Therefore, a reading age of 8.3 at age 11 recognises that a pupil has special educational needs; a reading age of 8.7, in these terms, means that the pupil is 'underachieving'!

This complex relationship is further blurred by the increasing recognition of disaffection and its impact on learning (Klein, 1999). At what point does the disaffection and underachievement of a Black Caribbean boy at a secondary school, who is increasingly resisting schooling (possibly as a result of what he sees as a racist experience), become an emotional or cognitive need, recognised as a special educational need meriting necessary additional resources organised by the SENCo? The greater probability is that he will be seen as a behavioural problem which may be 'dealt with' (or disciplined) through the pastoral system (head of year, head of house) rather than as a pupil whose experience of barriers to learning has left him behind in the great race to literacy and to A*–C grades at GCSE. He might, however, be helped through a more inclusive approach, possibly suggested by the SENCo. The following questions need to be addressed:

- What would be the difference in the school's response had our resistant pupil been a white working-class girl?
- How often is underachievement among pupils with statements for learning difficulties discussed in special or mainstream schools?

The current media discussion on underachievement risks focusing attention on the attainments of a small minority of able students (measured in A*–C grades at GCSE or A/AS-level) rather than reflecting on the wider wastage of potential skills and abilities among a greater number of pupils (Gillborn, 2001). Klein (1999) explores the difficult relationships between disaffection and SEN and, like Daniels, Visser, Cole and de Reybekill (1999), stresses the importance of recognising that not all disaffection or 'naughtiness' is an emotional or behavioural difficulty.

It is clear that, despite accusations of 'excuses', there is a strong direct association between social class and success in education (Gillborn and Mirza, 2000). Children without safe living conditions, food, warmth and clothing, let alone access to books, computers and other stimuli, and whose parents are stressed by poverty, are less likely to succeed at school. Mittler (2000) is explicit about class and economic links to underachievement, suggesting that:

> … boys are more susceptible to social disadvantage in early childhood, girls more vulnerable at adolescence. (p.58)

He further points out that:

> … at the age of seven, five times as many children from social class five had reading difficulties, as compared with those from social class one. (p.52)

Acknowledging gross inequalities in health and their social consequences, Mittler makes the link between children who experience social and economic deprivation, and those with special needs and illness or disability, and also shows that the poorer health suffered by ethnic minorities is a reflection of poverty. Put simply, with poorer health and poorer living conditions, pupils are more likely to have special educational needs. Corbett (2001b) recognises this and emphasises the need to see pupils holistically, within the wider community of their housing and leisure activities.

Culture clashes: inclusion or competition?

The statement of aims of most schools usually stresses that each pupil is valued as an individual and it is the intention of staff to help to fulfil her or his potential. Although an inclusive approach clearly supports this aim, there are major tensions between inclusive and competitive philosophies both in the government and in schools. Government advocates inclusion but simultaneously expects schools to achieve increasingly high academic targets. The prevailing culture in schools is influenced by government pressures to raise standards and to achieve targets set in literacy and numeracy, in order to appear in a favourable position in published league tables. In some schools, considerable resources have been provided for pupils whose performance falls just short of achieving the desired targets. Additional literacy support is sometimes given at KS2 to pupils who can be encouraged to move from level 3 to level 4 in time for Standard Assessment Tasks. Pupils whose attainment is well below national expectations have sometimes suffered comparative neglect, as their results do not impact on the league tables in the same way (Gillborn, 2001). The pressure on schools to set targets and to raise standards may well directly militate against the admission and inclusion of pupils whose academic performance will not prove sufficiently competitive. Gillborn (2001) effectively critiques the inherent conflict between the Government's expectation of inclusion and its recent Green Paper (DfEE, 2001) which encourages increased specialisation and the use of selection.

Connecting the disconnected: moving towards inclusive education

The Government has sought to increase the inclusion of pupils with special educational needs and disabilities in mainstream schools (DfEE, 1997; DfEE, 1998; DfEE/QCA, 1999; DfES, 2001) and to improve the provision for such pupils in mainstream and special contexts. Mittler (2000) argues that the inclusion debate has been reinvigorated by disability rights groups who have presented inclusion as a fundamental issue. For many, the word 'inclusion' suggests a necessary shift in the culture of mainstream schools to expect and welcome pupils with disabilities and learning difficulties. However, the publication of *Social Inclusion: Pupil Support* (Circular 10/99, DfEE, 1999) increased the 'catchment group' for discussions on inclusion to embrace pupils 'at risk of disaffection and exclusion' and recognised the impact of social and cultural disadvantage on learning. As O'Brien (1998) states:

> Inclusion is not only about eliminating discrimination for those who are cognitively or physically disadvantaged; it is also about improving provision for vulnerable children who suffer relentless economic and emotional deprivation. (p.151)

Mittler is even more specific; for him:

> ... the inclusion agenda ... challenges all forms of exclusion and discrim-
> ination, whether arising from society's response to disability, gender, race,
> sexual orientation or poverty and social disadvantage.
>
> Mittler, 2000, p.93

For the first time, and some twelve years after its introduction, the National
Curriculum (DfEE and QCA, 1999), implemented in September 2000, sets
out a 'statutory inclusion statement on providing effective learning opportunities for all pupils' (p.32), and acknowledges that pupils from certain
identified groups may be at a disadvantage unless curriculum planning is
specifically designed to meet their needs. These groups are:

- boys and girls;
- pupils with special educational needs;
- pupils with disabilities;
- pupils from all social and cultural backgrounds;
- pupils of different ethnic groups, including travellers, refugees and asylum
  seekers;
- pupils from diverse linguistic backgrounds.

A clear expectation is spelt out for staff to be aware of the requirements of the
equal opportunities legislation covering race, gender and disability, in order to
meet the full range of pupils' needs. It appears that the move towards inclusion
is simultaneously bringing about a consistency of approach to differing groups
and a recognition of the diverse needs of distinct groups of pupils. At the same
time, the new Code of Practice has come into place (DfES, 2001). We have yet
to see whether these changes will simply result in more rearranging of the ways
in which special education is delivered or whether they will:

> ... construct a form of education which is more equitable in itself and
> which will promote wider social equity.
>
> Dyson, 1997, p.153

Stephen Lawrence's legacy: the impact of the Macpherson report

As the disability rights movement has had a galvanising effect on national
inclusion policy, so special education may be said to have benefited from the
Stephen Lawrence Inquiry. Recommendations of the Stephen Lawrence
Inquiry (Macpherson, 1999) state that:

> ... consideration is given to amendment of the National Curriculum

aimed at valuing cultural diversity and preventing racism, in order better to reflect the needs of a diverse society. (Recommendation 67)

The Labour Government has ensured that 'institutional racism' is addressed through policy and action at all levels, from Ofsted and local education authorities to individual classrooms, through the Race Relations (Amendment) Act (2000). It has ensured that every school has been sent a copy of two publications which support self-evaluation through audit and a checklist; one specifically addresses racism in education (*Learning for All*, CRE, 2000) and includes audit statements relevant to pupils with SEN.

Diniz (1999) and Gillborn (2001) argue convincingly that the identification and assessment of the special educational needs of pupils from minority ethnic groups are affected by institutionalised racism. This is demonstrated, for example, by a willingness to attribute pupils' difficulties and disabilities to 'within-culture' factors rather than, for example, linking inadequate health-care provision for Pakistani and Bangladeshi children to the high numbers identified as having hearing loss and deafness (Ahmad et al., 1997), or a lack of awareness of heritage languages and cultures in schools and services, for example, the use of standardised SEN assessment tests with Asian children (Desforges, 1995; Cline, 1998). An increasing body of literature refutes the within-child explanations of the disaffection and exclusion of Black children, especially boys, and recognises the responsibility of schools to re-examine their cultures. Macpherson has brought the issues into the open: those in special education must recognise their own roles in bringing about greater equity for pupils from minority ethnic groups. Using the audits provided in *Learning for All* may help schools and LEAs to identify areas for change within their control.

The second publication, sent to all schools, the *Index for Inclusion* (Booth, Ainscow, Black-Hawkins, Vaughan and Shaw, 2000) addresses issues of equality and inclusion more broadly. At the same time, Ofsted (2000a) has published valuable guidance on evaluating educational inclusion and introduced compulsory training for all its inspectors, as a direct result of Macpherson's recommendation (Macpherson, 1999) that Ofsted be required to inspect the implementation of strategies by local education authorities and governors to 'prevent and address racism' (Macpherson, 1999, Recommendations 68 and 69). However, Ofsted's guidance wisely focuses on evaluating the inclusion of a wide spectrum of pupils, adding to those groups identified above (p.56):

- pupils from minority ethnic and faith groups;
- pupils who need support to learn English as an additional language;
- gifted and talented pupils;
- children 'looked after' by the local authority;
- others such as sick children; young carers; those children from families under stress; pregnant schoolgirls and teenage mothers;
- any pupils who are at risk of disaffection and exclusion. (p.1)

Notably omitted from all lists are gay and lesbian pupils, who remain a hidden and vulnerable minority in all schools and whose learning may consequently be disadvantaged (Rivers, 2000).

The emotional behaviour of children who belong to one of these groups may be affected both by the factor that makes them different (for example, their giftedness or the stress that they experience in their home situations), but also by their responses to school as a place that either recognises or ignores their 'differences', and enables them to learn.

Many children will 'belong' to more than one of the groups listed above, and in all there are likely to be children with special educational needs or disabilities. This point can be illustrated by asking you to define yourself: perhaps by sex, 'race', class, (dis)ability or impairment, age, marital status, role in the family, profession, skills, talents, size ... the list could go on!

- Which of these attributes defines you most distinctly in your own eyes?
- Which are most important in how other people define you?
- How have any of these attributes affected your learning as a child, as an adult and, subsequently, in your current job?

Each person's learning is affected by multiple factors, and there are implications for schools in turning inclusion policies into practice for pupils who have special educational needs and/or disabilities, and for whom barriers to learning are compounded by their gender, culture, class or ethnicity.

It may be that the term 'special educational needs' is no longer helpful, reflecting a 'within-child' or medical model to guide planning. O'Brien (1998), Mittler (2000) and Dyson (2001) all offer systemic approaches to planning which are far broader and more inclusive. Dyson (2001) emphasises the rights of children to a guarantee of concern for their individual progress, within an inclusive context where systemic planning is embedded in classroom practice. O'Brien (1998) focuses on the needs that are common to all, those that are relevant to a discrete group and finally to those features of planning which will be necessary for a few specific individuals. This way of thinking about a class or school which is mixed in terms of gender, ethnicity, social class and ability or disability, emphasises commonality while recognising difference, and includes all those within it. Teachers may then ask:

- What is it that all children need in order to participate and to learn? (common needs)
- What is it that this group of pupils needs – because they are (for example) boys and/or with Down's syndrome and/or with hearing impairments and/or from the Bangladeshi community and/or Muslims – that is distinctive or different? (distinct needs)
- What else is it that this individual needs which is specific to her or him? (specific/individual needs)

O'Brien (1998) points out that:

> ... the membership of groups highlights distinct needs ... an individual's membership of such groups has to be reflected positively in the curriculum and in classroom interaction. (p.148)

An excellent example of this practice is given by Corbett (2001b), describing how work with young trainees with learning difficulties addressed their needs specifically and holistically. But it is essential that we do not create divisions or hierarchies of disadvantage: inclusion policy and practice must recognise the complexities of individual experiences and address their impact on learning: what Corbett (2001a) calls 'connective pedagogy', that is, taking a holistic view of the pupil.

The experiences and outcomes of differing discriminations often have commonalities. If a teacher has low expectations of a child because of her or his sex, sexuality, ethnic or social background, cognitive or physical ability or disability, those expectations will potentially have a negative impact on the child's learning. If inclusion is a process of change that will enhance the learning experiences and achievements of all pupils, it must address areas of potential disadvantage coherently, and develop what Daniels et al. (2001) call 'pedagogies for equity' in education.

'Regardless of' or 'focused on' disadvantaged groups?

The needs of distinct groups can be met through what I shall call 'regardless of' and 'focused on' approaches. The introduction to the documents from QCA, *Planning, Teaching and Assessing the Curriculum for Pupils with Learning Difficulties*, illustrates the first approach. It declares that:

> ... the guidelines relate to all pupils aged between five and sixteen who have learning difficulties, regardless of factors such as their ethnicity, culture, religion, home language, family background or gender, or the extent of their difficulties. (p.4)

The curriculum opportunities and activities it advocates are applicable to all pupils but it does not recognise the distinct needs resulting from being part of a distinct group. For example, the suggestions for pupils at Key Stage 3 on learning about 'My body' refer to sanitary products and menstruation and masturbation but do not focus on gender and ethnicity issues in planning and teaching. The examples could have drawn attention to the importance of same-sex groups for discussions, or acknowledged the needs of male and female pupils who have been circumcised. Nor does the PSHE and Citizenship programme acknowledge the right of all pupils with learning difficulties to be seen as sexual beings; heterosexuality is assumed.

Although there is an advantage in policies and programmes which are intended to apply to all, there is a danger that if they do not identify the needs of particular groups or focus on specific examples, they will simply make no difference. As Gillborn, (2001) says: 'Color-blind policies tend to have racialised effects' (p.107). This lesson can be applied more widely: what is not specifically addressed will continue to damage pupils' opportunities. To be specific about the needs of distinct groups is not to undermine inclusion, as Mittler (2000) points out. Referring to the failure of what he calls 'colour blind' policies to meet the needs of children from ethnic minorities, he argues that:

> A conscious, focused attention on their needs is necessary to avoid marginalisation and unwitting discrimination. (p.77)

This statement applies equally to all disadvantaged groups and we need to be able to translate policy and programmes from the general inclusive principle to the specific relevant practice: to be cognisant of, and 'focus on', the learning of distinct groups within an inclusive context.

The principles and the questions: reviewing policy and practice

Schools that wish to address inclusivity and equity need to audit their current practice in order to identify where change is needed and where they can build on success. As long ago as 1988, Mortimore et al. (1988) held that:

> ... schools which are effective in promoting progress for one group of pupils (whether those of a particular social class, sex or ethnic group) will usually also be effective for children of other groups.' (p.217)

We could say that planning effectively for inclusivity promotes effectiveness; in the National Curriculum guidance (DfEE/QCA, 1999) three principles are explored that are described as 'essential to developing a more inclusive curriculum' and which all teachers are expected to address in their planning and teaching:

- The need to set suitable learning challenges for all pupils;
- The need to respond to pupils' diverse learning needs;
- The need to overcome potential barriers to learning and assessment for individuals and groups of pupils. (p.32)

For each principle, specific indicators and examples are given to help teachers to identify good practice.

These principles for inclusion knit well with the questions identified and addressed by Booth et al. (2000) in the *Index for Inclusion*:

- Who experiences barriers to learning and participation in the school?
- What are the barriers to learning and participation in the school?
- How can barriers to learning and participation be minimised?
- What resources are available to support learning and participation?
- How can additional resources be mobilised to support learning and participation? (p.14)

Teachers, governors, pupils and parents are invited to identify or address inclusive practice through questionnaires and indices for evaluating inclusion.

Ofsted (2000a) requires inspectors to consider three questions in order to evaluate inclusion which are pertinent and practical for staff to consider when devising policies:

- Do all pupils get a fair deal at school?

This relates to

- what benefits pupils get out of school, particularly their achievements;
- the opportunity to learn effectively, without interference and disruption;
- the respect and individual help they have from their teachers;
- pupils' access to all aspects of the curriculum;
- the attention the school gives to pupils' well-being;
- whether they and their parents are happy with the school.

- How well does the school recognise and overcome barriers to learning?

This is about

- the school's understanding of how well different groups do in school;
- the steps taken to make sure that particular groups are not disadvantaged in school and to promote their participation and success in learning;
- the school's strategies for promoting good relationships and managing behaviour;
- what the school does specifically to prevent and address racism, sexism and other forms of discrimination, and what it does about those cases of discrimination that do occur.

- Do the school's values embrace and inclusion and does its practice promote it?

The clues are

- how the values of the school are reflected in its curriculum, resources, communications, procedures and conduct;
- how people talk about and treat one another in the school;
- the leadership provided by senior staff and the consistency of staff behaviour;
- what the school intends and tries to do for 'people like me'.

Ofsted, 2000a, p.3

There is a coherence in these three documents which is both refreshing and challenging. The expectations made of teachers and schools are explicit and the process of change can be supported by using these self-audit opportunities to review, amend and monitor inclusive practice, and to ensure that all pupils 'get a fair deal'. Nevertheless, it is also true that the practice of equality needs adequate resourcing and we have yet to see whether and how this will be available by government.

The issues of equity, equality and SEN are inextricably bound together. It is clear that if schools are to become truly inclusive they must recognise both commonalities and distinctions between groups of learners who have hitherto been understood as belonging to separate spheres of SEN, 'race', gender and class. There is a need for a clear philosophy of education that embraces issues of both entitlement and equity (Corbett, 2001b) and sees the parts in relation to the whole and the whole as the sum of its parts: a holistic and 'connective pedagogy' (Corbett, 2001a). The approach to meeting the diverse needs of pupils and to overcoming obstacles to learning and achievement can no longer be sustained at an individual within-child level and must be systemic (O'Brien, 1998; Mittler, 2000; Dyson, 2001).

The key question for schools must be that posed by Ofsted: do all pupils get a fair deal at school? If the answer for some groups is 'No', what must be done to ensure that they do? Children deserve a guarantee of entitlement and equity in their education (Dyson, 2001) which will come about only when schools consider their definition of inclusive education, and work towards its reflection in the reality of daily life by honest and ongoing evaluation. The tools are available; audits and checklists (Ofsted, 2000a; Booth et al., 2000; CRE, 2000) are supplied to schools by the Government. However, unless there is willingness amongst staff, pupils, parents, governors, friends and neighbours of the school to carry out these audits, and a commitment by the whole school community to act on the findings and to bring about change, such audits will not impact on the daily experiences of children and young people. Macpherson said of institutional racism:

> It persists because of the failure of the organisation openly and adequately to recognise and address its existence and causes by policy, example and leadership.
>
> Macpherson, 1999, p.28

The same can be said of the exclusivity in education systems which leads to disaffection, failure and the waste of young lives and potential. 'Being equitable requires conscious consideration and effort' (Corbett, 2001b, p.118); schools must examine their leadership, policy and practice, whether at the micro level of the classroom where teachers' work reflects the inclusion statement of the National Curriculum (DfEE, 1999), or at the macro level of the impact of national and local government initiatives. Those involved with education must agree the changes necessary in what they actually do: for example, in curriculum content, teaching styles, organisation of teaching groups, deployment of resources, setting specific targets to recognise distinct needs and review policies for coherence and consistency. Effective monitoring and evaluation systems, including Ofsted, must ensure that all children do get 'a fair deal'. Inclusion will entail a shift in power, a review and redistribution of resources and a culture change that reconnects the disconnected, embracing distinct groups within a holistic educational philosophy for equity and achievement.

REFERENCES

Ahmad, P., Oxley McCann, A. and Plackett, C. (1997) 'Home-school liaison in multicultural schools in Cleveland', in J. Bastiani (ed.) *Home-school Work in Multicultural Settings.* London: David Fulton.

Arnot, M., David, M. and Weiner, G. (1999) *Closing the Gender Gap: Post-war Education and Social Change.* Cambridge: Policy Press.

Barrs, M. and Pidgeon, S. (1998) *Boys and Reading.* London: CLPE.

Bleach, K. (1998) *Raising Boys' Achievement in Schools.* Stoke-on-Trent: Trentham Books.

Booth, T., Ainscow, M., Black-Hawkins, K., Vaughan, M. and Shaw, L. (2000) *Index for Inclusion: Developing Learning and Participation in Schools.* Bristol: Centre for Studies on Inclusive Education (CSIE).

Brodie, I (2000) 'Children's homes and school exclusion: Redefining the problem', *Support for Learning,* 15 (1) 25–9.

Byers, R. (1999) 'The National Literacy Strategy and pupils with special educational needs', *British Journal of Special Education,* 26 (1) 8–11.

Cline, T. (1998) 'The assessment of special educational needs for bilingual children', *British Journal of Special Education,* 25 (4) 159–61.

Coard, B. (1971) *How the West Indian Child is Made Educationally Subnormal in the British School System.* London: Beacon Books (reprinted 1991, London: Karia Press).

Commission for Racial Equality (2000) *Learning for All: Standards for Racial Equality in Schools.* London: CRE.

Cooper, P., Upton, G. and Smith, C. (1991) 'Ethnic minority and gender distribution among staff and pupils in facilities for pupils with emotional and behavioural difficulties in England and Wales', *British Journal of Sociology of Education,* 12 (1) 77–94.

Corbett, J. (2001a) 'Teaching approaches which support inclusive education: a connective pedagogy', *British Journal of Special Education,* 28 (2) 55–9.

Corbett, J. (2001b) 'Is equity compatible with entitlement? Balancing inclusive values and deserving needs', *Support for Learning,* 16 (3) 117–21.

Daniels, H., Creese, A., Hey, V., Leonard, D. and Smith, M. (2001) 'Gender and learning; equity, equality and pedagogy', *Support for Learning,* 16 (3) 112–16.

Daniels, H., Hey, V., Leonard, D. and Smith, M. (1996) Equal to the challenge?, *Special!* Autumn, 15–16.

Daniels, H., Hey, V., Leonard, D. and Smith, M. (1999) 'Issues of equity in special needs education from a gender perspective', *British Journal of Special Education,* 26 (4) 189–95.

Daniels, H., Visser, J., Cole, T. and Reybekill, N. (1999) *Emotional and Behavioural Difficulties in Mainstream Schools.* Research Report No. 90. London: DfEE.

Department for Education and Employment (DfEE) (1997) *Excellence for all Children:*

Meeting Special Educational Needs. London: The Stationery Office.

Department for Education and Employment (DfEE) (1998) *Meeting Special Educational Needs: a Programme of Action.* London: The Stationery Office.

Department for Education and Employment (DfEE) (1999) *Social Inclusion: Pupil Support (Circular 10/99).* London: DfEE.

Department for Education and Employment (DfEE) and Qualifications and Curriculum Authority (QCA) (1999) *The National Curriculum Handbooks for Primary/Secondary Teachers in England.* London: DfEE/QCA.

Department for Education and Employment (DfEE) (2000) *Statistics in Education: Permanent Exclusions from Maintained Schools in England* (Issue 10/00). London: The Stationery Office.

Department for Education and Employment (DfEE) (2001) *Schools: Building on Success: Raising Standards, Promoting Diversity, Achieving Results.* (Cm 5050). London: DfEE.

Department for Education and Skills (DfES) (2001) *Special Educational Needs: Code of Practice.* London: DfES.

Desforges, M. (1995) 'Assessment of special educational needs in bilingual pupils: changing practice?', *School Psychology International,* 16, 15–17.

Diniz, F. A. (1999) 'Race and special educational needs in the 1990s', *British Journal of Special Education,* 26 (4) 213–17.

Dyson, A. (1997) 'Social and educational disadvantage', *British Journal of Special Education,* 24 (4) 152–7.

Dyson, A. (2001) 'Special needs education as the way to equity: an alternative approach', *Support for Learning,* 16 (3) 105–11.

Epstein, D., Elwood, J., Hey, V. and Maw, J. (1998) *Failing Boys? Issues in Gender and Achievement.* Buckingham: Open University Press.

Fisher, H. (2001) 'Achieving the best: gender and the Literacy Hour', *British Journal of Special Education,* 28 (1) 30–4.

Frater, G. (2000) *Securing Boys' Literacy.* London: The Basic Skills Agency.

Gerschel, L. (1998) 'Equal opportunities and special educational needs: equity and inclusion', in C. Tilstone, L. Florian and R. Rose (eds.) *Promoting Inclusive Practice.* London: Routledge.

Gillborn, D. (2001) 'Raising standards or rationalising education? Racism and social justice in policy and practice', *Support for Learning,* 16 (3) 105–11.

Gillborn, D. and Mirza, H.S. (2000) *Educational Inequality: Mapping Race, Class and Gender (a Synthesis of Research Evidence.* HMI 232). London: Ofsted.

Green, L. (1993) 'Possible gender bias within teachers' perceptions of pupils with special needs', *Support for Learning,* 8 (2) 78–80.

Gross, J. (1996) 'The weight of the evidence: Parental advocacy and resource allocation to children with statements of special educational need', *Support for Learning,* 11 (1) 3–8.

Henry, J. (2001a) 'Boy-friendly tests unfair say heads', *Times Educational Supplement,* 25/5/2001, p.3.

Henry, J. (2001b) 'Help for the boys helps the girls', *Times Educational Supplement,* 1/6/2001, p.5.

Hill, J (1994) 'The paradox of gender: Sex stereotyping within statementing procedures', *British Educational Research Journal,* 20 (3) 345–55.

Holland, V. (1998) 'Underachieving boys; problems and solutions', *Support for Learning,* 13 (4) 174–8.

Klein, R. (1999) *Defying Disaffection: How Schools are Winning the Hearts and Minds of Reluctant Students.* Stoke-on-Trent: Trentham Books.

Mac an Ghaill, M. (1994) *The Making of Men: Masculinities, Sexualities and Schooling.* Buckingham: Open University Press.

Macpherson of Cluny, Sir William (1999) *The Stephen Lawrence Inquiry (The Macpherson Report, CM 4262-1)*. London: The Stationery Office.

Male, D. (2000) 'Who goes to MLD schools?', *British Journal of Special Education*, 23 (1) 35–41.

McNamara, S. and Moreton, G. (1995) *Changing Behaviour: Teaching Children with Emotional and Behavioural Difficulties in Primary and Secondary Classrooms.* London: David Fulton.

Millard, E. (1997) *Differently Literate: Boys, Girls and the Schooling of Literacy.* London: Falmer Press.

Mittler, P. (1999) 'Equal Opportunities – for whom?', *British Journal of Special Education*, 26 (1) 3–7.

Mittler, P. (2000) *Working Towards Inclusive Education: Social Contexts.* London: David Fulton Publishers.

Mortimore, P., Sammons, P., Stoll, L., Lewis, D. and Ecob, R. (1988) *School Matters: the Junior School Years.* London: Open Books.

Newham LEA (2001) *Girls' Voices: Are they on the Agenda?* London: London Borough of Newham (The Girls' Project, Tunmarsh Centre, Tunmarsh Lane, E13 9NB).

Noble C. and Bradford, W. (2000) *Getting it Right for Boys ... and Girls.* London: Routledge.

O'Brien, T. (1998) 'The Millenium Curriculum: Confronting the Issues and Proposing Solutions', *Support for Learning*, 13 (4) 147–52.

Office for Standards in Education (Ofsted) (1993) *Boys and English.* London: Ofsted.

Office for Standards in Education (Ofsted) (2000a) *Evaluating Educational Inclusion: Guidance for Inspectors and Schools* (HMI 235). London: Ofsted.

Office for Standards in Education (Ofsted) (2000b) *The National Literacy Strategy in Special Schools 1998–2000* (HMI 238). London: Ofsted.

Office for Standards in Education (Ofsted) (2001) *The National Numeracy Strategy in Special Schools: an Evaluation of the First Year* (HMI 267). London: Ofsted.

Ollerton, M. (2001) 'Inclusion and entitlement, equality of opportunity and quality of curriculum provision', *Support for Learning*, 16 (1) 35–40.

Osler, A. (1997) *Exclusion from School and Racial Equality: Research Report.* London: Commission for Racial Equality.

Osler, A., Watling, R., Busher, H., Cole, T. and White, A. (2001) *Reasons for Exclusion (Research Report 244).* London: DfEE.

Pickering, J. (1997) *Raising Boys' Achievement.* Stafford: Network Educational Press.

Qualifications and Curriculum Authority (QCA) (1998) *Can Do Better: Raising Boys' Attainment in English.* London: QCA.

Qualifications and Curriculum Authority (QCA) and DfEE (2001) *Planning Teaching amd Assessing the Curriculum for Pupils with Learning Difficulties.* London: QCA.

Rivers, I. (2000) 'Social exclusion, absenteeism and sexual minority youth', *Support for Learning*, 15 (1) 13–18.

Rundell, S. (2001) 'How to improve his stories', *Times Educational Supplement*, 1/6/2001, p.28.

Scott, L. (2001) 'Adding drama! Sex and relationships for children with learning difficulties', *Sex Education Matters*, 24, Spring 2001, pp.4–5.

Sewell, T. (1997) *Black Masculinities and Schooling: How Black Boys Survive Modern Schooling.* Stoke-on-Trent: Trentham Books.

Shah, R. (1995) *The Silent Minority: Children with Disability in Asian Families* (Revised edition). London: National Children's Bureau.

Stewart, D. and Ray, C. (1001) Ensuring entitlement: sex and relationships education for disabled children. Forum fact sheet from Sex Education Forum and Council for Disabled Children. London: National Children's Bureau.

Tierney, T. and Dowd, R. (2000) 'The use of social skills groups to support girls with emotional difficulties in secondary schools', *Support for Learning*, 15 (2) 82–5.

Torrance, D.A. (2000) 'Qualitative studies into bullying within special schools', *British Journal of Special Education*, 27 (1) 16–21.

Troyna, B. and Siraj-Blatchford, I. (1993) 'Providing support or denying access? The experience of students designated as ESL or SN in a multi-cultural school', *Educational Review*, 45 (1) 3–11.

Vardill, R (1996) 'Imbalance in the numbers of boys and girls identified for referral to educational psychologists: Some issues', *Support for Learning*, 11 (3) 123–9.

Warner, R. (1999) 'The views of Bangladeshi parents on the special school attended by their young children with severe learning difficulties', *British Journal of Special Education*, 26 (4) 218–23.

Wilson, G. (2000) 'The effects of season of birth, sex, cognitive abilities on the assessment of special educational needs', *Educational Psychology*, 20 (2) 153–66.

Wright, C., Weekes, D. and McGlaughlin, A. (2000) *'Race', Gender and Exclusion from School*. London: Falmer Press.

Chapter 5

Policies for positive behaviour management

Ted Cole

In this chapter Ted Cole considers positive behaviour management from the perspective of the political, theoretical and
research agenda. He emphasises the importance of both
accepting and valuing pupils who challenge the system, and of
developing whole-school, positive behavioural policies which
help to build up staff confidence in managing difficult behaviour. Although there is an emphasis on those pupils who are
considered to have emotional and behavioural difficulties, his
examples demonstrate essential principles in action for work
with a range of pupils with special educational needs.

Does the advance of inclusion (Thomas, Walker and Webb, 1998; Tilstone,
Florian and Rose, 1998) hold good for pupils labelled as being disruptive or
having emotional and behavioural difficulties (EBD)? Clark, Dyson, Millward
and Robson (1999) noted intractable problems of behaviour even in the most
inclusive of settings. Research has underlined the severity of the management
problems posed by some pupils with learning and behavioural difficulties, the
stress caused to peers and staff, and the extensive demands on senior management time. Difficulties continue despite differentiated and appropriate
teaching and proficient behaviour management, but Ofsted reports indicate
that some schools in disadvantaged areas are more successful in managing
difficult behaviour than some in more affluent areas. What are the characteristics of successful schools and what policies do they operate to minimise the
segregation of pupils with learning and emotional and behavioural difficulties?

DEFINITIONS AND PARAMETERS

The government definition of EBD is given in Circular 9/94 (DfE, 1994b):

> Children with EBD are on a continuum. Their problems are clearer and
> greater than sporadic naughtiness or moodiness and yet not so great as to
> be classed as mental illness. (p.4)

Their differences range from 'social maladaptation to abnormal emotional stresses' (p.7); 'are persistent and constitute learning difficulties' (p.7), and children with EBD are seen as having problems in relationships. Cole (1998) noted that behaviour difficulties are usually accompanied by underachievement in class and sometimes by pronounced learning difficulties.

These pupils' difficulties can stem from both within- (sometimes including the biological or genetic) and without-child factors usually in interaction with each other and with a complicated ecosystem involving peers, family and neighbourhood influences (Cooper, Smith and Upton, 1994). In this chapter, 'pupils with EBD' is used not only for students with statements for EBD (and those on the Code of Practice Stages for learning difficulties associated with behaviour) but also for the far greater number of pupils termed 'disruptive' or 'having attention deficit disorder' (ADHD) or said to 'have mental health difficulties'. The epidemiology depends not only on local interpretations of national guidance but also on different professions' contrasting perspectives and traditions. The writers of one local education authority's behaviour support plan noted: 'The lively youngster in one setting can be deemed a major problem in another' (Cole, Daniels and Visser, 1999, p.22). Government statistics and LEA behaviour support plans appear to indicate that the number of pupils with significant EBD or those deemed 'seriously disruptive' amounts to 5% of the national school population (Cole et al., 1999).

CREATING AND MAINTAINING AN INCLUSIVE SCHOOL ETHOS

A prerequisite for effective mainstream policies for pupils with EBD and learning difficulties is the creation and maintenance of an appropriate inclusive school ethos. Daniels, Visser, Cole and de Reybekill (1998) noted that some schools are fortunate in having a history of 'looking after' at risk pupils, of forging close community links and working towards successful inclusion. In contrast, in schools where a suitable balance between stressing the academic and the pastoral has never been achieved (Galloway, 1990; Power, 1996), initiatives are necessary to bring about fundamental changes in attitudes and policies. In other schools, the quasi-market reforms of the 1980s and 1990s may have weakened their capacity for coping with pupils who challenge the 'standards' and published league table agendas (Parsons, 1999; McLaughlin and Rouse, 2000; Hallam and Castle, 2001).

In all schools, the quality, style and attitudes of leadership (in particular those of the head teachers) are crucial to creating and maintaining an inclusive ethos. One head stated, 'We are a comprehensive school', before stressing his duty to all children in his community, including those with learning and behavioural difficulties. In schools coping well with behavioural issues, statements such as this were an articulation of deeply held beliefs, and senior staff, imbued with inclusive values, possessed the skill and motivation to influence the attitudes and actions of their sometimes more-doubting colleagues. Many teachers and learning support assistants (LSAs) have become receptive to senior staff initiatives to engender positive behaviour management. Conversely, head teachers and senior staff are receptive to, and supportive of, teacher ideas and initiatives. There is evidence of a desire to experiment with reward systems and a common reluctance to reject pupils, for example, through the frequent use of fixed-term and permanent exclusions. Daniels et al. (1998a) noted that the direction, coherence and cohesiveness in these schools was generated by the leadership, but made possible by staff who were committed and caring towards their less gifted and more challenging pupils.

Research indicates that, when not in direct contact with children, staff spend time talking to colleagues about work-related topics or student needs to support each other; to provoke reflection and self-analysis; to explore new ideas and to help colleagues to learn new skills (Hopkins, 1997). As well as being 'talking' schools, they are 'learning' schools using the 'do-review-learn-apply' planning and practice cycle in most aspects of school life (Dennison and Kirk, 1990) including behaviour management. Practitioners were engaged in an on-going re-evaluation of their work through formal development days, training and advice from LEA support services or through staff working groups. Lessons learnt led to adjusted practice (Daniels et al., 1998) and Cole, Visser and Daniels (2000) provide further evidence of 'learning' schools. Teachers and learning support assistants (LSAs) are then willing to use their school's Behaviour Co-ordinators (BCos), details of whose roles are given below, to observe and discuss their classroom performance and to review school systems.

Behavioural difficulties are usually linked to underachievement and to learning difficulties (Daniels et al., 1998; Hallam and Castle, 1999; Cole and Visser, 2000). Missed schooling or social and emotional upsets are likely to be combined to make young people acutely aware of their recurrent failure in front of their peers. Their reaction is commonly 'fight' or 'flight', and help needs to be channelled diplomatically to address their learning difficulties. Close working between pastoral, subject and learning support departments is required although, too often, it seems that SENCos (Special Educational Needs Co-ordinators), heads of department and heads of year act separately, to the detriment of individuals and groups and ultimately to the ethos and effectiveness of the school. It is a feature of the 'good practice' schools in Daniels et al. (1998) that such divisions did not exist or at least that senior management was actively trying to bring the activities of pastoral and SEN staff closer together. An example was the placing of an assistant SENCo in each subject department in order to provide early specialist intervention for 'at risk' pupils and 'front-line' advice to subject specialists in differentiation techniques or behaviour management. In another school, in a staff meeting, the deputy head confessed to having just experienced a particularly difficult lesson with a new Year 9 pupil. The SENCo offered to see the young person immediately to establish what, if any, learning difficulties he had. This was their standard practice (Daniels et al., 1998).

The research underlines a predictable but crucial factor identified in the literature on behavioural difficulties (Redl, 1966; Cooper, 1993): schools coping well with 'difficult' children are characterised by having many talented and effective staff who are able to form helpful relationships with challenging young people. Cole, Visser and Upton (1998) listed the characteristics, as perceived by teacher respondents to a national survey, of successful teachers with pupils with EBD. They did not need to be masters of psychoanalysis or of therapies or different from good, committed mainstream staff. They should be well-organised, consistent, humorous, calm, enthusiastic; skilful in delivering their specialist subjects; set clear boundaries; flexible; understand 'behaviour' causation (Cole, 1998) and be empathetic to the young people. Talking to children with EBD elicited a similar view: they respect teachers who set firm boundaries, are skilful classroom managers and deliverers of their subject. More, however, is needed: a Year 10 girl with a statement for EBD described good staff as:

> ... teachers who understand you and take an interest in you. After you have finished your work they ask you how you are. They socialise. You get to like them.
>
> Daniels et al., 1998, p.83

A Year 10 boy who had recently 'come off' a statement for EBD compared good and bad teachers:

> They [the good] are polite and treat you with respect. If a teacher ... is in a foul mood or shouting at you, you do the same back.
>
> Daniels et al., 1998, p.83

A group of young people at a small rural secondary school commented:

> Staff are seen as friends and helpers to children and each other. The caring ethos has been absorbed by generations of children and teachers. Children show concern for other pupils and will say if another child is having a bad day and needs special attention or help.
>
> Daniels et al., 1998, p.20

For a school to minimise feelings of disaffection and resulting challenging behaviour, form tutors have to *embrace* and not *resist* their pastoral role as mentors and supporters (Cole and Visser, 2000; Munn, Lloyd and Cullen, 2000). In primary schools, there is more likely to be a tradition of caring and talking and of creating inclusive cultures in which all pupils and their families feel welcome. The challenge is clearly greater in large secondary schools, particularly those having catchment areas with a history of resistance to schooling and less local faith in teachers. Cultures can, however, be changed: pastoral staff and subject specialists can alter practice until they are perceived by pupils more as *pastors* than agents of punishment.

WHOLE-SCHOOL BEHAVIOUR POLICY

Relevant and 'lived' comprehensive whole-school behaviour policies help to minimise EBD (DES, 1989; Daniels et al., 1998). Such policies should:

- be succinct but detailed and in written form;
- used as a vehicle for promoting desired staff practice;
- contain school pro formas;
- give explanatory notes as well as flow-charts for referrals;
- make the links explicit between pastoral, subject and special needs departments;
- be seen as a resource to be consulted by teachers in times of need;
- be open, consultative and ongoing if reflection and self-evaluation amongst staff is to be promoted and the stakeholders are to feel 'ownership' of the process.

There can be teacher resistance to the regular use of such policies (Daniels et al., 1998) and, where this happens, policy documents need to be used as the basis for ongoing staff development, referred to by senior staff periodically as particular issues arise throughout each school year and not allowed to gather dust at the back of teachers' cupboards. All school staff (including administration and caretaking staff) should be involved (see Box 1). In the long term, *imposed* policies tend to be subverted, circumvented or ignored.

Box 1: Creating and maintaining a whole-school behaviour policy in a six-teacher primary school

Despite a positive Ofsted report that praised the behaviour of pupils and might have prompted the school to rest on its laurels, it was felt beneficial to review the behaviour policy. Pupils, full-time teachers, part-time teachers, LSAs, midday supervisors, governors and parents were all actively involved in a review of existing policy over a period of months. This happened in discussions in class, in formal meetings and in informal discussions in breaks and after school. A revised draft policy was widely circulated before final approval by the school governors. The result was a policy owned by all stakeholders. Research in the school suggested that the consistency and cohesion of the staff in the operation of this policy contributed to the inclusion of children on the SEN register for behavioural reasons.

Daniels et al., 1998

Useful advice on the content of behaviour policies has been given by DES (1989), Ofsted (1993), DfE (1994a) and Clarke and Murray (1996). Box 2 shows the contents of an exemplary policy observed in a large secondary school (Daniels et al., 1998).

Box 2: The content of a whole-school behaviour policy

A whole-school behaviour policy should describe:

(a)   the mission statement and the general aims of the school;
(b)   the rights and responsibilities of staff, pupils and parents;
(c)   the school's Code of Conduct/rules;
(d)   approaches to the encouragment of good behaviour;
(e)   routines and staff responsibilities;
(f)   'Cause for Concern', 'Incident Forms' and other pro-forma devised with the help of the school psychologist;
(g)   sanction and reward systems;
(h)   pastoral support systems;
(i)   links to other school policies;
(j)   advice on working with parents.

The consistent application of agreed policies is crucial as emotional and behavioural difficulties are exacerbated by uncertain and unpredictable policy application. In Daniels et al. (1998), senior staff worked hard to ensure that all staff applied agreed policies thoroughly in, for example, the use of:

• 'positive behaviour' credit and certificate systems;
• systems for reporting worrying or unacceptable behaviour;
• records of the interventions used;
• behaviour report and monitoring forms;
• supervision rosters for break times ;
• rules for movement of pupils through buildings;
• attendance registers, their maintenance and the follow up of absentees.

The need for some sanctions was seen in all schools, the emphasis of which was on the reinforcement of desired behaviours and it was evident that staff should ensure that they model the values and attitudes they wish to see permeating their own communities.

PROFICIENT CLASSROOM MANAGEMENT

Positive behaviour policies should encourage teachers to review their own practice and to identify their sometimes unwitting part in creating challenging behaviour. In addition, senior managers should be proactive in creating school climates in which reviews of practice are embedded and in which skilled help can easily be sought, without feelings of failure or blame, to tackle identified weaknesses.

Classrooms in EBD schools which bring together groups of pupils that have been highly disruptive in mainstream settings are not infrequently quiet, purposeful environments with little outward sign of disturbance (Laslett, 1977; Cole et al., 1998). Similarly, in mainstream settings, some pupils with EBD (including some said to have ADHD and who are not taking psycho-stimulants such as 'Ritalin') behave well for some teachers, but are severely disruptive for others. Clearly, disruptive behaviour is often situation-specific, relating in part to how the adults in school settings act. Jordan (1974) (cited in Smith and Laslett, 1993) identified 'deviance-provocative' and 'deviance-insulative' teachers. Identifying and 'where possible' rectifying teacher shortcomings is an aspect of school life to which more time and resources should be devoted as pupils with EBD tend to be the first to respond with disruptive behaviour to inappropriate or unskilled teaching. These children often lack patience, become easily frustrated, have short attention spans and low anger thresholds, give up on tasks and are frightened of new work. Unless they are taught skilfully, these factors will readily come into play, particularly if the style of teaching exacerbates the low self-esteem of many pupils with EBD and 'shows them up' in front of their peers.

Conversely, they can respond well to proficient teaching (Ofsted, 1999) and in Daniels et al. (1998) teachers were observed successfully controlling and motivating pupils with EBD. These teachers were confident presenters of their subject and masters of basic classroom craft, clearly possessing Kounin's (1970) 'withitness'! They were skilled in the use of eye-contact for engaging interest or of 'the look' to express disapproval; they used varying tone of voice and an appropriate choice of language, sometimes blended with humour to defuse situations or to stop minor disruptions. They anticipated and avoided trouble through diversionary tactics or low-level interventions that did not provoke pupil resentment. They tended not to be desk-bound but moved around the room as appropriate, thereby exercising 'proximity control' (Redl and Wineman, 1952). Their craft contrasted with the limited repertoires of less effective teachers who were clearly in need of training and development as DfEE (1997) stressed.

One structured approach to practical on-site teacher development is Birmingham LEA's 'Framework for Intervention' (FFI) scheme (City of Birmingham Education Department, 1998; Daniels and Williams, 2000; Cole et al, 2000). At the heart of FFI are LEA advisory teachers and on-site

Behaviour Co-ordinators (BCos), who urged class teachers first to look at their own basic practice before searching for an 'explanation' of a child's perceived misbehaviour 'within the child'. Disruptive behaviour can too readily be seen as the outward manifestation of inner disturbance or of a medical condition, such as wrongly diagnosed ADHD (Elliott and Place, 1998; Baldwin, 2000). Making such a diagnosis should be resisted, at least until after the teacher, supported by the BCo, has checked the key elements of the total *behavioural environment* including the teacher's own contribution (see Box 3).

Box 3: Checking the behavioural environment

1) How is the 'difficult' child influenced
   - by the school's rules/expectations?
   - by what happened in a previous lesson or break time?
   - by the rest of the class?
2) How does the class enter the classroom before the start of the lesson?
3) Are the seating arrangements suitable for what I am teaching?
4) Are the children grouped in the most appropriate way?
5) Are the necessary materials and equipment readily accessible to the pupils?
6) Is heating, lighting and ventilation suitable?
7) Am I giving clear instructions in an audible and 'non-grating' voice?
8) Am I teaching at an appropriate level: not too hard, not too easy?
9) Am I modelling the suitable use of polite language?
10) Am I providing variety and pace in my lessons?

Where FFI is well established, both newly qualified and experienced teachers have found it useful to ask themselves the questions posed in Box 3 while completing a detailed Behavioural Environmental Checklist (BEC) about the impact of wider school life upon this class, as well as the teacher's own practice. Often the BCos are asked to observe the lessons. A Behavioural Environment Plan (BEP) is then constructed, not to target the individual child but rather the teacher's management of the whole problematic class, and events outside the classroom that may be influencing difficulties within it. Completing BECs and BEPs, supported by the BCo, are described as Level One interventions. Some evidence shows that these can obviate the need to develop interventions targeted at individual pupils, which initially cause concern to the teacher (Cole et al., 2000). If the Level One intervention proves unsuccessful, the focus can then turn to the individual child and Level Two approaches. For example, the construction of individual behaviour plans, peer or mentor support schemes, interventions from specialist staff or anger management training. The provision of time and the creation of structures for BCos (and in large schools, Assistant BCos) to operate effectively requires resources and at least medium-term LEA support. The Birmingham system has relied on time-limited government grants, but the indications are that this is a fruitful approach worthy of imitation and perhaps meriting the employment of some of the funding made available to tackle social exclusion under, for example, Pupil Retention Grants (DfEE, 1999).

Other research work (Hallam and Castle, 1999; Cole and Visser, 2000) suggests the potential of advisory teachers in developing classroom practice. Staff self-support and development groups run along the lines of Teacher Support Teams (Creese, Daniels and Norwich, 1997) can also be invaluable.

CURRICULAR FACTORS

An effective teacher can make almost any subject interesting to pupils with EBD. Certainly Shakespeare (tales of lust, excitement and violence?) does not have to be an obstacle and can be brought alive by imaginative teachers. Likewise, religious education, music and modern foreign languages, viewed by senior staff of the nation's EBD schools as the most difficult subjects to deliver *circa* 1996/7, ceased to be a problem when skilled specialist practitioners sympathetic to the problems of pupils with emotional and learning difficulties were employed in some schools (Cole et al., 1998). However, teachers who perhaps are not 'born to the profession' or are required to teach outside their subject specialism predictably find behaviour management and student motivation easier when they are allowed flexibility of approach, sometimes outside a statutory framework. Where possible that which is taught and the manner of teaching should play to their students' areas of relative strength, as well as their interests outside the classroom (particularly for Years 9 through to 11). Schools should explore and develop policies that take these factors into account without sacrificing rigour or challenge or becoming patronising to their students.

Somewhat surprisingly, the notion of a general National Curriculum was not seen as an obstacle to effective practice with pupils with emotional and learning difficulties. Instead, senior staff tended to recognise that it had increased the range and quality of education offered in special and mainstream schools (Cole et al., 1998). Aspects of different subjects (for example, creative writing in English or algebra in Mathematics), however, did evoke criticism from some mainstream teachers. In Cole et al. (1998) and Daniels et al. (1998) there was support for recent reductions in the number of subjects that had to be taught and for the Green Paper's (DfEE, 1997) and Programme of Action's (DfEE, 1998) encouragement of more vocational and practical subjects and links with colleges of further education for pupils in Key Stage 4. Such a policy is sensible, subject to the important proviso that it is not used as an excuse for offering an undemanding, alternative curriculum not linked to national accreditation. Our data suggests many successful placements of KS4 pupils in well-organised FE colleges, sometimes leading to GNVQs and directly paving the way to lasting employment. A Year 10 girl with EBD described her enjoyment of a GNVQ beauty 'taster course' at the local FE college (Daniels et al., 1998)

The head teacher of a school that had retained a grammar school image and was noted for good examination results, argued for curricula that played to many pupils' 'natural propensities' for the practical and the verbal rather than the abstract and the written (Daniels et al., 1998). There is not unanimity on this argument, however, and the head teacher of a large inner-city comprehensive thought he had 'turned round' his school by ridding it of its vocational, 'boys' secondary modern approach'. At this school the emphasis on academic entitlement for all students had increased, and teacher expectations of the capabilities of their pupils risen. Clearly an appropriate balance has to be struck between the academic and the vocational and the written and the verbal, but with an emphasis on flexibility and responsiveness to individual pupil capabilities and, perhaps, local circumstances. Where a balance is managed in relation to curriculum delivery, there can be a marked reduction in behavioural difficulties.

MANAGING THE BEHAVIOUR OF INDIVIDUAL PUPILS

Strategies adopted in 'good practice' schools to target the specific challenges presented by individual pupils were refinements of 'normal' behaviour systems and approaches used across their schools (Daniels et al., 1998) for pupils without notable EBD. Whenever possible, strategies were instigated against a backdrop of a policy of early identification and intervention and an additional key factor is the ability of back-up staff to offer a swift 'catcher' and support system when a class teacher needs to ask a pupil to leave the class. Behaviour management is unlikely to be successful if it is not part of a wider set of supportive relationships between pupils and key staff.

Behaviourist-learning approaches are useful. Commonly they involve careful observation and tallying of behaviours on frequency charts, and specific target setting linked to clearly defined reinforcements. Reward systems can range from points or merit certificates through lunchtime use of computers to small sums of money or vouchers for shops, the choice being made in negotiation with the pupil (Daniels et al., 1998a). Schools can also offer a mixture of extrinsic rewards and verbal reinforcement (adult approval and praise) sometimes given at weekly award assemblies. School policies should stress the dictum 'Catch Them Being Good' (Madsen et al. cited in Cole et al., 1998) and outline the rewards on offer, as well as stressing the principles sketched in Box 4.

Box 4: Reward principles

- *Rewards have to be earned.* Pupils will not respect rewards perceived as unearned, nor respect staff who give them too freely. Rewards can become appeasement.
- *Rewards must relate to clear, agreed targets.* Targets should be specific, limited in scope to maintain a child's focus, realistic, negotiated and agreed as worthwhile by the child. Global injunctions on a child's Behaviour Plan or Report Card 'to behave' or 'be good' are of very limited use.
- *Rewards must be given at appropriate time intervals.* Large rewards offered half-termly or weekly may not work as well as small rewards offered daily or twice daily or after the attainment of targets for a particularly problematic lesson with a particular teacher. Flexible time scales offer more chances for 'forgiveness' of the pupil.
- *Praise should be delivered appropriately.* Praise can take the form of lavish words. Some pupils, however, may be embarrassed by public praise (Hanko, 1994; Rogers, 1994), but will respond to non-verbal communication (for example, a 'thumbs up' or nod of the head). Praise might best be offered away from a student's peer group (for example, in a head of year's office).
- *Rewards should come from a 'significant other'.* Rewards or sanctions given by teachers perceived as hostile or indifferent are likely to be ineffective (Daniels et al., 1998).

Pupils with emotional and learning difficulties can usually accept sanctions perceived by them as fair, unless they have become substantially alienated from the school community and have very poor relationships with most staff. Sanction systems must avoid being mechanistic and punitive, thereby failing to achieve the necessary balance between overall fairness and allowing for individual capacity and difference. Rigidity of application can be a danger for simplistic interpretations of, for example, *assertive discipline* (Canter, 1990; Daniels et al., 1998). Sanction systems must be accompanied by regular monitoring, which does not need to be punitive, by staff who are 'significant others'. A head teacher was observed in a secondary school sitting next to a child at school dinner to chat to him informally as well as to check with him the entries on his lesson report card (Daniels et al., 1998), the 'message' being that it was the pupil's bad behaviour alone that had been criticised.

Beyond the application of a school's formal behaviour systems, school policies must create opportunities for talking and listening to 'at risk' young people. Staff interviewed as part of Daniels et al. (1998) frequently referred to the difficult home circumstances and the emotional turmoil of most of the pupils considered to have EBD. They tended to be knowledgeable and sympathetic to these wider problems, had gained their understanding through contact with the child's family or carers or through ongoing contacts in school with the children themselves. Time had been found for these children, and time is essential for successful work with children with EBD whatever the setting. Positive relationships had been nurtured by regular communication between teachers, support and (sometimes) administrative staff and the vulnerable and disruptive and staff made a point of stopping for a brief chat with pupils with EBD in the corridors, or before or after 'problem' lessons. These frequent 'naturalistic' interactions, part of sharing the same 'life-space' (Cole et al., 1998), are used to reassure and to remind pupils with EBD that they are valued and that they remain part of the school community despite the challenging behaviour they often present.

When difficult problems do occur, it is essential that assistance for the class teacher is on hand immediately from experienced staff, as it is vital that class teachers do not feel alone, without recourse to help, in extreme situations and that other pupils do not experience excessive disruption and inappropriate behaviour. Cole et al. (1998) and Daniels et al. (1998) found such 'catcher systems' to be widely valued. Their role was to remove and counsel seriously disruptive pupils, to calm down others in the aftermath of tantrums or fights, and it was found that 'the calm after the storm' of serious classroom or break time incidents could be used to provide 'emotional first aid' (Redl, 1966) to an upset pupil with serious emotional difficulties. Children can be most open to sharing confidences and listening to the opinions of valued staff when the immediate storm of an emotional outburst has subsided (Redl and Wineman, 1952).

Given the central part played by LSAs in enabling inclusion, a sensitive approach to offering learning support is necessary and some pupils, usually those with moderate learning and behavioural difficulties, seem to be at ease with the presence of an LSA beside them. These pupils in secondary schools may well have grown used to such an arrangement in their primary schools and were reported to be heavily reliant upon, and to expect and to enjoy the presence of, their LSA (Daniels et al., 1998). In contrast other pupils disliked LSA support as they interpreted it as a highly visible sign of their difficulties, which 'showed them up' in front of their peers. Schools need policies that are understood and followed in relation to learning support (Thomas et al., 1998; Lorenz, 1998; Lacey, 2001).

Box 5: Offering classroom support sensitively

An underachieving Year 10 pupil, formerly on an EBD statement, appreciated:

- a teacher who managed to brief the pupil about lesson content ahead of class;
- other staff who would wait until the other pupils were engaged in quiet writing before discreetly moving to his table to offer support.

An LSA described her strategy: she made a point of sitting close to a girl who liked her in close proximity. For another child, the LSA would bide her time and wait until the teacher was moving round a room offering support to other children so that it was not unusual or stigmatising for her to go over and offer to be a scribe for the child who was uneasy about her presence (Daniels et al., 1998).

Valuable support can also be offered by staff or volunteers not directly employed by the school. Girls sometimes found it useful to talk to the school nurse and both boys and girls to peripatetic EBD teachers or to youth workers (Daniels et al., 1998; Cole and Visser, 2000). At one school, Bengali children received counselling from a Bengali EWO (Education Welfare Officer). 'At risk' black pupils are disproportionately included in the exclusion figures (Osler, 1997; Osler, Watling, Busher, Cole and White, 2001) and often appreciate support from black staff. The value of adult mentors is increasingly being recognised, particularly where the mentor shares the same ethnic heritage (DfEE, 1999; Cole and Visser, 2000).

Flexible curricular organisation and timetabling is also important. Full inclusion with their regular class for every lesson was judged to be against some children's medium- and long-term interests. Given the degree of their underachievement and/or disruption in some lessons, or unsatisfactory relationship with particular teachers, some withdrawal was judged wise (Daniels et al.1998). Ideally, children's timetables should reflect their individual needs and capabilities. In practice, a compromise is sometimes needed to give overwrought staff and the pupils' peers respite from some children's extreme behaviours.

Finally, it is advisable to consider the physical environment as a prop to the management of a few pupils' more extreme behaviour. A comfortable *physical and private space* (a room or an area) can be a haven or sanctuary for a few pupils when in throes of a damaging behavioural outburst. It can be part of children's individual behaviour plans, understood by the subject teachers, as an escape from the classroom or playground when:

- they are having difficulty in controlling their anger or emotions;
- they feel the need for 'time out' from peers who are goading them;
- they need to talk with specialist staff;
- a subject teacher decides that the child's behaviour has become too disruptive.

Pupils can return from this sanctuary to rejoin their usual groups when in a calmer mood.

CONCLUSION

The policies and practices described above will help children and staff, but it is recognised that no easy prescriptions can be offered for schools serving neighbourhoods where there are acute social problems and an entrenched culture of disaffection and dissatisfaction with education. Schools can, and often do, make a difference (Mortimore, Sammons, Stoll and Ecob, 1988) but it was discouraging to hear a teacher say of a school serving a disadvantaged community, 'You have to like the children, like the work and like being here' (Daniels et al., 1998, p.53), clearly implying that some staff in this school, probably through tiredness and chronic disappointments, did not. Similarly worrying was the comment, 'You can talk to staff here' by a Year 10 pupil (Daniels et al., 1998, p.84). Sadly, this was a novel experience for him and contrasted with his previous schools from which he had been excluded. Inclusion can only advance when sufficient skilled and committed staff win the respect and liking of pupils and create school communities of which they want to be a part. Data repeatedly indicate that once pupils and their families reach the firm conclusion that a school has little to offer and sometimes has rejected them, there will remain intractable problems, perhaps only solvable by a move to another mainstream school or to a contrasting 'segregated' setting (Cole et al., 1998; Cole and Visser, 2000).

This is only partly a criticism of some teachers as staff can be forced by school traditions and government diktat to move away from fulfilling a pastoral role adequately and to work in an anti-inclusionary way. A generation ago, Balbernie (Foreword to Millham, Bullock and Cherrett, 1975) portrayed successful work with difficult young people as 'the art of making oneself available in relationships for others'. Such strategies can be achieved only if staff are enabled to create time and space for talking and listening to pupils as a central part of their professional role, without detracting from skilled and rigorous teaching. In secondary schools in particular this has been a difficult challenge since long before the introduction of the National Curriculum and the 'marketisation' of education (Leavold, 1984; Cole, 1989), but the reforms of the 1980s and early 1990s probably exacerbated the situation (Booth, Ainscow and Dyson, 1998; Cole, 1999; McLaughlin and Rouse, 2000). Nevertheless, some schools meet the challenge better than others and their policy and practice must be shared.

REFERENCES

Baldwin, S. (2000) 'How should ADHD be treated: a discussion with Paul Cooper', *The Psychologist*, 13 (12) 598–602.

Booth, T., Ainscow, M. and Dyson, A. (1998) 'England: inclusion and exclusion in a competitive system', in T. Booth and M. Ainscow (eds.) *From Them to Us*. London: Routledge.

Canter, L. (1990) 'Assertive discipline', in M. Scherer, I. Gersch and L. Fry (eds.) *Meeting Disruptive Behaviour*. London: Macmillan.

City of Birmingham Education Department (1998) *The Framework for Intervention*. Birmingham: City of Birmingham Education Department.

Clark, C., Dyson, A., Millward, A. and Robson, S. (1999) 'Theories of inclusion, theories of schools: deconstructing and reconstructing the inclusive school', *British Educational Research Journal*, 25 (2) 157–77.

Clarke, D. and Murray, A. (1996) *Developing a Whole School Behaviour Policy: a Practical Approach*. London: David Fulton.

Cole, T. (1989) *Apart or A Part? Integration and the Growth of British Special Education*. Milton Keynes: Open University Press.

Cole, T. (1998) 'Understanding challenging behaviour: prerequisites to inclusion', in C. Tilstone, L. Florian and R. Rose (eds.) *Promoting Inclusive Practice*. London: Routledge.

Cole, T. (1999) 'Defining and developing proficient education for pupils with emotional and behavioural difficulties in special and mainstream schools'. Unpublished PhD dissertation. University of Birmingham.

Cole, T., Daniels, H. and Visser, J. (1999) *Patterns of Educational Provision Maintained by Local Education Authorities for Pupils with Behaviour Problems* (A report sponsored by the Nuffield Foundation). Birmingham: University of Birmingham.

Cole, T. and Visser, J. (2000) *EBD Policy, Practice and Provision in Shropshire LEA and Telford and Wrekin LEA*. Birmingham: University of Birmingham.

Cole, T., Visser, J. and Daniels, H. (2000) *The Framework for Intervention: Identifying and Promoting Effective Practice* (Second Evaluation Report). Report commissioned by the City of Birmingham Education Department. Birmingham: The University of Birmingham.

Cole, T., Visser, J. and Upton, G. (1998) *Effective Schooling for Pupils with Emotional and Behavioural Difficulties*. London: David Fulton Publishers.

Cooper, P. (1993) *Effective Schooling for Disaffected Students*. London: Routledge.

Cooper, P., Smith, C. and Upton, G. (1994) *Emotional and Behavioural Difficulties*. London: Routledge.

Creese, A., Daniels, H. and Norwich, B. (1997) *Teacher Support Teams*. London: David Fulton.

Daniels, A. and Williams, H. (2000) 'Reducing the need for exclusions and statements for behaviour', *Educational Psychology in Practice*, 15 (4) 221–7.

Daniels, H., Visser, J., Cole, T. and de Reybekill, N. (1998) *Emotional and Behavioural Difficulties in the Mainstream* (Research Report RR90). London: DfEE.

Dennison, B. and Kirk, R. (1990) *Do, Review, Learn, Apply: a Simple Guide to Experiential Learning*. Oxford: Blackwell.

Department for Education (1994a) *Pupil Behaviour and Discipline* (Circular 8/94). London: DFE.

Department for Education (1994b) *The Education of Children with Emotional and Behavioural Difficulties* (Circular 9/94). London: DFE.

Department for Education and Employment (1997) *Excellence for All Children: Meeting Special Educational Needs* (Green Paper Cm 3785). London: The Stationery Office.

Department for Education and Employment (1998) *Meeting Special Educational Needs: a Programme of Action.* London: DfEE.

Department for Education and Employment (1999) *School Inclusion: Pupils' Support* (Circular 10/99). London: DfEE.

Department of Education and Science (1989) *Discipline in Schools: Report of the Committee of Enquiry* (The Elton Report). London: HMSO.

Elliott, J. and Place, M. (1998) *Children in Difficulty: a Guide to Understanding and Helping.* London: Routledge.

Galloway, D. (1990) *Pupil Welfare and Counselling.* London: Longman.

Hallam, S. and Castle, F. (1999) *Evaluation of the Behaviour and Discipline Pilot Projects (1996–99)* (Supported under the Standards Fund Programme: Research Report, RR163). London: DfEE.

Hallam, S. and Castle, F. (2001) 'Exclusion from school: What can help prevent it?', *Educational Review* (Special Issue: Inclusion in Practice), 53 (2) 169–79.

Hanko, G. (1994) 'Discouraged children: when praise does not help', *British Journal of Special Education*, 21 (4) 166–8.

Hopkins, D. (1997) 'Improving the quality of teaching and learning', *Support for Learning*, 12 (4) 162–5.

Kounin, J.S. (1970) *Discipline and Group Management in Classrooms.* New York: Krieger.

Lacey, P. (2001) 'The role of learning support assistants in the inclusive learning of pupils with severe and profound learning difficulties', *Educational Review* (Special Issue: Inclusion in Practice), 53 (2) 157–67.

Laslett, R. (1977) *Educating Maladjusted Children.* London: Granada.

Leavold, J. (1984) 'A sanctuary for disruptive pupils', in M. Lloyd-Smith (ed.) *Disrupted Schooling: the Growth of the Special Unit.* London: Murray.

Lorenz, S. (1998) *Effective In-Class Support.* London: David Fulton Publishers.

McLaughlin, M. and Rouse, M. (2000) (eds.) *Special Education and School Reform in the United States and Britain.* London: Routledge.

Millham, S., Bullock, R. and Cherrett, P. (1975) *After Grace – Teeth.* London: Chaucer.

Mortimore, P., Sammons, L., Stoll, L. and Ecob, R. (1988) *School Matters.* Wells: Open Books.

Munn, P., Lloyd, G. and Cullen, M. (2000) *Alternatives to School Exclusion.* London: Paul Chapman.

Ofsted (1993) *Achieving Good Behaviour in Schools.* London: HMSO.

Ofsted (1999) *Principles into Practice: Effective Education for Pupils with EBD.* London: Ofsted.

Osler, A. (1997) 'Drama turns into a crisis for blacks', *Times Educational Supplement*, 10 October 1997.

Osler, A. , Watling, R., Busher, H., Cole, T. and White, A. (2001) *Reasons for Exclusion from School* (Research Brief 244). London: DfEE.

Parsons, C. (1999) *Education, Exclusion and Citizenship.* London: Routledge.

Power, S. (1996) *The Pastoral and the Academic: Conflict and Contradictions in the Curriculum.* London: Cassell.

Redl, F. (1966) *When We Deal with Children.* New York: Free Press.

Redl, F. and Wineman, D. (1952) *Controls from Within.* New York: Free Press.

Rogers, B. (1994) *Behaviour Recovery: a Whole-school Program for Mainstream Schools.* London: Longman.

Rose, R. (2001) 'Primary school teacher perceptions of the conditions required to include pupils with special educational needs', *Educational Review* (Special Issue: Inclusion in Practice), 53 (2) 147–56.

Smith, C. and Laslett, R. (1993) *Effective Classroom Management: a Teacher's Guide*. London: Routledge.

Thomas, G., Walker, D. and Webb, J. (1998) *The Making of the Inclusive School*. London: Routledge.

Tilstone, C., Florian, L. and Rose, R. (1998) (eds.) *Promoting Inclusive Practice*. London: Routledge.

Chapter 6

Effective multi-agency work

Penny Lacey

In this chapter, Penny Lacey considers the advantages and disadvantages of multi-agency work and outlines some radical
solutions to current challenges. She identifies key factors in
drawing up policies for effective collaborative work.

Although there are many individuals who are committed to multi-agency
collaboration, they are often thwarted by the ways in which different agencies
are conceived and run. Equally, at a service level, there are agencies whose policies clearly state that they desire to collaborate with others, but individuals
have neither the time nor the inclination to turn policy into practice. Bringing
together policy and practice in effective multi-agency work remains as much
of a challenge at the beginning of this century as it did in the second half of the
last. Individuals and services have tried to overcome barriers to collaboration
and their efforts will form the basis of this chapter. Although there has been
relatively little research published, there is sufficient to begin to draw together
the factors that seem to help or hinder multi-agency collaboration.

The first section of this chapter will focus on policies at national and local
levels, in a search for some of the reasons why so many difficulties arise in
multi-agency work. This will be followed by an examination of examples of
effective practice particularly in the pre-school years. The final section contains
a suggestion for a radical restructuring of education to counteract some of the
difficulties common in multi-agency work.

POLICIES ON MULTI-AGENCY WORK

Pupils with learning difficulties are likely to be known to several agencies and the
services (organised by these agencies) will have varying amounts of contact with
them and their families. Pupils with multiple disabilities may be on the caseload
of many professionals, some of whom may be in contact with each other; others
may be working in isolation (Lacey, 2001). All the agencies are likely to have

policies that relate to multi-agency work; some may claim to be working in a close professional relationship. Policies for multi-agency work can be found at all levels from Government legislation through local government to individual services and they often contain ideas that are very difficult to put into practice. For example, Government papers on special educational needs contain many references to the need for agencies to work together to meet children's needs:

> There must be close co-operation between all the agencies concerned and a multi-disciplinary approach to the resolution of issues.
>
> DfE, 1994, p.3

> Effective collaboration between LEAs, social services departments and health authorities is essential.
>
> DfEE, 1997, p.71

Other agencies have similar policy statements, for example the Children Act 1989 states that:

> District Health Authorities, LEAs, grant maintained schools and City Technology Colleges must comply for a request from a social services department for assistance in providing services for *children in need*.
>
> DoH, 1989, Section 27

The Children Act is typical of human services legislation in this country in that following this exhortation to work together, there is a 'get-out' statement:

> ... so long as the request is compatible with their duties and does not unduly prejudice the discharge of their functions ...
>
> DoH, 1989, Section 27

Consequently there is a reduced expectation of collaboration between agencies to work together as there is no *right* for children and their families to have their services working together; it is only *preferable*.

The *Code of Practice on the Identification and Assessment of Pupils with Special Educational Needs* (DfE, 1994) is similarly facilitative, but not prescriptive:

> ... representatives of LEAs, social services departments and the health service may choose to meet on a reasonably regular basis to plan and co-ordinate services.
>
> DfE, 1994, para. 2.40

Therefore, at the highest level, it possible to see why it is difficult to translate policy into practice. Although agencies might like to meet to co-ordinate their work, they have *permission* to refuse to work with others if their resources are limited. There have been times when the low level of social services' resources has threatened relationships with other agencies as there have not been sufficient social workers to respond to requests to attend annual reviews or to contribute to transition plans for pupils in their last years in school.

In 1997 the DfEE commissioned research into inter-agency work between education, health and social services from the University of Newcastle (Dyson, Lin and Millward, 1998). Researchers were asked to identify obstacles to effective inter-agency co-operation in the context of the Code of Practice; to establish models of effective practice; and to recommend ways in which co-operation and decision-making can be improved. The results suggest that effective inter-agency work depends on:

- efficient information management within, and between, agencies;
- specific locations and opportunities within which to develop (for example, close proximity or a shared project);
- a clearly defined focus, significant to all agencies;
- shared aims between agencies, powerful enough to counter their very different core purposes;
- individuals who can create an agenda for working together.

These factors are suggested as being in a 'virtuous circle' of co-operation. Efficient communication leads to trust which makes it more likely that professionals will work together on the same project or in the same premises with the same aims.

Although the researchers make recommendations for improvements they are cautious in their expectations of great changes in the near future. The difficulties caused by the separate statutory bases of the agencies and their professional cultures arising from different professional training are likely to remain for some time to come. It would be very exciting to be able to foresee a single agency for children or for people with disabilities and difficulties. It is unlikely, however, that joint agencies, dedicated to the needs of children with special needs and their families, will be set up immediately.

The recommendations from the research (Dyson et al., 1998) are:

- individual and local initiatives should be encouraged as there is no one blueprint for effective inter-agency work;
- agencies should exchange regularly updated information with each other;
- there should be a unified approach to assessment to reduce overlap and frustration about information transfer;
- a data system should be set up that is common to all agencies;
- a policy on sharing confidential information should be drawn up;

- a vision for inter-agency work should be published by each agency as a basis for building up common aims and activities;
- common training needs across agencies should be identified and staff should meet these together;
- initiatives such as shared premises for agencies should be encouraged;
- joint setting of targets, monitoring and evaluation should be established;
- agencies should review their procedures for responding to the concerns of parents.

Although modest, the recommendations may be difficult to implement especially by agencies hard pressed to fulfil their prime duties and who need to withdraw from peripheral activities in order to maintain their central work.

MULTI-AGENCY WORK IN PRACTICE

From the previous section, it is clear that the Government is committed to encouraging or enabling collaboration between agencies to meet the needs of children with disabilities and difficulties. Its policies constantly refer to multi-agency work and it has facilitated working together through initiatives such as joint finance, partnership programmes, action zones and the transfer of funds from one agency to another. Against this background, what does multi-agency work look like in practice at the beginning of the new century? What is being achieved and what are the major obstacles to effective working?

Although many of the successes in inter-agency work are to be found in early years practice, there are also inadequacies. For example:

> The speech and language therapist from the pre-school team visited the home of a boy with learning difficulties. As the therapist assembled the resources for a communication assessment, the mother's disbelief grew and eventually she exclaimed, 'The Portage worker did that assessment last week!'

Members of effective teams communicate regularly with each other, agree on procedures, have common aims and plan their work jointly. Such collaboration is lacking in the example and it is clear that the two professionals were working completely independently of each other with the consequent difficulties of overlap or 'slipping through the net'.

In contrast, for example:

A speech and language therapist, an occupational therapist and a physiotherapist are employed to work in the same centre to assess the needs of young children with multiple disabilities. Each is trained to conduct assessments not only in his or her own discipline but, at a basic level, in the other two disciplines. Thus one therapist can take almost complete responsibility for a new referral, removing the need to pass the child from one therapist to another. Each child is discussed by all three therapists using video or one-way window observations and 'hands-on' sessions can be arranged if there is a particularly intractable challenge.

The principles that drive the sort of joint-working practised by these three therapists arise from the frustrations felt by families, who are referred from agency to agency, none of whom seem willing to talk or to take responsibility for co-ordinating services.

Keyworking

Recently there has been a particular interest in structures that reduce the difficulties experienced when different agencies are working with one family. A popular model is *keyworking*, and the Joseph Rowntree Foundation has funded a project to set up, monitor and evaluate keyworker services in two local authorities (Mukherjee, Beresford and Sloper, 1999). The results of pre-project research indicated that although many professionals find themselves unofficially working as keyworkers, there were very few official keyworker services. The UK SOFTY (Support Over First Two Years) survey (Limbrick-Spencer, 2000) confirmed this finding, and parents were asked what support they needed when they had a very young child with multiple disabilities. Parents wanted:

- emotional support, especially someone to talk to who had some counselling skills;
- information about their child's condition given at a pace that parents can manage and in language they can understand;
- information about services, that can help parents to understand what is available;
- easy access to what is needed, rather than having to battle for services;
- the co-ordination of services, to manage an array of appointments and information;
- the whole picture in order to ensure that the family's needs were being seen as a whole.

Limbrick-Spencer (2000) is clear that the response to the needs of the parents in the survey is a keyworker approach: one person who could meet the needs identified in the six areas given above.

During the Rowntree project (Mukherjee et al., 1999) six elements of keyworking were developed:

- proactive, regular contact;
- a supportive, open relationship;
- a family-centred approach;
- working across agencies;
- working with families' strengths and ways of coping;
- working for the family rather than the agency.

To be effective, these six elements should be supported by training and supervision in an organisational context where there is a commitment to multi-agency working and inter-agency structures.

From the research, it is clear that the presence (officially or unofficially) of a keyworker is not going to produce inter-agency collaboration on its own. The provision of a keyworker must be part of a package which aims to improve collaboration between professionals in the pre-school phase. It is also important for the various agencies to be housed in the same locality, making both communication and collaboration easier. Despite these apparent advantages, recent research suggests that placing services in close proximity does not always guarantee efficient collaboration (Wigfall and Moss, 2001).

Campus multi-agency work

More than the Sum of its Parts? is a report on a multi-agency child-care network carried out by Wigfall and Moss (2001). The research was focused on the Coram Community Campus, where a group of ten voluntary and statutory organisations are physically sited to provide a 'one-stop shop' for local families in the King's Cross area of Camden. The organisations include KIDS (a special needs charity), TreeHouse (a small school for children with autism), the Thomas Coram Early Childhood Centre (a 108-place nursery maintained by Camden LEA) and the King's Cross Homelessness Project (run on a voluntary basis).

Two of the aims of the study were to describe and evaluate the development of a campus model of service as a multi-agency child-care network and to assess its replicability. The researchers were particularly interested in exploring how such a network could be set up and the difficulties that need to be addressed. The results of the study suggest that after two years much had been achieved in encouraging services to work together more closely, but much more had to be done before the network became more than just a collection of services sharing a site. There appeared to be three constraints to the greater integration of services (Wigfall and Moss, 2001, pp.72–3):

1. Each service had its own perspective, agenda, structure and aims which makes it difficult to find the right amount of collective action and identity.
2. Little time or space has been given over to joint activities or training.
3. There are many demands on and initiatives for individual services which make it difficult for them to look outwards to other agencies despite Government encouragement of 'joined-up thinking'.

A few families in the King's Cross area are using the campus as envisaged, and are acquiring trust in individual services from which they gain confidence to move around other services in order to derive benefits that might not have been possible without the campus structure. It was disappointing to the researchers that more families were not exploiting the potential but they conclude that this may be due to a lack of awareness at this early stage of development, and suggest that families will have to learn how to use the facilities.

The study (Wigfall and Moss, 2001, pp 74–5) concludes with a set of conditions needed for enabling similar child-care networks to work:

1. a joint vision, shared principles and corporate strategic planning;
2. a democratic approach to implementation through a co-ordinating agency, good communication systems and open consultation;
3. dedicated resources such as time for the change process, staff development and shared activities, funding, statutory support, quality staff and a process of evaluation.

An underlining factor, evident from this study, is the need for time dedicated to setting up and maintaining joint working. It is not sufficient to put people together and to expect them to work together effectively.

MULTI-AGENCY WORK IN SCHOOLS

Many of the points made about the pre-school years apply equally to the school years when it should be easier for multi-agency work to be established as a consequence of the stable basis provided by the school. Unfortunately there are many instances of poorly co-ordinated practice during the school years where speech and language therapists work in isolation with individual pupils and provide little information for teachers, or where specialist teachers for sensory impairments devise individual pupil programmes which teachers do not implement.

The Code of Practice (DfES, 2001) requires all maintained schools to publish information on their arrangements for working in partnership with LEA support services, health and social services, the connexions service and any relevant voluntary organisations. There is a suggestion that service level agreements and contracts between schools and services would be helpful, together with the use of these outside agencies as consultants and as in-service advisers. Other proposals for specific responsibilities include the co-ordination of the health provision for individual children with SEN by the school medical officer.

As stated earlier, written policies do not necessarily lead to effective practice, especially when they allow 'get-out clauses'. Effective practice requires facilitation. For example:

> a primary school that is additionally resourced to take pupils with a range of special educational needs has negotiated with the speech and language therapy service for a concentrated, but intermittent, input from the therapist. The therapist spends two full days in the school every half term, assessing new referrals, working with staff on writing speech and language programmes for individuals and groups of pupils, giving in-service training and demonstrating activities with both individual pupils and with groups. The school buys in supply staff to provide non-contact time for teaching staff and the timetable is modified to provide suitable periods for working with individual pupils and groups. The therapist is also available for telephone consultations on a weekly basis.
>
> Two teaching assistants (one for each key stage) and the SENCo have been given responsibility for working with the speech and language therapist, ensuring continuity at classroom as well as school level. The SENCo is responsible for organising the two day visits and making sure that the needs of the pupils and staff are met as far as possible. In association with teachers and teaching assistants she determines priorities for the visits of the speech and language therapist and together they plan the timetable for the two days.
>
> They ensure that all the individual and group objectives for speech and language therapy are addressed on a regular basis, they check that resources are available and they liaise with the SENCo over changing needs. Classroom teachers have overall responsibility for implementing speech and language therapy objectives and are allocated non-contact time for discussions with the SENCo and the assistants to ensure efficient practice.

In the example, specific support is given to enable teachers, teaching assistants, the SENCo and the speech and language therapist to collaborate as it is recognised that joint work is only possible if:

1. time is allocated for joint discussions (by both the school and the therapy service);

2. funds are available for releasing school staff to talk;
3. school staff and therapists work side-by-side;
4. the timetable is arranged to enable both talking and joint working;
5. school staff are sufficiently comfortable with meeting pupils' speech and language needs as part of their daily work;
6. the therapist is available to answer queries at set times when not in the school;
7. someone (in this case the SENCo) takes overall responsibility for organising the joint work;
8. school staff are committed to working jointly with visiting professionals.

However well joint work, such as this, is organised, there is still the feeling that a rather small sticking plaster is being placed on a gaping wound. Circumstances in schools make it very difficult for time to be allocated specifically for multi-agency work.

RESTRUCTURING EDUCATION

It is evident that the call to work in partnership across agencies in the school years is fraught with difficulties. A commitment to collaborative teamwork has enabled schools and services to explore ways of working together but such arrangements depend on good will and on the problem-solving skills of individuals. If the inclusion of pupils with special educational needs is to become successful it is imperative to ensure that multi-agency work is fully effective; one of the major difficulties is the shortage of time for school and service personnel to work, talk and train together.

A lack of time was identified as one of the stress factors for teachers in a survey conducted by Kyriacou (2001), who found that a quarter of teachers regard teaching as 'very' or 'extremely stressful'. He also identified 'high workload', 'coping with change', 'dealing with colleagues, administration and management', 'role conflict' and 'poor working conditions' as contributing to their stress. Esteve (2000) suggests that there was a transformation in the role of the teacher over the final years of the twentieth century. He identifies fast-moving social, political and economic changes which contribute to the differing expectations of teachers and teaching in the new century. He points to the fact that teachers are expected to do more than merely encourage cognitive development in pupils. Human, emotional and moral values had been taught at home in the past, and anti-social behaviour, disability and difference were dealt with in segregated settings.

Esteve (2000) goes on to intimate that by being required to adopt other roles, teachers lack sufficient time to do anything well. Battery and Wright (2000) echo this view and suggest that in the UK teachers are being controlled and directed, and feel they are only able to implement directives.

Tranter (2000), discussing the 1998 Government consultation paper 'Teachers Meeting the Challenge of Change', suggests that although the document claims to be concerned with the modernisation of the profession, it is really about incentives for the ambitious and the controlling powers of surveillance.

In Spring 2001, the *Times Educational Supplement* reported for several weeks on the call for a 35-hour week for teachers. It cited many instances of exhausted teachers who work long hours, in one case 66 hours a week (Mansell, 2001), and of the impossible workload associated with an excess of paperwork. The public still sees teachers as part-time workers with long holidays, whereas the reality is very different. Most regularly work evenings, weekends and during school holidays. Letters to the *Times Educational Supplement* frequently mention their lack of a social life and the frustrations of excessive demands.

Additional pressures result from multi-agency work which makes yet another claim on their time and it is understandable that teachers are reluctant to take on pupils with needs over and above those they are already struggling to meet. The inclusion of all pupils into the school community is time-consuming and, although teachers are pleased that others are taking an interest in pupils whose needs they alone cannot meet, they have little time or energy for collaborative working. Many hope that eventually they will be allowed to get on with the primary job of educating classes of pupils.

What can be done to change the situation? The following questions need to be considered:

- Should teaching time be completely reorganised?
- Should teachers work a notional 9am–5pm day throughout the year, with evenings and weekends off and five weeks holiday like the rest of the workforce?
- How could such changes help teachers to work with outside agencies and in-school support staff?

The current system of terms and holidays was adopted in the nineteenth century to respond to the demands of the agricultural industry. At the time it was assumed that teachers would work in isolation in classrooms with groups of pupils and *pass on* knowledge. Circumstances are different now and teaching makes different demands. Working with other adults is common and the closed classroom door is a relic of the past.

How would the new school year work for teachers? Currently teachers and pupils work for 39 weeks per year and have 13 weeks holiday. If teachers worked for an extra eight weeks when pupils were not in school, this would bring them to a total of 47 weeks; the number of working weeks which equates with other comparable jobs. These extra eight weeks would be available for undertaking work which is difficult to fit into the current way of working, such as curriculum development, planning, training and collaborative teamwork.

It is not being suggested that teachers should work even longer hours than is already the case. They would work more weeks in the year, but the hours would be spread more evenly. It is envisaged that they would work no longer than the notional 9am–5pm day but the extra number of days worked would enable them to rid themselves of the exceedingly long hours worked during the current term times. This change would allow teachers and other professionals to find mutual time to work together uninterrupted by the immediate demands of teaching.

Obviously, some work with other agencies, such as the assessments of pupils, cannot be undertaken during vacations, but it may be possible to keep discussions to a minimum during 'classroom time' and to timetable in-depth discussions at the end of the six-week teaching block. There will always be emergencies (dealings with the police or social services) but these would be the exceptions rather than the rule. The advantages of such collaborative working are that:

- school staff would have specific times set aside for joint planning, report writing and the exchange of information;
- preparation for collaborative work would be carried out in the vacation and teachers would no longer experience unexpected visits to the classroom by members of outside agencies;
- social services case conferences could be held during vacations, enabling teachers to attend.

Support for this pattern of working could take many different forms and would, for example, require the following:

1. a telephone for every teacher;
2. the flexibility to contribute to occasional evening meetings such as parents' evenings or governors' meetings in return for half days off in the vacation;
3. the flexibility (and trust) to be able to work at home as well as in school during vacations;
4. responses to official documents to be timed to fall in with vacations;
5. other agencies to plan their work to fit in with the new patterns;
6. professional development providers to run courses during vacations.

Many of the traditional ways of working would disappear under this proposed system and, although the current generation of teachers could find the change hard, once established it would help to create a satisfactory way of working for all.

CONCLUSIONS

The content of this chapter has ranged over different aspects of multi-agency work. It began with an examination of Government policy on agencies working in partnership and considered examples, none of which were fully satisfactory, of effective working. The final section developed a proposal for restructuring using a collegial approach to the meeting of needs. If inclusion, involving multi-agency work, is to become a reality, radical changes are essential.

It is hoped that the many questions raised will have stimulated discussions and will lead to changes for the better. Schools now, however, need to devise their own policies for multi-agency work, within which certain requirements would seem to be essential.

1. Agencies should share physical space (if not permanently, then regularly through frequent meetings).
2. A co-ordinator or keyworker is required to bring together the different agencies and to drive forward the partnership.
3. Partners should have common aims (for individual pupils and for the partnership).
4. Time must be made for talking together, working jointly, training each other and evaluating the partnership.

Without these requirements, it is unlikely that multi-agency work will be effective. Each agency and its representatives must feel secure and confident in working with others. When professionals feel overstretched and underskilled it is unlikely that they will welcome the chance to form partnerships with professionals who work in different ways. It is hoped that this chapter has helped to counteract negative feelings and has provided a positive picture for multi-agency work in the twenty-first century.

REFERENCES

Battery, M. and Wright, N. (2000) 'The directed profession: teachers and the state in the third millennium', *Journal of In-service Education*, 26 (3) 475–86.

DfE (1994) *The Code of Practice on the Identification and Assessment of Special Educational Needs.* London: HMSO.

DfEE (1997) *Excellence for all Children: Meeting Special Educational Needs.* London: DfEE.

DfEE (2000) *SEN Code of Practice on the Identification and Assessment of Special Educational Needs and SEN Thresholds: Good Practice Guidance on Identification and Provision for Pupils with Special Educational Needs* (a Consultation Document). London: DfEE.

DfES (2001) *Special Educational Needs: Code of Practice.* London: DfES.

DoH (1989) *The Children Act.* London: DoH.

Dyson, A., Lin, M. and Millward, A. (1998) *Effective Communication Between Schools,*

LEAs and Health and Social Services in the Field of Special Educational Needs. London: DfEE.

Esteve, J. (2000) 'The transformation of the teacher's role at the end of the twentieth century and new challenges for the future', *Educational Review*, 52 (2) 197–207.

Kyriacou, C. (2001) 'Teachers' stress: directions for future research', *Educational Review*, 53 (1) 27–35.

Lacey, P. (2001) *Support Partnerships: Collaboration in Action*. London: David Fulton.

Limbrick-Spencer, G. (2000) *Parent Support Needs: The Views of Parents of Children with Complex Needs*. Birmingham: Handsel Trust.

Mansell, W. (2001) 'Exhausted new recruits' plea to Blunkett', *The Times Educational Supplement*, 13 April.

Mukherjee, S., Beresford, B. and Sloper, P. (1999) *Unlocking Key Working: An Analysis and Evaluation of Key Worker Services for Families with Disabled Children*. Bristol: The Policy Press.

Tranter, S. (2000) 'First among equals – is this possible?', *School Leadership*, 13 (22).

Wigfall, V. and Moss, P. (2001) *More than the Sum of its Parts? A Study of a Multi-agency Child Care Network*. London: National Children's Bureau.

Chapter 7

Towards inclusive therapy

Policies and the transformation of practice

Christopher Robertson

This chapter is concerned with ways in which therapy for children with learning difficulties can be integrated into mainstream educational provision. Christopher Robertson discusses how good practice can be developed and how mainstream schools might use the knowledge and skills associated with specialist practice in ways that move beyond simply 'transplanting' expertise. At the centre of the approach outlined is the perspective of the child, rather than his or her needs as perceived by therapists and teachers. It is also argued that this approach needs to be underpinned by systematic policy and planning at national, regional and local levels.

Other children play, but you do 'therapy'. Other children develop, but you are 'trained'.

Mason, 1992, p.27

More physiotherapists, occupational therapists and speech therapists should be available in the community and be able to come to young people's homes outside school hours where possible.

Educable, 2000, p.59

These two quotations characterise the experiences of therapy for some young people and adults with disabilities. In the first, Mason questions the purpose of therapy, implying how it differentiates and possibly discriminates between children. In the second, *Educable*, a group of young students with disabilities who undertook research into their own educational and related experiences, do not question the role of therapy in their lives, but query its place as part of the range of educational activities that constitute the school day. These are legitimate concerns about the nature and provision of therapies provided by occupational, physio- and speech and language therapists working, in the main, for health authorities.

This chapter is concerned with how therapies of this kind can be transformed to support inclusive educational and related development for children and young people with learning difficulties. Initially it will be argued that orthodox therapy, of the kind referred to here, is worthwhile although some authors have questioned the value of therapy and rehabilitation as a normalising obsession (Oliver, 1996, p.100), whereby 'curing' becomes a millenarian aim for some professionals rather than something that is beneficial to the recipient. My own view is that therapy, like teaching, can become too focused on issues of control. It is by shifting the locus of control, however, to one where pupil voice and participation are seen as being of prime importance (Clough and Barton, 1998; Robertson, 2001a) that we can fully use the developmental, preventative and palliative potential of therapy in a way that is integral to education. Although this chapter will focus on issues primarily concerned with mainstream schools, the underlying imperative of listening to children's views and being guided by them is one that is applicable to more inclusive forms of practice wherever they take place. It is of course important to note that the 'how' and 'where' of therapy provision, if negotiated between those involved, may be provided in places other than schools and at times outside the normal school day. A recently published White Paper on education, *Schools: Achieving Success* (Department for Education and Skills, 2001b) rhetorically, at least, recognises a more flexible role for schools whereby:

> ... they will be able to provide community services such as health and social care, child-care, after school study and community learning so that they are a 'dawn 'til dusk' resource for the community.
>
> Department for Education and Skills, 2001c

Consideration is also given to the new approaches to therapy provision which have built on the good practice that has emerged in recent years. Consequent education policy, such as the Green Paper *Excellence for All Children: Meeting Special Educational Needs* (Department for Education and Employment, 1997) led to the commissioning of significant research (Law, Lindsay, Peacey, Gascoigne, Soloff, Radford, Band and Fitzgerald, 2000; Law, Lindsay, Peacey, Gascoigne, Soloff, Radford and Band, 2001) that mapped and scrutinised therapy provision. Although it focused on children with speech and language needs, it also identified strengths and weaknesses that might be extrapolated to occupational therapy and physiotherapy policy and practice and:

> reveals a severe shortage of speech and language therapists, characterised by high caseloads, problems of recruitment and retention of therapists and wide variations in levels of services to mainstream schools.
>
> Miller, 2001, p.248

At the same time it shows that therapists and teachers can, and do, work effectively and innovatively to support children and that these 'ways of working' do not necessarily involve the simple replication or 'transfer' of approaches developed in specialist settings.

Also fundamental to this chapter is the argument that effective therapy provision in mainstream schools for children with learning difficulties has been the subject of neglect, at least in the United Kingdom. Literature that discusses 'support' for inclusive practice tends to focus particularly on the role of learning support assistants (see, for example, Farrell, 2001), or that of local education authority support teachers and advisers. Nevertheless the important role that learning support assistants have to play in developing inclusive practice (Department for Education and Employment, 2000), as indirect providers of therapy services, needs to be appraised and monitored in the context of a clearer conception of what counts as good-quality therapy provision, as captured in the following:

> Hannah's physiotherapy sessions took place for about fifteen minutes just before lunch on Thursdays. The sessions were in the morning when she was less tired, with the same classroom support helping to ensure consistency for Hannah. The physiotherapy programme was outlined by the physiotherapist who visited approximately once a term to assess Hannah's progress and determine any changes to the regime.
>
> Wise and Glass, 2000, p.40

In describing how they, as learning support assistants, supported the mainstream inclusive placement of Hannah, Wise and Glass provide an excellent description of how education professionals and therapists can work together effectively. At the same time, their observations raise issues about the nature of professional expertise and how we evaluate the effectiveness of therapy provision.

Finally, it is suggested that there is an urgent need to reframe our thinking about the interface between special educational needs provision and the delivery of other services that provide therapy for children and young people. Inclusive educational provision (regardless of what we might think about its quality) is already the norm in many parts of the UK. Currently, for example, over 1.8 million children in England have identified special educational needs, 356,000 more than in 1997. Over 60% of children with statements attend mainstream schools, and fewer than 90,000 children attend maintained special schools (Department for Education and Employment, 2001b). The vast majority of children with learning difficulties, who require therapy provision, are likely to be educated in their local mainstream schools. The implication is that therapy provision in education needs to be organised in ways that are responsive to organisational complexity across all phases and sectors of education. As Fish (1989) noted, this necessitates considering *what* is required of services rather than focusing on the traditional modes of delivery so often associated with discrete and separate forms of provision.

POLICY AND PRACTICE IN SCHOOLS

A good starting point for thinking about how education service professionals and therapists can work effectively together is provided by Graham and Wright (1999) who have devised a collaboration scale that can be used in a variety of educational contexts, and as part of school improvement planning and practice. For example:

> 'In mainstream, it can be a tool for managers to identify the kind of support class teachers and SENCos require in their attempts to make provision for pupils with physical disabilities and other SEN, based upon multi-professional advice.' (p.40)

The scale consists of twenty indicators grouped under three main headings of planning activities, sharing activities, and goal achieving activities (Box 1).

Using such indicators to develop and maintain effective, pupil-focused practice has traditionally been regarded as easier to achieve in special school settings (Graham and Wright, 1999; Wright and Kersner, 1999), and there is worrying evidence concerning the nature and availability of certain kinds of therapy-linked provision for children with complex learning and communication difficulties in mainstream schools. Clarke, McConachie, Price and Wood (2001), for example, in a recent study of how children's augmentative and alternative communication (AAC) needs are met, note that: 'system users in mainstream schools *may* be at risk of failing to reach their potential for progress in the development of communication skills' (p.52). This would seem to be because patterns of support are not well matched to learning contexts and that pupils placed in mainstream schools are less likely to receive adequate levels of therapy provision than similar children in special schools. To improve this situation, the development collaborative approaches of the kind referred to here (and those described by Lacey in her chapter in this book) are essential, but need to be accompanied by a significant increase in the levels of therapy provision available to mainstream schools.

Despite the difficulties, examples of good practice, where therapy and education are well integrated in inclusive contexts, can be found in many parts of the country, and are likely to increase as experience of meeting the needs of children with learning and related difficulties grows. At Cleves School (Alderson, 1999) in the London Borough of Newham, long-standing inclusive practices, underpinned by the local authority's commitment to developing inclusive provision, are ordinary, routine and characterised by good-quality communication. A member of staff at the school, Debbie (deputy head and a SENCo), conveys this well:

> Speech and language therapists usually work with one or two children, or with groups. If they write a programme for a child, they are not here

Box 1

Planning activities

- Co-planning the implementation of the curriculum with other professionals to ensure the work of all professionals is incorporated and meets the needs of pupils.
- Deciding with others who will carry out aspects of pupils' programmes.
- Agreeing who will co-ordinate the implementation of programmes.
- Agreeing how an integrated programme will work.
- Planning and developing overall therapy provision within the school.
- Joint ongoing assessments of pupils' needs.
- Developing a monitoring system to ensure that information about pupils is shared.

Sharing activities

- Discussing realistic demands on professionals' time and or use of equipment.
- Communicating with other professionals regularly by telephone, email, or in writing.
- Giving a knowledge of my 'role' to others and explaining the contribution I make to meeting the needs of pupils.
- Talking to other professionals regularly to share knowledge and expertise.
- Sharing responsibility with other professionals for all aspects of the pupils' development.
- Participating in wider activities of the schools (for example, social events).
- Informal regular liaison to exchange information.
- Trying to use a common 'jargon free' language that can be understood by professionals, parents and pupils.

Goal-achieving activities

- Agreeing various short-term goals to achieve common longer-term aims for pupils.
- Identifying and agreeing an overall common goal for each pupil.
- Ensuring that when pursuing my goals for the pupil that they are relevant to the overall agreed common goal for that pupil.
- Acknowledging the importance of particular methods used by different professionals to achieve identified goals.
- Knowing and understanding the goals of other professionals and how they contribute to the overall goal.

    Adapted from Graham and Wright, 1999, pp.38–9

every day so it would be one of the school staff who does the programme and it is important that the speech therapist passes that information and the techniques and methods on to a member of staff. So we encourage them to train and work with staff about particular aspects of the children's programmes. They liaise with the curriculum support teacher but also with the rest of the staff. They assess children and offer their expert advice about what children need and then they teach us programmes which anyone can use.

Alderson, 1999, p.56

Similar approaches to occupational therapy and physiotherapy characterise inter-professional practice at Cleves, and are framed within facilitative and effective policies that ensure inclusive patterns of working are appropriately resourced. Notable too is the recognition of the value of equivalent expertise. Inclusive education clearly needs to be located within educational contexts and cultures that are welcoming (Booth, Ainscow, Black-Hawkins, Vaughan and Shaw, 2000), but it also needs to be built upon foundations of specialist knowledge, skills and understanding (Robertson, 2001b).

At Trafalgar Infant School, such expertise clearly becomes 'shared knowledge' between therapists, teachers and learning support assistants (Wise and Glass, 2000):

The speech and language therapist wanted Hannah to work on her tongue control. It was suggested that I encourage Hannah to use her tongue, rather than her fingers, to move food around her mouth. She was also reminded to close her mouth as she ate. This had the advantage of making eating less messy for her.

And:

She positioned her frame by the toilet door, supporting herself on the door frame as she walked into the toilet ... She always used the same toilet as a handle had been positioned on the wall to help steady her as she pulled her pants down and when she was sitting on the toilet. (pp.45–6)

By working closely with therapists, and using their own detailed knowledge of a pupil's personal needs, personality and physical environment, two learning support assistants (job-sharing) show how effective informal professional networks of practice can be. As Corbett notes:

... there is no great mystique to becoming an effectively inclusive school. It is about a shared vision by the school team (teachers, LSAs, governors, and parents); enthusiastic leadership by committed, experienced and skilled senior teachers; appropriate levels of resourcing; and an open

> receptivity to learning new skills and trying out whatever strategies seem to be useful. (2001a, p.58)

At the same time, Dessent (1996) highlights the value of having a designated, responsible member of staff in a school, someone who co-ordinates the convergent policy and practice of education and therapy. This would seem to be a natural role for the special educational needs coordinator (SENCo), although, as Simmons (1994) and Tomlinson (1996) point out, SENCos seem to have a burgeoning set of responsibilities that are increasingly difficult to fulfil. The revised *Special Educational Needs Code of Practice* (Department for Education and Skills, 2001a) offers no comfort, outlining as it does expanded SENCo duties. The solution would seem to be an expansion of the responsibilities of other teachers in this area (Ferguson, 2000), and the enhancement of opportunities for professional development that focuses on inter-professional collaboration and its impact on educational practice. Any such developments would, however, be much more likely to prove effective if they were built on foundations of a system of initial teacher education that took inclusive education seriously (Robertson, 1999). As Garner (2000) starkly, but accurately, notes, 'without concerted attention to the pervasive shortcomings of ITE, the pursuit of inclusion is an irrelevance' (p.115). No doubt, despite the difficulties of providing inclusive infrastructures, schools will seek and provide imaginative responses to the problem of working collaboratively with therapists. Similarly, therapy services can and will continue to strive for more coherent multi-agency practice at a local level. Topping, Gascoigne and Cook (1998), for example, have outlined a model that can bring together well-focused support for children with communication difficulties in educational settings, enabling mainstream teachers to liaise with a 'lead professional' rather than an array of advisers and experts who are hard to find, let alone bring together.

Another way of addressing the need to provide high-quality multiprofessional support for children with learning difficulties is through the radical re-development of some specialist provision in line with national policy which aims to promote further inclusion *with* special schools (Department for Education and Employment, 1997; 1998). The Somerset Inclusion Project (Bannister, Sharland, Thomas, Upton and Walker, 1998; Thomas, Walker and Webb, 1998) provides a possible template for how it can take place, what an inclusion service looks like and what it does. Three broad responsibilities for a teacher co-ordinator in the service are outlined: the curriculum, liaison and management. Under the heading of 'liaison':

> The teacher co-ordinator also liaises with physiotherapists, speech and language therapists, and parents at regular planning meetings and arranges all the annual review processes. He or she also provides a focus for external agencies (educational psychologists, school transport,

occupational therapists and LEA staff) and arranges informal meetings, when necessary, which take two forms:

1) informal liaison at hand-over times, at break-times, at lunchtimes and at the beginning and end of the school day;
2) a formal weekly meeting to discuss, to review and to set targets.'

Bannister et al., p.68

At one level this description of role would seem to duplicate or overlap with that of the SENCo. However, because SENCos are already likely to be working to or beyond full capacity, and because a teacher co-ordinator of the kind referred to here will have a specialist background (for example, in work with pupils who have severe and/or profound and multiple learning difficulties), there are good reasons for thinking that such a model could augment and improve the inclusive capability of schools. With enhanced staffing support of this kind there might also be a stronger expectation that innovative transformative practice could be developed involving education service professionals and therapists seeking new and more effective ways of working together. This might take the form, for example, of collaborative support networks for clusters of schools (Evans, Lunt, Wedell and Dyson, 2000) within which therapy services could be provided effectively and coherently, perhaps overcoming deep-seated difficulties associated with pupil transition. The development of such approaches appears consonant with the current policy in England that advocates the value of developing families of schools and local educational communities (Department for Education and Skills, 2001b). Such supportive networks would also make the 'flow of communication' between professionals easier (Wright and Kersner, 1998), and of a kind that is genuinely concerned with a 'sharing of knowledge on different perspectives of child development' (Whittaker, 1997, p.391).

LOCAL AND REGIONAL APPROACHES TO DEVELOPING INCLUSIVE THERAPY PROVISION

As commentators like Lindsay (1997) and Cole (1999) have observed, whether we like it or not education often seems to embrace different value systems at one and the same time, which operate in tension with each other. On the one hand, policies for inclusion and equality of opportunity are espoused, premised on a human rights perspective. On the other, specialisation in schooling, choice and diversity are seen as central to the overarching aim of creating a world-class and highly competitive nation. As the tensions appear to arise from policy dissonance (and this shows no sign of disappearing), it would seem appropriate to focus on developing inclusive multi-professional practice at regional or local levels where approaches to development can take account of particular contextual issues. For example, an inner city borough and a large rural LEA will provide very different contexts for planning policy provision, although, at the same time, both contexts can plan for inclusive provision and practice. The models developed to achieve this end, however, may well look very different. Lindsay has argued for:

> A more targeted approach, based on mainstream schools with specialist integrated resources for some children, together with other children individually included into 'local' schools, meets the aims of mainstreaming, access to a broad and balanced curriculum, opportunity for collaborative and mutual learning for all, and the efficient use of resources for the benefit of greater numbers of children. (1997, p.58)

Box 2

I CAN Early Years Programme

The I CAN educational charity is currently setting up and running a number of Early Years Excellence Centres designed to meet the needs of a wide range of young children experiencing communication difficulties. The programme aims to:

- reduce the numbers of children entering school with severe and complex speech and language difficulties;
- enable those children who do enter school with such difficulties, to embark successfully on their primary education.

The intervention approach used is intensive and requires teachers and speech therapists to work together. Children attend the centre either for a morning or afternoon session five days a week and receive two speech and language therapy inputs during each session, in either one-to-one or small group settings. The children also attend nursery classes and their specialist input is seen as closely linked and not as something different, or added on (Evans, 2001, p.13). The I CAN model of intervention endeavours to make sure that children's needs do not go unmet in the early years, and that children's severe and complex learning difficulties/communication problems are identified and intervention programmes are put in place.

The I CAN model is an interesting example of how the voluntary sector is working with LEAs at a local level, but within an overall national framework (twenty centres are being established in different parts of the country). Each centre costs £155,000 to set up (funded by I CAN) and after two years LEAs are committed to funding the provision for at least three more years.

Coram Community Campus

This is another early years focused multi-agency provision developed in London. The Campus provides a range of local services for families of young children, including those with special educational needs, and operates as a network of family and children's services created from a public/private partnership. A recent study of multi-agency practice at the project (Wigfall and Moss, 2001) has shown that despite grouping a range of professionals together in what might be seen as ideal conditions to provide support for children and their families, collaborative multi-agency practices were not well developed. Seemingly, the complex organisational structure of the service network made the integration of individual professional practices difficult and not everyone involved was aware of the overall principles of the network.

This example highlights how an overall vision of how collaborative practice will work is required if such activity is really to be 'more than the sum of its parts' (Wigfall and Moss, 2001). Education professionals and therapists who have the opportunity to work more closely together within inclusion services will need to be aware of the possible pitfalls of such organisational models.

Such an approach is often criticised by those who advocate that inclusion can only be called 'inclusion' when all children attend their local schools. The difficulty with this view is twofold. Firstly, the idea of 'local' is increasingly difficult to make sense of as parents make choices about the schools that they wish their children to attend. In addition, the concept of school as the only place in which education can occur is being challenged by e-learning and the use of the internet. Secondly, a 'local only' approach is almost certainly going to prevent some children (those with complex learning difficulties, for example) from receiving adequately resourced education and therapy, or the associated expertise. Box 2 shows two examples of how targeted local initiatives are emerging and having an impact, but are also presenting difficulties.

Local initiatives in developing inclusive education and therapy provision, important as they are, will always 'represent a piecemeal approach' (Law et al., 2001, p.137). A regional approach to overcoming fragmentary practice is developing through the *Special Educational Needs Partnerships* networks now operating across eleven regions in England (Department for Education and Skills, 2001e). As recent government guidance on inclusive schooling notes, with regard to inter-agency activity, 'One of the Partnerships' four strategic areas of work is to develop through collaborative working more inclusive policies and practices.' (Department for Education and Skills, 2001f, para.17, p.8). The impact of these regional partnerships warrants evaluation but is certainly promising. There is a need for these local and regional initiatives to operate within a wider national strategy and policy framework.

A NATIONAL PERSPECTIVE

Despite concerns in the previous section about apparent contradictions in government education policy and the consequent difficulties for anyone involved in planning inclusive educational services, there is good news on the provision of speech and language therapy services for children.

In its *Meeting Special Needs: A Programme of Action* (Department for Education and Employment, 1998) the Government set out its agenda for improving the achievements of children with special educational needs over a three-year period, and promised to address serious and long-standing concerns about the quality of the available speech and language therapy services. Two major research projects (Law et al., 2000; Department for Education and Employment and Department of Health, 2000) have produced a wide ranging set of thirty-one recommendations which, if acted upon, should have a major impact on inconsistencies in the speech and language therapy provision. Although space precludes a detailed analysis of their findings and recommendations, Box 3 lists those which convey their significance, and encourage the reader to consider how they might also be applied to the development of other therapy services of particular relevance to the needs of many children with learning difficulties.

Some of these recommendations have already led to important practical developments. For example, the Department for Education and Employment awarded £188,000 to *I Can* to develop, with others, a joint professional development framework for teachers and speech and language therapists during 2001 (Edelman, 2001, p.8). The Department has also made targeted Standard Funds available to services for children with speech and language needs, although, as Law et al. (2001) point out, whether this money has reached the appropriate services in a climate of highly devolved funding is uncertain. More positively, this education/health training initiative is being extended through the Standards Fund to cover other therapies normally provided by health authorities in educational contexts. Other recommendations connect well with recent thinking about pedagogy in the field of learning difficulties and illustrate the value of interdisciplinary thinking. Watson (2001) has outlined principles of social constructivist teaching, and these, with their emphasis on classroom dialogue, resonate well with the idea of a National Speaking Strategy that is embedded in the daily practice of schools.

The recommendations that have yet to be implemented, perhaps not surprisingly, are those that call for coherent planning from national to local levels and those that challenge shortfalls in funding. It is also unclear how the recommendations as a whole apply to children with severe and profound and multiple learning difficulties, some of whom are likely to have a legitimate claim on speech and language therapy services throughout their school careers. A task for those directly involved in this field is to ensure that implicit messages in the recommendations about the needs of children with learning difficulties are made explicit. Such action will prevent exclusive practices arising by default because

Box 3

A) Selected recommendations from the report: *Provision for Children with Speech and Language Needs in England and Wales* (Law et al., 2000). That:

- there should be a renewed emphasis on the role that speech and language therapy plays in mediating all the child's experiences in school and at home (*Rec. 1*);
- the greater part of the provision for school-aged children with speech and language needs should be embedded within the curriculum and take the child's educational context into consideration (*Rec. 2*);
- services work together to appraise the level and type of inequities in existence, and put appropriate mechanisms in place to address these inequalities (*Rec. 3*);
- a funding stream be explored that runs from the DfEE (now DfES) to LEAs (co-ordinated by both DfEE and DH), for the commissioning of services to children with speech and language needs within educational contexts (*Rec. 4*);
- LEAs act as lead commissioners through NHS providers of SLT services for children in educational contexts (*Rec. 5*);
- SLT managers offering services for children with speech and language needs should be in a position to negotiate appropriate models of service delivery (*Rec. 6*);
- new joint funding partnerships be exploited to provide pooled designated budgets for services for children with speech and language needs (*Rec. 7*);
- the level of funding in general be considered in the light of the apparent shortfall between reasonable levels of provision and what is currently available (*Rec. 8*);
- specific funding needs to be earmarked for areas of unmet need, namely provision for children in secondary schools, those with emotional and behavioural difficulties, and those for whom English is an additional language (*Rec. 9*);
- structures be put in place to enable joint strategic planning across Trusts and LEAs (*Rec. 12*);
- trusts and LEAs jointly review the implementation of processes to improve practitioner level collaboration (*Rec. 13*);
- national and local mechanisms be put in place to monitor the level of collaboration and disseminate effective collaboration (*Rec. 14*).

Note: A useful summary of this report can be found in an article by Law et al. (2001).

B) Selected recommendations from the report *Provision of Speech and Language Therapy Services to Children with Special Educational Needs: Report of the Working Group* (Department for Education and Employment and the Department of Health, 2000)

- the Teacher Training Agency should re-emphasise the importance of communication within initial teacher training modules dealing with speaking and listening, and encourage joint training opportunities for student teachers and therapists (*Rec. 3*);
- support for specialised INSET provision for teachers, learning support assistants and speech and language therapy assistants should be provided to all English LEAs through the DfEE's Standards Fund programme (*Rec. 4*);
- the DfEE should encourage organisations active in the area of communication difficulties to bring forward good practice case studies to share with teaching staff and SLTs on training courses (*Rec. 6*);
- consideration should be given to promoting greater opportunities for further specialised training at postgraduate level. This might entail a modular form of provision linked to the practical needs of LEAs and trusts and leading to an MA/MSc/MEd award (*Rec. 8*);
- the group recommends that Government should consider expanding the drive on literacy to embrace a National Speaking Strategy for Schools, building on and enhancing speaking and listening aspects of the curriculum, together with a focus on pupils aged 3–4 and provision for targets (*Rec. 9*).

some children's needs are not seen to be *primarily* related to communication and interaction. As the revised *Special Educational Needs Code of Practice* reminds us:

> Children will have needs which may fall into at least one of four areas [of need], many children will have inter-related needs. The impact of these combinations on a child's ability to function, learn and succeed should be taken into account.
>
> Department for Education and Skills, 2001a, para 7.52, p.85)

The provision of effective and inclusive therapy services for children with learning difficulties is likely to be enhanced when wider environmental barriers are removed and, as a consequence, children are able to participate fully in their school communities, and staff (including therapists) are able to work in conditions that optimise opportunities for learning. Box 4 shows some significant developments in policy, funding and practice that should be helpful to schools and therapists.

Box 4

The Disability Rights Code of Practice (Schools) 2002
(Disability Rights Commission, 2001)
The Code will be implemented in September 2002 and it will explain new duties that extend the Disability Discrimination Act 1995 to cover every aspect of education. Paragraph 1.1 (p.5) states that:

> The duties make it unlawful to discriminate, without justification, against disabled pupils and prospective pupils, in all aspects of school life.

The Code should encourage LEAs and schools to consider ways in which they will make their facilities accessible to children with disabilities and will encourage schools to be proactive and to anticipate problems before they arise. It, together with other parts of the *Special Educational Needs and Disability Act 2001*, places a duty on schools and local education authorities to improve the accessibility of their schools to children with disabilities.

Schools Access Initiative (SAI)
(Department for Education and Employment, 2001a)
In March 2001, the Department for Education and Employment announced an expansion of the Schools Access Initiative, making £220 million available to improve access for disabled children in English schools (for example: £1,045,800 to Birmingham LEA; £460,000 to Cornwall LEA and £260,000 to York City LEA). The benefits of this initiative have been described in a research study commissioned by the National Union of Teachers and Scope (Price Waterhouse Cooper, 2001), although consideration of integrated therapy provision is not addressed in any detail.

New school developments
Bishop (2001), an architect and consultant on innovative educational design, has described recent examples of school building developments that: 'show a range of creative solutions for widely differing SEN and budgets' (p.63), which illustrate how specialist requirements (for example, multi-purpose PE and physiotherapy facilities) can be built into revamped schools. The Department of Education and Skills (2001d) has also produced guidance on inclusive school design, although, as Garner (2001) notes, it seems to take a very optimistic view of the funds that might be available to create the exemplar buildings described.

More positively, developments in architecture influenced by principles of universal design (Imrie, 1996; Napolitano, 1996; Van Rooyan,
1997; Weisman, 1992) show how both new and old buildings can be
made accessible to a wide range of people with differing needs and can
also be aesthetically pleasing, 'readable' and welcoming environments. As Marks (1999) points out, these approaches also reflect
ideas espoused by proponents of the social model of disability (for
example, Finkelstein, 1980; Oliver, 1990).

The important points are that accommodation for therapy provision in education settings can be inclusive, that good quality provision is not cheap and that
it should be aesthetically pleasing to its users rather than being purely functional.

Notwithstanding political shifts that impact on educational practice, there
would appear to be grounds for thinking inclusive practices, which bring
education and therapy services together for the education of *all* children, are
being supported by significant policy developments at a national level. There
is a continuing need, however, to address the detail of inclusive practice, and
in ways that ensure some groups of pupils are not disadvantaged or subjected
to invisible forms of exclusion even though their needs are met superficially in
mainstream schools. Developing and sustaining good practice, as a recent
international study of inclusion in eight countries shows (OECD, 1999),
requires systematic policies that operate at national, regional and local levels
and focus on inclusive learning contexts and the services that can make them
work effectively.

CONCLUSION

As Law et al. (2001) note, the development of inclusive therapy provision
requires action and research at school, local authority, regional and national
levels. Good practice, although sporadic, exists, and we can learn from it.
This chapter has considered the nature of this practice and its relation to
policy. Underpinning such practice is the idea that professionals, from both
education and therapy service backgrounds, should view their roles in terms of
how they can empower children with learning difficulties and French emphasises its importance:

Professionals in such a situation serve as a resource to disabled people as
they strive to reach their own goals. They do not attempt to dominate, to
take control, or to 'manage' disabled people but rather to act as 'supportive enablers' actively sharing their expertise and knowledge while learning
from their disabled associates...

French, 1997, p.348

As Robertson (2001a) points out, this has now become a requirement of professional practice in educational contexts and the revised *Special Educational Needs Code of Practice* (Department for Education and Skills, 2001a) includes a chapter on pupil participation. In a sense this new obligation is a formal and helpful challenge to the kind of paternalism associated with therapy provision for children and adults with learning difficulties (Walmsley, 1997). It also indicates that the concerns of Mason and the *Educable* research group referred to at the beginning of this chapter can be addressed, and that therapy can be provided in inclusive educational contexts in ways that are not simply 'training activities'. Professionals with holistic orientations to practice (Eckersley, 1993) will place a child's perspective on therapy in education at the heart of their work and therefore focus on how entitlement and equity can be achieved (Corbett, 2001b). The policy developments referred to in this chapter support this struggle for entitlement and equity, but we need more of them, and fewer of those which seem to prioritise *exclusive* rather than *inclusive* practices.

REFERENCES

Alderson, P. (ed.) (1999) *Learning and Inclusion: The Cleves School Experience*. London: David Fulton.

Bannister, C., Sharland, V., Thomas, G., Upton, V. and Walker, D. (1998) 'Changing from a special school to an inclusion service', *British Journal of Special Education,* 25 (2) 5–69.

Bishop, R. (2001) 'Designing for special educational needs in mainstream schools', *Support for Learning,* 16 (2) 56–63.

Booth, T., Ainscow, M., Black-Hawkins, K., Vaughan, M. and Shaw, L. (2000) *Index for Inclusion*. Bristol: Centre for Studies on Inclusive Education.

Clarke, M., McConachie, H., Price, K. and Wood, P. (2001) 'Speech and language therapy provision for children using augmentative and alternative communication systems', *European Journal of Special Needs Education,* 16 (1) 41–54.

Clough, P. and Barton, L. (eds.) (1998) *Articulating with Difficulty: Research Voices in Education*. London: Paul Chapman Publishing.

Cole, P. (1999) 'The structure and arguments used to support or oppose inclusion policies for students with disabilities', *Journal of Intellectual and Developmental Disability,* 24 (3) 215–25.

Corbett, J. (2001a) 'Teaching approaches which support inclusive education: a connective pedagogy', *British Journal of Special Education,* 28 (2) 55–9.

Corbett, J. (2001b) 'Is equity compatible with entitlement? Balancing inclusive values and deserving needs', *Support for Learning,* 16 (3) 117–21.

Department for Education and Employment (1997) *Excellence for All Children: Meeting Special Educational Needs*. London: The Stationery Office.

Department for Education and Employment (1998) *Meeting Special Educational Needs: a Programme of Action*. Sudbury: DfEE.

Department for Education and Employment (2000) *Working with Teaching Assistants: A Good Practice Guide*. London: DfEE.

Department for Education and Employment (2001a) '£50M for access in Schools', press release on the Schools Access Initiative by the DfEE, 13 March. http://www.dfee.gov.uk/pns/.

Department for Education and Employment (2001b) *Special Educational Needs in Schools in England: January 2001* (provisional estimates). www.dfee.gov/uk/statistics/DB/SFR/.

Department for Education and Employment and the Department of Health (2000) *Provision of Speech and Language Therapy Services to Children with Special Educational Needs (England)* (Report of the working group). Annesley, Nottingham: DfEE.

Department for Education and Skills (2001a) *Special Educational Needs: Code of Practice.* London DfES.

Department for Education and Skills (2001b) *Schools: Achieving Success*, Government White Paper. London: The Stationery Office. http://www.dfes.gov.uk/achievingsuccess.

Department for Education and Skills (2001c) 'Far reaching reform to put the pupil first and enable every school to succeed', Press release 5 September. http://www.dfes.gov.uk/pns/.

Department for Education and Skills (2001d) *Inclusive School Design* (Building Bulletin 94). London: The Stationery Office.

Department for Education and Skills (2001e) *SEN Regional Partnerships.* http://www.dfes.gov.uk/sen/index.cfm.

Department for Education and Skills (2001f) *Inclusive Schooling: Children with Special Educational Needs*, Statutory Guidance, November 2001, Ref: DfES/0774/2001. Annesley, Nottingham: DfES Publications.

Dessent, T. (1996) *Options for Partnership between Health, Education and Social Services*, NASEN policy options for special educational needs seminar series. Tamworth: NASEN.

Disability Rights Commission (2002) *Disability Rights Draft Code of Practice (Schools): New duties (from September 2002) not to discriminate against disabled pupils and prospective pupils in the provision of education and associated services in schools, and in respect of admissions and exclusions.* Manchester: Disability Rights Commission. http://www.drc-gb.org.

Eckersley, P. (ed) (1993) *Elements of Paediatric Physiotherapy*. Edinburgh: Churchill Livingstone.

Edelman, G. (2001) 'Learning and developing skills together', *Communicate*, Spring/Summer, 89.

Educable (2000) *No Choice: No Chance. The Educational Experiences of Young People with Disabilities*. Belfast: Save the Children and Disability Action.

Evans, J., Lunt, I., Wedell, K. and Dyson, A. (1999) *Collaborating for Effectiveness: Empowering Schools to be Inclusive*. Buckingham: Open University Press.

Evans, L. (2001) 'Sun, moon and stars', *Special Children*, 136 (March) 12–15.

Farrell, P. (2001) 'Special education in the last twenty years? Have things really got better?' *British Journal of Special Education*, 28 (1) 3–9.

Ferguson, D. (2000) 'Preparing teachers for the future', *The OnPoint Series*. Oregon: National Institute for School Improvement, University of Oregon. http://www.edc.org/urban.

Finkelstein, V. (1980) *Attitudes and Disabled People: Issues for Discussion*. New York: World Rehabilitation Fund.

Fish, J., (1989) *What is Special Education?* Buckingham: Open University.

French, S. (1997) 'Defining disability: its implications for physiotherapy practice', in S. French (ed.) *Physiotherapy: a Psychosocial Approach* (2nd edition). Oxford: Butterworth Heinemann.

Garner, P. (2000) 'Pretzel only policy? Inclusion and the real world of initial teacher education', *British Journal of Special Education,* 27 (3) 111–16.

Garner, P. (2001) 'Inclusive school design' (Building Bulletin 94). A review, *Special*, Autumn, 51.

Graham, J. and Wright, J. (1999) 'What does 'inter-service collaboration' mean to professionals working with pupils with physical disabilities?', *British Journal of Special Education*, 26 (1) 37–41.

Imrie, R. (1996) *Disability and the City: International Perspectives*. London: Paul Chapman Publishing.

Law, J., Lindsay, G., Peacey, N., Gascoigne, M., Soloff, N., Radford, J., Band, S. and Fitzgerald, L. (2000) *Provision for Children with Speech and Language Needs in England and Wales: Facilitating Communication Between Education and Health Services* (Research Report RR239). London: Department for Education and Employment. Also available as a research briefing on http://www.dfee.gov.uk/research/.

Law, J., Lindsay, G., Peacey, N., Gascoigne, M., Soloff, N., Radford, J. and Band, S. (2001) 'Facilitating communication between education and health services: the provision for children with speech and language needs', *British Journal of Special Education,* 28 (3) 133–41.

Lindsay, G. (1997) 'Values, rights and dilemmas', *British Journal of Special Education*, 24 (2) 55–9.

Marks, D. (1999) *Disability: Controversial Debates and Psychosocial Perspectives*. London: Routledge.

Mason. M. (1992) 'Internalised oppression', in R. Rieser and M. Mason (eds.) *Disability Equality in the Classroom: a Human Rights Issue*. London: Disability Equality in Education.

Miller, C. (2001) Review of two recent research reports: 'Provision for Children with Speech and Language Needs in England and Wales: Facilitating Communication between Education Health Services' and 'Provision of Speech and Language Therapy Services to Children with Special Educational Needs (England)', *Child Language Teaching Therapy*, 17 (3) 247–52.

Napolitano, S. (1996) 'Mobility impairment', in G. Hales (ed.) *Beyond Disability: Towards an Enabling Society*. London: Sage in association with the Open University Press.

OECD (1999) *Inclusive Education at Work: Students with Disabilities in Mainstream Schools*. Paris: OECD.

Oliver, M. (1990) *The Politics of Disablement*. Basingstoke: Macmillan.

Oliver, M. (1996) *Understanding Disability: From Theory to Practice*. Basingstoke: Macmillan Press.

Price Waterhouse Cooper (2001) *Within Reach: an Evaluation of the Schools Access Initiative* (A report for SCOPE and The National Union of Teachers). London: National Union of Teachers.

Robertson, C. (1999) 'Initial teacher education and inclusive schooling', *Support for Learning*, 1 (4) 169–73.

Robertson, C. (2001a) 'Pupil participation and the revised Code of Practice', *SLD Experience,* 30 (Summer) 2–5.

Robertson, C. (2001b) 'The social model of disability and the rough ground of inclusive education', in T. O'Brien (ed.) *Enabling Inclusion: Blue Skies … Dark Clouds?* London: The Stationery Office.

Simmons, K. (1994) 'Decoding a new message', *British Journal of Special Education*, 21 (2) 59.

Thomas, G., Walker, D. and Webb, J. (1998) *The Making of the Inclusive School*. London: Routledge.

Tomlinson, S. (1996) 'Conflicts and dilemmas for professionals in special education', in C. Christensen and F. Rizvi (eds.) *Disability and the Dilemmas of Justice*. Buckingham: Open University Press.

Topping, C., Gascoigne, M. and Cook, M. (1998) 'Excellence for all children: a redefinition of the role of the speech and language therapist', *International Journal of Language and Communication Disorders*, 33 (Supplement) 608–13.

Van Rooyan, J. (1997) 'There's no such thing as a building', *New Squiggle: The Newsletter of Squiggle Foundation*, 1 (Autumn) 5–6.

Walmsley, J. (1997) 'Learning difficulties: Changing roles for physiotherapists', in S. French (ed.) *Physiotherapy: A Psychosocial Approach* (2nd edition). Oxford: Butterworth Heinemann.

Watson, J. (2001) 'Social constructivism in the classroom', *Support for Learning*, 16 (3) 140–7.

Weisman, L. (1992) *Discrimination by Design*. Champaign, UL: University of Illinois Press.

Whittaker, C. (1997) 'Key issues in the psychological development of the child: implications for physiotherapy practice', in S. French (ed.) *Physiotherapy: A Psychosocial Approach* (2nd edition). Oxford: Butterworth Heinemann.

Wigfall, V. and Moss, P. (2001) *More than the Sum of its Parts? A Study of a Multi-Agency Childcare Network* (Joseph Rowntree Foundation Study). London: The National Children's Bureau.

Wise, L. and Glass, C. (2000) *Working with Hannah: A Special Girl in a Mainstream School*. London: RoutledgeFalmer.

Wright, J. and Kersner, M. (1998) *Supporting Children with Communication Problems: Sharing the Workload*. London: David Fulton.

Wright, J. and Kersner, M. (1999) 'Teachers and speech and language therapists working with children with physical disabilities: implications for inclusive education', *British Journal of Special Education*, 26 (4) 201–5.

Part II

Policies into practice through two core subjects

Chapter 8

Raising standards in mathematics

Jill Porter

In this chapter Jill Porter identifies some of the difficulties that
teachers face in developing the mathematical understanding of
pupils with special educational needs. The effective teaching of
pupils with a range of learning difficulties is not only dependent
on staff having an in-depth knowledge of the subject, but also
on having detailed knowledge of progression in mathematical
understanding. She argues that, without this knowledge, in
attempting to raise standards staff may be unaware that pupils
may be losing previously acquired skills and are unable to apply
their learning meaningfully. She stresses that policies should
lead to the uncovering of such anomalies and poses questions
useful to staff in the formulation of policies.

Mathematics is an aspect of learning that creates anxiety. People who otherwise
have good self-esteem and view themselves as successful achievers feel waves of
panic when asked a mathematical question. Children in primary schools view
how clever their classmates are in relation to their achievements in mathematics (Hunter, Turner, Russell, Trew and Curry, 1993). Does this reflect the
teaching policies of the past or is it integral to the subject matter? It is, of
course, traditionally a subject in which comparisons are easily made: in the past
children have followed schemes that are hierarchically organised and which are
seen to sum up the differentials in their progress and as a consequence they
may be divided into sets for most of their school life. Children have, therefore,
been constantly reinforced in their view of their own attainments. In many
ways it can be argued that the introduction of the National Numeracy Strategy
(DfEE, 1999) with its emphasis on whole-class work, together with concerns
about 'over differentiation', may well be breaking many of these traditions. It
is, however, not only teaching methods but also some of the characteristics of
the subject that can create difficulties for pupils unless the teacher is aware and
takes appropriate actions. In this chapter the particular issues that inform
schools' policies and practices are discussed.

The National Numeracy Strategy was introduced in September 1999 to all schools with primary aged children. It followed the setting up of a National Numeracy project involving some 18 LEAs, drawing on both the research literature and practice in other countries. The target was to raise achievements with the objective that 75% of 11 year olds should reach age-related standards (or better) by 2002 (DfEE, 1998). The design principles reflected a concern that it should largely follow the structure of the National Literacy Strategy with a regular lesson of mathematics using a 'blend' of methods and an emphasis on oral and mental work. Particular attention was to be given to teachers knowing how to 'illustrate, demonstrate, and explain mathematical concepts' (DfEE, 1998, p.22) through sustained interactions, especially in whole-class settings. Such a strategy should also have an impact on parents and draw on their perceptions of the importance of numeracy. From the outset, reference was made to teachers in special schools with the clear expectation that they would be included in the training and that primary and special schools would cluster together to share ideas and experiences, ideally led by a mathematics teacher.

The Strategy, however, gave out mixed messages. Reference was made to evidence from a project which suggested that those pupils who were delayed would catch up if they were kept with the whole class. Indeed the original guidance cautions against too much differentiation as teachers were seen to give too much time to managing 'troublesome' pupils and not enough to the teaching of mathematics. In the same document, however, it was recognised that some pupils will experience more severe difficulties including:

> ... memorising and recalling facts ... an inability to understand and apply methods of calculating and visual/spatial difficulties in representing and interpreting mathematical information.
>
> DfEE, 1999, para.123

For those pupils, it was envisaged that there was a need for individualised work in the middle section of the lesson (whilst also pointing to the importance of learning from others). It was, therefore, being suggested to teachers in mainstream schools that in the majority of instances too much concern was being given to pupils' difficulties: treat them similarly and pupils will reach similar levels of attainment. The implication for special schools was that some pupils, at least, would require work to be well linked with their Individual Education Plans (IEPs).

There can be no doubt that attitudes and expectations are an important element in raising achievement and studies have repeatedly pointed to the wide variations in achievement in mathematics. Interestingly, it is a subject in which pupils included in mainstream have been found to make greater gains owing to its pivotal place within the curriculum. The introduction of the National Curriculum and, more recently, the National Numeracy Strategy

(NNS) has encouraged teachers to consider its relevance for all pupils, including those at the earliest stages of learning. The review by Ofsted of the first year of the NNS is optimistic about its influence on the attainment of pupils with special educational needs (Ofsted, 2000, 2001). A small-scale study that I carried out reflects the progress that can be made by *all* pupils given access to a daily lesson in mathematics. While all pupils made gains, some areas of learning were lost in the course of the year (Porter, 2001a). This suggests that in raising achievement we need to pay attention to both new learning and old learning and reflects broader concerns that have been expressed more generally in relation to pupils with Down syndrome (Wishart, 1996). It should not be assumed that pupils will automatically retain previous knowledge and skills. Policies and planning need to reflect this concern as much as ensuring that pupils continue to make new achievements.

THE IMPORTANCE OF MATHEMATICS

Schools' policies and practices will raise expectations when teachers are confident in understanding both the nature and importance of mathematics. The new curriculum guidelines (QCA, 2001) emphasise the role of mathematics in relation to developing children's understanding of their world and facilitating access to other areas of learning. It underpins their abilities, for example, in:

- seeing and using relationships;
- comparing and contrasting along a number of dimensions;
- imposing an order;
- the recognition of patterns;
- recognising relationships in time and space;
- modelling and representation;
- forecasting and probability;
- problem solving.

Many mathematical skills in everyday life are taken for granted by most of us. When I lose my diary I automatically scan my desk for something that is blue, rectangular and thin, recognising it when I spy the edge of it peeking out from under papers and other books, and rejecting other similar items that are the wrong size or colour. Equally I automatically perceive that a video is missing when there are two resting on the table where once there were three. Such knowledge enables me to anticipate that one may thankfully have been returned to the video shop. These examples demonstrate how mathematical skills and understanding of a very basic nature are woven into everyday tasks that are meaningful and goal directed for me as an individual. They highlight the importance of recognising that mathematical understanding is not something that has to be developed using particular material in specific environments. Research has identified how children develop and utilise mathematical skills and understanding that are functional to their own contexts. A famous example of this is the way in which the street children in Brazil learn to make quite complex calculations as sellers of candy (Saxe, 1991). This is often referred to as informal understanding, as is the knowledge and understanding gained by pre-school children. One of the challenges for teachers of pupils with learning difficulties is to capitalise on this informal understanding, and to harness children's own interests to encourage the development of strategies that can be generalised across contexts.

Policies need therefore to reinforce positive attitudes and expectations for the whole range of pupil achievement. In particular they need not only to aid teachers in recognising early developments but also to emphasise their relevance to, and impact on, daily life.

Policy audit question

In what ways does your school's policy for mathematics foster high expectations of the achievements of all pupils?

In what ways does it promote an understanding of the significance of early developments of mathematical skills and understanding?

UNDERSTANDING CHILDREN'S DIFFICULTIES

We have long been used to adopting an interactive definition of special needs and, as elsewhere in the curriculum, it is important with mathematics to think about children's difficulties in the context of the type of learning environment that is presented. Historically there have been wide differences in pupils' achievements in mainstream schools with a gap of as much as five years between the achievements of pupils leaving primary schools. (This variation is also evident in pupils in special schools, and should probably be of equal concern.) The NNS specifically aims to reduce these differences and in order to do so we need to take into account the nature of pupils' difficulties and to ensure that the teaching strategies we adopt do not inadvertently create problems.

It has been useful in considering pupils' difficulties to make a distinction between what they can do and what they understand: between the conceptual understanding and the procedural skills. Whole-class teaching requires special thought as, moving through a syllabus where the understanding is largely hierarchically ordered, the teacher needs to ensure that *all* pupils have grasped the necessary understanding. Pupils who miss key elements, either through ill health or poor attendance, and pupils who need more time to consolidate learning may be hindered in their progress because they have not achieved the foundations on which later understanding is based. Pupils who have not understood the principles of counting, for example, and that in whatever way you process the items for counting the number will remain the same, may be unable to use the skill to develop strategies of adding and subtracting at some later stage. Pupils' difficulties may be hard to identify in oral work where they may supply the right answer from someone else's whispered insights. They will not, however, be able to explain how they reached an answer. Additionally, it is often the errors they make, and do not detect, which provide evidence that earlier understanding has not been achieved.

> Raymond is reluctant to count objects placed in front of him. He is highly anxious when asked to do anything that he feels will be difficult. He is also easily distracted from the task and gently rocks from side to side in the chair, focusing on the light. He will put away the cups and will count them as he does so. From this we learn that he can produce the sequence one to six to tag objects. When objects are put out in a line, however, he double counts items or skips over them. His skill at this stage is limited to particular contexts that reinforce the one-to-one tagging of items. The teacher has chosen to concentrate on contexts that are meaningful and relevant to Raymond and that will give him practice in saying the number sequence and extend it over time to more items.
>
> Simon, unlike Raymond, counts with very little encouragement up to 60 and beyond. He is a very verbal pupil. He recognises the numerosity of small amounts, so can label sets of two, three and four. He can use his knowledge of the sequence of numbers to count large sets of objects. If he makes a mistake he does not recorrect himself but has learnt to start again. He has not, however, made the link between knowing the cardinality of a small set and counting. When asked to give the teacher four of his items, he gives them all, counting each in turn into the teacher's outstretched hand. With prompting he can remember how many were wanted, so the problem is not that he has forgotten. Even when the teacher closes her eyes and says, 'Tell me when I have four in my hand', he continues to give all. In order to promote this understanding the teacher uses role reversal and asks him how many he wants. She also reduces her requests to very small sets of one and two and occasionally three.

A common difficulty for all children is in moving between their informal understanding, based in concrete situations, to formal understanding of abstract and symbolic contexts. Hughes (1986) provides us with numerous examples of how young children's understanding can be limited by the context in which they are asked to perform. This does not imply that children can only apply their understanding when they are provided with real items but they need to be able to picture or form mental representations to understand what they are being asked to do. An example from Hughes's book demonstrates how confused a child can be when asked to add two amounts and there is no referent: 'two what? asks Ram'. Equally children are able to succeed on tasks in which the same sum is acted out by inserting bricks in a tin. Even though the child is unable to see the results of the addition it is still a concrete situation and he or she is able to add the two sums. It continues to be a concern that there is a separation between what is formally taught as mathematics in school and its application to 'authentic' events in the real world (Hughes, Desforges and Mitchell, 2000).

Leanne has experienced difficulty in learning the sequence of number words which even now she does not say clearly, and she often does not articulate the initial sound. The teacher works on activities that promote an understanding of numbers that is not reliant on producing a sequence of count words. The teacher uses a 'surprise party box' (the sort that children are given with a small present when leaving a party). Leanne watches as the teacher puts first one and then a second identical small toy in the box. She then takes one of the toys out, closes the box and shakes it. She asks Leanne to guess how many toys are in the box. Leanne thinks and raises one finger. Leanne is invited to look in the box and see if she is correct. The procedure is repeated but this time to portray an addition-sum, one add one. Leanne again correctly indicates the number of items in the box.

Pupils may not only experience difficulty with a conceptual understanding of numeracy, and many will experience specific difficulties that interfere with acquiring mathematical skills and understanding. Two areas are particularly implicated: language and working memory. Studies of children with specific language difficulties, and those with auditory impairment, highlight the role of spoken language and its impact on children's development (Donlan, 1998; Nunes and Moreno, 1998). Children in nursery settings are provided with a rich environment in which number words are used in a wide variety of practical and concrete contexts. Language in mathematics comes to develop special and precise meanings, and children are usually gradually inducted into those that centre around activities (including play, games and routines) through interactions with adults, siblings and peers. Additionally, inner speech comes to play an important role in monitoring problem-solving behaviour. It is likely that for many children with language difficulties, whatever their source, visual processes will play a more important role.

The second area highlighted is that of working memory: the short-term store that allows us to hold information in mind whilst we perform some mental operation on it. If, for example, a child is asked to give eight items, he has to hold the number eight in mind whilst he simultaneously counts out, one, two, three, four etc., until he reaches a match for the target number. If this parallel task is well practised and easily executed the demands on memory are lessened. There is, however, evidence that even at the earliest stages of learning the count words, the child may have problems in remembering the sequence (Porter, 1999). This may be particularly true of children who have problems in distinguishing between the sounds or who have auditory sequential memory difficulties. Once again it is likely that visual cues may support pupils better than oral cues and reduce the load on memory.

The separation of conceptual understanding and procedural skills limits the meaningfulness of pupil attainment. The development of skills, without understanding, results in their limited application. They need to be well practised to be remembered, hence the choral chanting of tables. These skills can be used in routine contexts but are less likely to be spontaneously generalised to new situations. Moreover, when mistakes are made, if there is no conceptual understanding and therefore no way of predicting a reasonable outcome, they are less likely to be spotted. It would be wrong, however, to downplay the role of skills. For example, unless children have acquired the skills for counting flawlessly they will be held back in reaching a conceptual understanding of the invariance of number as they may well reach a different number when they recount a set of items or events. Rote knowledge can also be important in that it can provide short-cuts that demand little attention and working memory; it therefore frees up attention to perform additional or sequential mental operations. The ideal is to have both systems working in tandem.

In summary, children's difficulties with mathematics can fall within any, or indeed all, of the following and may be relatively transient or longer lasting:

- lacking an understanding of the foundations underpinning what is being taught;
- being unable to apply informal understanding to abstract contexts;
- anxiety;
- language;
- information processing skills, particularly working memory;
- applying skills in new contexts;
- opportunities to practise and consolidate learning.

Knowledge and understanding of the potential difficulties suggests that we can reduce the problems children encounter through:

- considering carefully the context in which we present the mathematics, using concrete situations and linking the abstract to the practical;

- ensuring that children's learning of skills is linked with the development of understanding;
- recognising the child's emotional response to the task and adopting teaching styles and activities in order to reduce them;
- listening for evidence that children are unclear about the language we use and adjusting our language accordingly;
- thinking of ways in which we can reduce the load on working memory – for example, through using visual cues to serve as reminders and sharing parts of the task until the child is fluent in the execution of these skills.

IDENTIFYING DIFFICULTIES

The kinds of errors that children make have long been taken as an indication of where they are encountering particular difficulties. The focus in mathematics has shifted from thinking about whether the pupil produced the right (or wrong) answer to considering the process that children use to get there; in other words, what thinking was evident. For many pupils with learning difficulties it can be instructive to talk with them about how they reached a particular answer. For others, however, they will not have the metacognitive skills to identify the strategy they used or the language skills necessary to describe it. It therefore rests with the teacher to set up contexts in order to shed light on their difficulties.

In an attempt to understand children's difficulties it is useful to look at the contexts in which they succeed: their strengths; what they can do and the strategies they use; the contexts in which they have difficulty; where their strategies fail and what sorts of errors they make. Ideally, in order to plan one's teaching, it is also helpful to identify the contexts in which the child will succeed with support. An important element in devising these contexts is to consider situations which remove sources of stress for the child. Children are unlikely to be able to demonstrate what they can do if they are feeling highly anxious and are aware that they cannot do what is required. One way to help them is by using games where the fun element counteracts the pressure. Another equally successful strategy, however, is to change roles with the child, so that in effect he or she becomes the teacher; thus asking him or her to spot the mistakes that others are making, or to instruct another child, provides an enabling context for demonstrating understanding. It also effectively removes some of the procedural demands and allows access to underlying understanding. Simplifying the procedures also helps, for example using smaller numbers, providing supportive material and using a familiar context as well as sharing the task.

There is a twin focus to assessment: thinking about the pupils' understanding and skills and also thinking about how the teaching contributes to their learning. It can, for example, be instructive to listen to our language, the instructions we provide, the demonstration we give, the type of feedback we provide to pupils and what other interaction and dialogue form part of the teaching. The periodic use of video together with a school ethos which promotes joint problem solving can help to provide insights into what can be a puzzling and seemingly inexplicable profile of attainment.

Rashid is a recently arrived refugee and has been in the school for less than one term. Rashid is a timid, anxious child working closely with a peer, who speaks his language and English. They are both completing a worksheet in which they have to make sets of five, using buttons, and writing the corresponding numerals in the boxes to indicate a variety of sums that make five. It is not clear to the teacher how much Rashid understands of the task. She has no way of knowing what instructions and explanations he has received from his peer as their almost completed worksheets have similar entries. The teacher spontaneously introduces a game to them and they have to complete one worksheet, but rather than selecting the numeral from the table, Rashid holds them in his hand and offers them to his peer to select one. Rashid then has to say if the numeral matches the set of buttons, and whether his peer is correct. Rashid's role is thereby changed to tutor and the teacher is better able to check his understanding without requiring a verbal response. In order to further check his understanding of the task, she takes a turn in the game, partitioning the buttons differently, but choosing an incorrect corresponding number.

Schools' policies need to promote the identification of pupils' difficulties to enable teachers to uncover the particular difficulties that children are encountering and to match their teaching provision accordingly. In some instances, this process may be facilitated through promoting collaboration with teachers with particular expertise within the school or by drawing either on wider LEA personnel or other specialist teachers.

Policy audit question

Do school policies facilitate teachers in understanding pupils' difficulties with mathematics? Do they, for example, draw attention to the distinction between skills and understanding? Do they encourage teachers to examine the types of responses pupils make, including their errors, and the strategies they use to approach mathematical situations?

Are whole-school systems in place to access specialist knowledge where this might support the understanding of pupil needs and access to the curriculum?

PROGRESSION FOR PUPILS WITH LEARNING DIFFICULTIES

Pupils who experience a significant difficulty in learning are likely to make slower progress and to have a lower ceiling on their learning. It does *not*, however, indicate that they will stop making progress or even that the pace of learning will decelerate. Whilst learning in mathematics is generally conceived as hierarchical, pupils can achieve the same outcome using different underlying skills. For example, they may demonstrate an understanding of 'more' and 'less' using perceptual skills that guide them perfectly well in their decision-making. As with Leanne, they may demonstrate an understanding of adding and subtracting (even when they cannot actually see the items) and be able to indicate how the outcome will change. Alternatively pupils may use their skills and understanding of counting to make similar judgements. As elsewhere in the curriculum, progression is also identifiable through children applying their skills and understanding to new contexts, ones that will slightly alter the constraints in which they are applied. Progression is also pinpointed in the curriculum guidelines (QCA, 2001) through pupils increasingly being able to share their awareness and knowledge with others and, with time, being able to reflect on the strategies (whether mental or physical) that enabled them to reach that conclusion. Attainment for many mainstream pupils is usually achieved by children being able to work in increasingly abstract contexts but this may be inappropriate for some pupils with learning difficulties where our aim is to ensure that what they are acquiring is a set of useful problem-solving skills that can be applied in individually relevant situations. We need to ensure that not only is this awareness of progression demonstrated through our practices, but also given value in the way that we record and recognise achievements.

The revised edition of *Supporting the Target Setting Process* (DfEE, 2001) provides summary statements of pupils' achievements that are subject specific from Level 4 onwards. It is, however, possible to recognise mathematical achievements in pupils who are working below that level and the following section provides some insight into how robust some of the early mathematical developments may be.

Pupil progression at the earliest stages

It is easy to get caught up in thinking that even the earliest stages of mathematics revolve around learning the skills of counting and formalising the properties of objects. If our curriculum for mathematics is to be inclusive of all pupils, it must demonstrate our recognition of its importance to achieving a broader understanding of the world. We know, for example, that number is an important property across a range of species; indeed it may promote survival where predators are concerned. Number, or numerousness, provides important cues in the environment, enabling us to predict and anticipate and to take appropriate action.

Clearly we become sensitised to these cues as they gain meaning.

Research shows that infants as young as five months are able to represent and reason about number (Wynn, 1992). They can, for example, discriminate between displays that differ only in relation to number, providing the quantities are small. This ability is not limited to visual discrimination as similarly they have been found to discriminate between the auditory sequence of two and three drumbeats and between the physical actions of a puppet jumping two or three times. In a series of ingenious studies using a puppet and a screen, young infants have been found to predict the outcome of adding and subtracting one, to one and two puppets. The infant, as judged by an independent observer, demonstrates surprise when he sees one puppet join another puppet, but the screen goes back to indicate that instead of two puppets, inexplicably (courtesy of a trap door), there is only one.

Older infants have been found to retrieve objects that they can no longer see by making an appropriate number of reaches, thus further demonstrating the ability to represent and reason about number. This sequence of awareness of number and reasoning through to simple actions and problem-solving behaviour can inform our teaching of pupils who are unlikely to develop conventional approaches to counting. Research has been carried out to investigate contexts to promote problem solving in pupils with complex needs (Porter, 2001b). In case-study work it became clear that contexts for pupils at the earliest stages need to be tailored individually to their needs and interests. A vital element is to find situations which will arouse children's interest and hold their attention in order to encode numerical information: for example, pupils need to sustain their *looking* if they are to register that more than one item is available. The context also needs to invite a response that is within the pupils' repertoire. As elsewhere, staff need to share their knowledge and experience with pupils in order to use it to promote learning. This individualisation requires a curriculum that draws attention to the ways in which children's awareness and understanding develop, but does not prescribe the activities through which this can be achieved.

Policy audit question

Does the school's curriculum for mathematics support staff in understanding progression within the curriculum? For example:

Does the curriculum make explicit the mathematical nature of early learning? Does the curriculum promote the application of mathematical skills and understanding to a range of everyday situations that would be meaningful to the pupil? Does the curriculum support the development of pupils' communication about mathematical activities? Is the mathematics curriculum linked to the development and application of problem solving?

GOOD PRACTICE IN THE NATIONAL NUMERACY STRATEGY

Evaluations of the NNS are only just beginning to be published and, whilst the evidence supports the view that pupils have gained, it is unclear what practices account for this. An early evaluation of the strategy highlighted that, nationally, pupils were making gains probably due to the increased emphasis that schools were giving to the subject as it was too soon for the strategy itself to have made a significant impact (Earle, Fullan, Leithwood, Watson, with Jantzi, Levin and Torrance, 2000). There is always a danger that, in seeking to demonstrate progress in raising standards, any sign of pupils' understanding is taken as achievement. Hughes, Desforges and Mitchell (2000) point to the emphasis within the NNS on calculation and computation with the danger that application becomes an optional add-on. It is possible that the pupils who are working most slowly miss these options in the pressures to raise standards. As has already been argued, it is essential for pupils with learning difficulties to have opportunities to consolidate and generalise their learning and to apply it to real-life contexts. If we cannot assume this spontaneous transfer in mainstream pupils we certainly cannot do so for pupils with complex or significant needs. Recording and reporting systems must reflect this need, including school-wide target setting. Whilst it may look impressive on paper that pupils are moving up the P scales, if they are losing earlier skills and understanding or are unable to apply their learning in a meaningful way, the school is gaining at their expense.

Research suggests that we need to be cautious in enabling children to have time to consolidate learning. A distinction must be made, however, between repetition of the same lesson and activity and opportunities to practise learnt skills. The example below illustrates how one special school has ensured that the timetabling of topics enables children to return to areas more frequently; time will reveal the appropriate balance. It is, however, likely that teachers will want to consider how recently acquired skills and understanding can be applied to other events and activities during the day. What has become routine could be regularly extended to incorporate new areas through introducing the unexpected.

Harris and Thompson (2000) describe an approach to the NNS which was evolved during the pilot of the Numeracy project. They outline how they started by being clear about the priorities and how they used this information to plan the broad topics across their two-year Key Stage band. Their planning ensured that by covering four topics a term, pupils would regularly revisit areas of learning. This whole-school approach to planning and recording also reduced the load on the individual teacher. Each would plan a block of work, including the activities and the resources for a week, and pass the plan on to the next teacher who would individualise it as appropriate to capture the range of needs within the class. In this way planning gains an accumulative benefit of the creativity and expertise of teachers across the key stage. Harris and Thompson (2000) cite the advantages to pupils of concentrating for a week on one maths concept and its associated vocabulary and, when this topic is revisited in a month, assessing what understanding the pupil has retained. Teachers are consequently able to tailor future work to the needs of their pupils. An evaluation of the progress made by those pupils about whom there was concern suggests that this framework has advantages. Pupils can encounter a range of mathematical activities and experience an appropriately broad curriculum, whilst at the same time the retention of their understanding is monitored. Although most researchers agree that the breadth of activity that is available to pre-school children supports their developing conceptual understanding, we do not yet know the extent to which pupils with learning difficulties benefit from copying this approach.

It is likely that pupils will be supported by learning support assistants or teaching assistants (LSAs or TAs), whose role is crucial. They require an understanding of how learning will occur, not simply what activity will be carried out, as it is easy for mathematics to be reduced to a series of activities or tasks that can be ticked as achieved. If, however, staff do not know how to support pupil learning, they can provide help that will enable the child to 'do' the activity, but unfortunately no learning will occur. Dialogue and demonstration, rather than physically helping the child to succeed, form an important part of this teaching. Although it may seem to be a poor use of resources, 'team-teaching' can enable assistants and teachers to share practices and insights into the success and difficulties that pupils (and staff) encounter. Where this is not possible, it is vital that the teacher and the assistant take time to talk on a regular basis and that they share opportunities for INSET.

Policy audit question

Is there provision within the school to examine the effectiveness of current teaching strategies, including the adopted framework of the NNS, for *all* pupils including those who might be described as having additional or significant learning difficulties?

Is provision in place for examining the progress of particular groups of pupils and for analysing what factors are supporting or impeding their progress? For example, schools might want to consider those pupils with challenging behaviour or those with additional language or communication needs and to examine how effectively additional support within the classroom is used, or the balance between different types of activities?

A recent survey of effective teachers of numeracy carried out by King's College London for the Teacher Training Agency (TTA) highlighted the importance of teachers having 'a rich network of connections between different mathematical ideas' and of having strategies to help pupils to make these connections. Such a process calls for teacher confidence and high expectations (rather than qualifications in mathematics). The report also highlights the importance of mathematics-specific, continuing professional development as well as effective teachers working closely with others in planning and evaluating approaches to teaching. Schools need to develop practices that are conducive to promoting this expertise in *all* staff. Raising standards must not simply be seen as children acquiring higher skill levels, but must be targeted towards developing important mathematical thinking tools which can be applied in contexts that are meaningful in daily life. Policies must be in place to ensure that such tools are developed.

REFERENCES

DfEE (1998) *Numeracy Matters* (The Preliminary Report of the Numeracy Task Force). London: DfEE.

DfEE (1999) *The National Numeracy Strategy*. Sudbury: DfEE.

DfEE (2001) *Supporting the Target Setting Process* (revised March 2001) (Guidance for effective target setting for pupils with special educational needs). Nottingham: DfEE.

Donlan, C. (1998) 'Number without language? Studies of children with specific language impairments', in C. Donlan (ed.) *The Development of Mathematical Skills*. Hove: Psychology Press.

Earl L., Fullan, M., Leithwood, K., Watson, N., with Jantzi, D., Levin, B. and Torrance, N. (2000) *Watching Learning: OSIE/UT Evaluation of the Implementation of the National Literacy and National Numeracy Strategies*. Sudbury: DfEE.

Harris, M. and Thompson, J. (2000) 'Let's do it! Numeracy at Hawkesbury Fields School', *SLD Experience*, 26 (Spring) 13–15.

Hughes, M. (1986) *Children and Number*. Oxford: Blackwell.

Hughes, M., Desforges, C. and Mitchell, C. (2000) *Numeracy and Beyond: Applying Mathematics in the Primary School*. Buckingham: Open University Press.

Hunter, J., Turner, I., Russell, C., Trew, K. and Curry, C. (1993) 'Mathematics and the real world', *British Educational Research Journal*, 19 (1) 17–26.

Nunes, T. and Moreno, C. (1998) 'Is hearing impairment a cause of difficulties in mathematics?' in C. Donlan (ed.) *The Development of Mathematical Skills*. Hove: Psychology Press.

Ofsted (2000) *The National Numeracy Strategy: the First Year*. London: DfEE.

Ofsted (2001) *The National Numeracy Strategy in Special Schools*. London: DfEE.

Porter, J. (1999) 'Learning to count: a difficult task?' *Down Syndrome Research and Practice*, 6 (2) 85–94.

Porter, J. (2001a) 'Including pupils with severe learning difficulties in the Numeracy Strategy'. www.isec2000.org.uk/abstracts/papers_p/porter_1.htm.

Porter, J. (2001b) 'Assessing awareness and coding of numerosity in children with severe and profound learning difficulties (Three exploratory case studies)', *BPS Centenary Annual Conference*, 28–31 March 2001, Glasgow, Poster presentation.

QCA, (2001) *Mathematics: Planning, Teaching and Assessing the Curriculum for Pupils with Learning Difficulties*. London: QCA.

Saxe, G.B. (1991) *Culture and Cognitive Development: Studies in Mathematical Understanding.* Hillsdale, NJ: Lawrence Erlbaum.

TTA (1999) *Effective Teachers of Numeracy.* A research project by King's College, London sponsored by the Teacher Training Agency. www.teach-tta.gov.uk/numeracy 20/09/00.

Wishart, J. (1996) 'Avoidant learning styles and cognitive development in young children', in B. Stratford and P. Gunn (eds.) *New Approaches to Down Syndrome.* London: Cassell.

Wynn, K. (1992) 'Addition and subtraction by human infants', *Nature*, 358 749–50.

Chapter 9

Policies for promoting literacy
Including pupils with severe and profound and multiple learning difficulties

Richard Byers and Linda Ferguson

> This chapter begins with a brief historical overview of the teaching of literacy to pupils with severe and profound and multiple learning difficulties; provides a detailed commentary on the implementation of the Literacy Hour for these pupils in a specialist context; and closes with reflections on the challenges that practitioners face.

The tensions that exist between inclusive ideologies and the drive to raise standards are well-known, and seeking to address individual needs through specialist approaches adds a further challenge to this complex and potentially volatile mix. This chapter sets out to explore these challenges using the implementation of the National Literacy Strategy in general, and the Literacy Hour in particular, as a study in inclusivity. It is important to investigate the possibility of reconciling the curricular interests of the majority with the special educational needs of the few by focusing on pupils with severe and profound and multiple learning difficulties. We chose these pupils as they are the learners we know best and, by looking at a particular case, they can help us to understand issues in the education of wider groups of learners.

LITERACY FOR PUPILS WITH SEVERE AND PROFOUND AND MULTIPLE LEARNING DIFFICULTIES

Reading for social survival and alternative and augmentative strategies

The history of literacy teaching for pupils with severe and profound and multiple learning difficulties is relatively brief and comparatively recent, as these pupils were considered 'ineducable' prior to 1971. When they did gain access to schools, albeit special schools for the 'educationally subnormal (severe)', in the early 1970s, the teaching of literacy was not considered to be a priority. Teaching in special schools at that time was based on narrow behaviourist principles and tended to concentrate on what were often called 'life skills' in order to prepare young people for personal and social 'independence'. Where literacy was taught, the social relevance of reading and writing was emphasised, for example, the 'notes on the education of mentally handicapped children' developed by the staff of Rectory Paddock School (1981) state that 'reading should be given a practical significance whenever possible'. Examples of reading such as recipes or bus timetables are given and the notes develop the notion of a 'functional sight' vocabulary of socially useful words which pupils could learn to recognise. The Rectory Paddock materials suggest that the 'mentally handicapped child' (who would be recognised today as having 'severe learning difficulties') can be helped to recognise these socially useful words using three strategies clearly drawn from the teaching of reading in mainstream education:

- the shapes of whole words;
- a 'limited number' of phonic cues;
- information obtainable from the context.

Alongside these mainstream approaches to the teaching of 'functional literacy', staff in specialist contexts began to make use of approaches to literacy which provided alternatives to standard text or augmentative prompts. Van Oosterom (1991), for example, makes reference to the use of diacritical marks; extended alphabets; colour codings; or symbolic accentuation to support pupils' reading. She also records staff using 'pictorially based symbolic systems' or 'rebuses', such as those explored by Devereux and van Oosterom (1984) and the staff of Blythe School (1986) and, later, by Detheridge and Detheridge (1997). These parallel tendencies (the desire to mimic the mainstream of education and the development of highly specialised approaches, some involving the early use of an emerging computer-based technology) characterise the history of teaching literacy to pupils with learning difficulties over the final years of the twentieth century.

The introduction of the National Curriculum in 1988 in England and Wales had a major impact upon the curriculum for pupils with severe and profound and multiple learning difficulties. Staff in special schools began, often for the first time, to seek access to a range of subject areas for their pupils, although attitudes to the teaching of literacy did not immediately change. Hassell (1990) discusses a 'social sight vocabulary' which pupils with learning difficulties might use in order to read 'for information'; the examples Hassell offers involve identifying the contents of a tin of beans; finding out what is on television; or scanning the menu for a take-out meal. Van Oosterom's (1991) early response to the challenge of creating access to the National Curriculum for pupils with learning difficulties continues to focus upon the importance of 'functional literacy'. Ackerman and Mount's (1991) work promotes the relationship between literacy and life skills, and vocational activities (particularly for senior pupils) and stresses perceived links between communication and literacy. In addition, Ackerman and Mount emphasise the role of information and communication technology, including concept keyboards and touch screens, used in association with tactile cues, signs and symbols in developing a 'whole language' approach to the creation of a 'literate environment' in schools for pupils with severe learning difficulties.

The National Curriculum Council's (NCC, 1992) work on teaching subjects to pupils with severe learning difficulties provides guidance, under attainment target sub-headings, on all aspects of English. Building on Ackerman and Mount's work, the NCC booklet adopts an eclectic approach to the use of signs, symbols, and information and communication technology (ICT) in support of pupils' reading and writing. Interestingly, the NCC material also emphasises the importance of communication as a cross-curricular skill: communication skills include 'use of body language'; the acquisition and use of language, including 'speech or signing'; using 'pictures/drawings, signs/symbols and, eventually, words'; and 'reading and writing as a means of communicating ideas'. Developments since 1992 have built upon these multi-modal initiatives and in this sense other forms of communication can build towards literacy. Fergusson (1994), for example, describes a 'total communication environment' in which various forms of communication co-exist alongside the use of photographs and rebus symbols on a 'communication continuum' which is seen as leading finally to the written word.

The National Literacy Strategy and the revised National Curriculum

The *Programme of Action* (DfEE, 1998a) has accelerated tendencies to move away from separate, specialised schooling for pupils with severe learning difficulties and towards a more integrated provision; social and locational inclusion; and inclusive approaches to curriculum planning. The National Literacy Strategy (NLS) *Framework for Teaching* (DfEE, 1998b), presented as another inclusive initiative, encouraged many schools for pupils with severe learning difficulties in England to consider the provision of a daily session dedicated to literacy for the first time. Guidance on teaching, *Children with Special Educational Needs* (DfEE, 1998c), designed to supplement the *Framework for Teaching*, suggests that the difficulties experienced by most children with special educational needs 'can generally be overcome through normal teaching strategies'. A small minority of pupils, including those who are the focus for this chapter, may, suggests the guidance, benefit from:

- different levels of work;
- work at a different pace;
- access to alternative or augmentative systems, including signs, symbols and the use of electronic aids.

Some pupils, the guidance acknowledges, 'may be learning to communicate through eye pointing or gestures, beginning to use objects of reference or symbols, matching pictures or symbols to objects or recognising that written words have meaning.' (p.114). The guidance does not state unequivocally that, for some pupils, it is appropriate to work on these kinds of objectives within the Literacy Hour, but it does encourage staff to use the *Framework for Teaching* 'flexibly' for pupils with severe or complex difficulties.

Berger, Henderson and Morris (1999) are much more forthright about this possibility and acknowledge that practitioners need to ensure that there is a 'clear focus on literacy instruction' and that an 'appropriate amount of time' is allocated to teaching focused upon the National Literacy Strategy Learning Objectives, but they go on to argue that access to reading and writing is achieved, for pupils with severe, complex and profound learning difficulties, 'through the development of language and communication'. Berger et al. go further and propose that the development of communication and listening skills is 'an essential step towards reading and writing' for pupils with severe and profound learning difficulties, and that work on communication and listening skills will enable these pupils 'to be fully included' in the Literacy Hour.

In QCA/DFEE's (2001) guidance on *Planning, Teaching and Assessing the Curriculum for Pupils with Learning Difficulties*, staff are reminded of the 'expectation' that they will implement a 'daily dedicated Literacy Hour'. The guidance also emphasises, however, the flexibility available to staff to develop the curriculum in ways that are appropriate to the needs of the pupils they teach and stresses the importance of communication in the curriculum for pupils with learning difficulties. Enabling pupils to 'interact and communicate' is given as the first example of an appropriate aim for their curriculum. Learning English is described as encompassing 'all aspects of communication' and staff are encouraged to interpret the idea of reading as incorporating 'any activity that leads to the derivation of meaning from visual or tactile representations'; and writing as including 'any activity that communicates and records events'. The guidance also highlights the importance of teaching the key skill of communication, which is broken down into a continuum of illustrative outcomes, similar to those given by Berger et al. (1999), which range from 'responding to ...', 'communicating with ...' and 'interacting with others' through to 'the application of emerging literacy skills'. The key skills, the guidance suggests, may be addressed through targets set in pupils' individual education plans and therefore 'opportunities for developing the key skill of communication can be provided across the curriculum as well as through English sessions and classes which focus on literacy' (p.5).

This guidance, we suggest, gives staff working with pupils with severe and profound and multiple learning difficulties a very clear set of messages about the role of communication in the curriculum; about the relationships between communication and literacy; and about the relationships between class time dedicated to curricular objectives and the integration of targets focused on priorities in learning for individual pupils. In the following case study, we explore the issues experienced in an all-age special school setting out to implement the Literacy Hour for pupils with severe and profound and multiple learning difficulties. The commentary is written from the perspective of the staff involved and we include vignettes to show how individual pupils with severe and profound and multiple learning difficulties respond to their inclusion within the approach to the Literacy Hour adopted in this school.

The Literacy Hour – an issue of access

> It is by being treated as communicators that we become communicators.
> Goldbart, 1994, p.16

The staff, in the past, had viewed communication as a cross-curricular subject and offered access to literature in a fairly *ad hoc* manner. We still believe that the ability to receive and initiate communicative interactions, thereby exerting some control over the environment, is fundamental to the quality of life of pupils. The staff also acknowledge that, in refining their attempts to communicate, pupils are likely to use a range of modes of communication, and they believe that it is important to value all modes of communication equally and to support and assist each pupil to make full use of the modes at his or her disposal. The role of the adult is perceived to be crucial when interpreting and responding to the many subtle cues offered by pupils who are functioning at a pre-intentional level of communication (Coupe O'Kane and Goldbart, 1998), including those with profound and multiple learning difficulties.

Following the prescribed two-day, mainstream-focused training for the National Literacy Strategy in 1998, it was decided to review the school's position on the teaching of English. An objective review of its communicative practice suggested that, although the school continued to uphold its policy of perceiving communication as a cross-curricular subject, the consequence may be a reduction in the focus and range of structured teaching opportunities. It was also acknowledged that there has been a tendency to regard the assessment of communicative skills as the province of the school's speech and language therapists, which has had the effect of reducing the confidence of teaching staff in their ability to understand and use communicative cues in a differentiated way to reflect individual pupil's skills.

It was decided to view the implementation of the National Literacy Strategy as an opportunity to re-commit staff, in policy terms, to the centrality of communication within the curriculum. It was agreed that the development of communication and listening skills constituted an essential step towards reading and writing for pupils with severe and profound and multiple learning difficulties (Berger et al, 1999) and that it established communication as a core strand in the model of the Literacy Hour. The opportunity was also used to explore a broader definition of literacy; to provide meaningful access for all pupils; and to increase the staff's involvement in the process of assessment.

The structure of the Literacy Hour

In July 1998, it was decided to embrace the Literacy Hour as a whole-school initiative and to adopt its balance of whole-class and small-group/individual teaching activities; the splitting of the hour into four segments; and its implementation on a daily basis. As the majority of pupils do not read or write (although many use symbols as a communicative mode) it was agreed to redefine the segments within the hour, in line with the policy decisions noted above, in order to promote meaningful participation for all pupils.

The first fifteen-minute, whole-class segment was entitled 'focused communication', which served to remind teachers of the importance of actively engaging and focusing each pupil from the beginning of the session. Objects and rebuses, which were known to be motivating for each pupil and which offered a dynamic (yet accessible) way of providing individual pupils with the opportunity to ask for a turn to participate, were used. This segment was seen as offering time to learn a new vocabulary (related to object or conceptual development) and as providing an arena for exploring objects soon to be referenced in shared text work. It was crucial that each pupil was enabled to perceive a role for himself or herself within the segment. Food, puppets, sensory and stimulating objects, in addition to the relevant rebuses, were used to reflect varying interests and ages.

The next segment, entitled 'shared text', continued the theme of whole-class teaching and offered an opportunity for pupils to practise emergent literacy skills where appropriate. Staff were encouraged to use familiar texts from a range of genres in ways that would be meaningful for all pupils.

The second half of the hour was divided between 'guided communication' (which allowed for small-group and individual teaching opportunities) and a plenary session lasting for ten minutes. The 'guided communication' section was assessment led and often reflected existing targets relating to pupils' individual priorities; thus, for some pupils functioning at a pre-intentional level of communication, it gave an opportunity to record their responses to a range of stimuli and to agree possible meanings. For other pupils, it provided a context in which to practise the linguistic programmes devised by the speech and language therapists and offered, for those pupils achieving at the highest levels, opportunities to practise phonic and writing tasks.

Recording sheets, for each of these sections, were completed on a daily basis, offered a detailed overview of pupils' performance across the week and enabled staff to review targets (both IEP and non-IEP related) regularly. For example, Katherine's IEP target of 'eye pointing to a named object from a choice of two with 75% success' was carried out in the guided communication section while the non-IEP targets 'to raise her hand to ask for a turn' and 'to look at the book when it was placed on her table' were practised within the focused communication and shared text sections respectively.

The last ten-minute or 'plenary section' proved to be the most problematic. Many pupils found it difficult to be reflective about their work or, indeed, to offer an opinion, and consequently the adults, who had been working with the pupils, were invited to provide a commentary on each learner's achievements. Pupils brought an example of their work or an object of reference back to the group in order to support the adults' descriptions of the tasks undertaken.

Creating access to the Literacy Hour

From the outset of the planning for the Literacy Hour two principles were crucial, that:

- all pupils should have equal access to, and involvement in, the work;
- whole-class teaching activities should accommodate the diversity within the class group rather than clustering pupils with similar prior achievements together across groupings.

It was therefore vital that those staff who were supporting pupils with profound and multiple learning difficulties understood their role should be 'enabling' and offered sufficient time for each pupil to initiate participation in the activity rather than overwhelming him or her with physical and verbal prompts.

One of the most useful aspects of the Literacy Hour for pupils with profound and multiple learning difficulties is the opportunity for practice. By using objects of reference and encouraging active participation within each session many pupils have begun to develop a perception of themselves as active learners. Using the same format on a daily basis (while altering the resources to retain the pupils' interest, but ensuring adequate exposure to facilitate learning) has empowered many pupils to develop an awareness of routines within the hour and to establish an individual behaviour with which to ask for 'a turn' to participate in the activities.

In order to demonstrate some of the strategies used to make the Literacy Hour accessible to the full range of pupils in a class, each segment of the hour will be discussed and then illustrated by a short case study of how particular pupils have engaged with the work.

Focused communication

Sessions begin by offering the class an opportunity to 'ask' to check their individual timetables. Once timetables (constructed from objects or rebuses) are checked, with all responses being valued and acted upon, everyone assembles in the particular area of the classroom where the object of reference for literacy work (a red box) is waiting on the table. At the table, everyone is offered the opportunity to take an object and/or symbol from the box. Staff are vigilant in watching for, and reporting, any movement (reflex or controlled) made by their pupils and will reinforce these behaviours by saying, for example: 'Elizabeth wants a turn to look in the box.'

The work progresses by choosing objects from the red box, which are named for the pupil and then offered for individual exploration. Where appropriate, pupils are asked to select objects from the box using function or attributes, for example, 'Can you find an object that is blue?' Pupils then have to listen for the name or attribute of their object in order to return it to the red box.

> Initially Emma, aged ten years, would move her right hand voluntarily but not purposefully. By focusing on this movement, we began to ask her to move her arm to tell us when she wanted to take a turn. Adult attention and turn taking became immediate consequences of her arm movement and, over several months, she moved from being fairly passive in communicative interactions to moving her arm purposefully to request a turn or a chocolate or a cup of tea. Over two years these skills have been extended and generalised outside the Literacy Hour and Emma is now perceived as someone who is active within the communicative process.

During the two and a half years that we have been teaching the Literacy Hour, we have observed a significant proportion of our pupils with profound and multiple learning difficulties using particular body movements and/or vocalisations to gain attention. Through continuous practice, there has been an increase in the intentionality/purposefulness of such movements evidenced both within and beyond the context of the Literacy Hour.

Shared text

The challenge of this section was twofold:

- to find ways of accessing texts and making them as meaningful as possible for those pupils with profound and multiple learning difficulties;
- for teachers to develop a wider understanding of the range of skills which could be classified as 'emergent literacy skills'.

It was also very important to ensure that the sharing of stories retained a sense of intimacy and promoted active listening on the pupils' behalf although the context was now that of a whole-class structured teaching activity.

Initially stories were used with which individual teachers were comfortable and added a 'storysack' approach to augment the text. In this way, pupils were able to choose and retain objects which were then referenced and re-referenced as the story progressed. Other pupils in the class were encouraged to turn a page, find the front of the book or visually track the adult's finger moving left to right across the text.

> Katherine, aged eight years, showed little interest in books but had always taken note of what her friend Ben liked to do. By positioning the pupils next to each other and using the same adult to access the text, staff began to notice slight changes in Katherine's responses to stories. She began 'to still' when it was Ben's turn to look at the book and to turn the page. After a few weeks she, too, would move her gaze to look at the book when it was offered and she has now learned to listen to parts of the story and to move her hand when she hears her chosen object mentioned in the story or poem.

As the staff have become more confident in shared text work, they have evolved a modular approach to the coverage of fiction, non-fiction and poetry. Issues of age appropriateness have been addressed by making books, following favourite recipes and videos in addition to using authors such as Roald Dahl and Shakespeare.

Guided communication

The transition from whole-class to small-group teaching activities allows a change in venue for the pupils and an opportunity to 'tune out' of the earlier tasks. For this segment, the learning support assistants in the classroom adopt a teaching rather than a supportive role, working with two or three pupils consistently across a half term.

Guided communication provides a context in which to practise IEP targets closely linked to the assessment of pupils' receptive and expressive language skills and to programmes generated by the speech and language therapists.

> Alistair, who is ten years old, has severe learning difficulties and is registered blind. He has always demonstrated a reluctance to explore objects and was highly tactile-defensive. His priority areas for working within guided communication reflected his level of linguistic functioning (single element level both expressively and receptively) and the need for him to learn to explore objects independently.

Through continuous practice within the Literacy Hour and by offering him a supportive and motivating (to Alistair) adult as a partner, he is now able to find, and explore independently, two objects placed in front of him and identify the one requested by the adult with 50% accuracy. He will also choose an object from the red box (in the focused communication work), remove it and place it on the table without resorting to throwing it; and has extended his early literacy skills by tactually scanning two moon symbols in an attempt to find the one which represents 'A'.

The plenary session

Staff have chosen to retain this session in their daily work as it is important to remind pupils of the work they have undertaken and to reflect upon their performance either independently or by using the adult who worked with them as an advocate. The plenary session is a whole-class activity which offers pupils with profound and multiple learning difficulties another opportunity to engage with an item from their guided communication work. It is also a time to receive focused adult attention, to participate in whole-class reflection and to celebrate success.

From policy to practice

This case study shows practitioners engaging in a radical reappraisal of both policy and practice. In responding to an initiative from the centre, originally designed to raise standards in the mainstream of education, colleagues in the special school in this case study have found opportunities to reaffirm some existing priorities; to reassess some accepted policy positions; and to develop new ways of working. In summary, their policy commitments entailed reasserting the centrality of some ideas, including the following:

- learning to communicate has a fundamental role to play in enhancing the quality of life for pupils and students with profound and multiple learning difficulties;
- communication has a key cross-curricular role in the curriculum for these learners;
- pupils and students with severe and profound and multiple learning difficulties are likely to use a range of modes of communication and all communicative behaviours will be seen as having equal value and will be fostered and supported.

Responses to the new initiative required new policies, including:

- all pupils having equal access to, and opportunities to participate in, the Literacy Hour;
- whole-class teaching elements of the Literacy Hour will entail working with highly diverse groups of pupils, and staff will meet the challenge of making the Literacy Hour inclusive and resist the temptation to create separate teaching groups of pupils with similar prior achievements;
- the approach to the implementation of the Literacy Hour must therefore be multi-modal and founded on what is already known about effective communication and literacy work;
- the development of communication skills must be seen as constituting an essential step towards reading and writing as well as being a key priority in its own right;
- communication will have a core role in the implementation of the Literacy Hour.

Some policy positions needed to be revised or reassessed in the light of experience of the new initiative, for example:

- promoting communication is an inter-disciplinary responsibility and demands inter-agency collaboration;
- inter-agency communication and shared practice, particularly in the area of assessment, must be improved;
- there is a need to work together, across agency boundaries, in order to explore and develop broader definitions of literacy and an expanding range of approaches to teaching the Literacy Hour.

We applaud the flexible approach taken by colleagues in the case study, in response to centrally defined policy, who did not turn their backs on the new initiative. They used the implementation of the Literacy Hour as an opportunity to take a fresh look at established ways of working and to drive policy and practice forward in new, more inclusive directions. These initiatives may support others in reviewing their approaches to the teaching of literacy and the development of more inclusive practice and, in conclusion therefore, we would like to draw together a number of points about the teaching of literacy, and the use of the Literacy Hour as a means of instruction, for pupils with severe and profound and multiple learning difficulties.

Practice needs to continue to move on from the approaches to literacy teaching (common in specialist contexts prior to the introduction of the National Literacy Strategy) which were often focused on the passive copying of text and which perpetuated a narrow emphasis on a social sight vocabulary. Pupils with severe and profound and multiple learning difficulties should, like their peers, be supported in exploring the full breadth of experiences related to literacy and literature and, where possible, should be enabled to learn to read and write for information, instruction and pleasure, as well as for social survival. It is clear that literacy skills are important as an aspect of personal, social and academic development; as a factor that helps to empower individuals with learning difficulties seeking to participate in a literate society; and as an element in promoting the key skill of communication in its widest sense. The question of how literacy is to be taught most effectively, however, to pupils with severe and profound and multiple learning difficulties remains.

Strategies adopted and adapted from the mainstream

In responding to this question, some authors emphasise the relevance and efficacy of traditional mainstream approaches to teaching literacy to pupils with learning difficulties. Ackerman and Mount (1991) and van Oosterom (1991), for example, suggest that the 'proto-reading' and 'proto-writing' activities with which children in the mainstream of education engage (such as learning about directionality; producing early forms of writing through purposeful scribble; developing concepts about print such as the beginning and end of books; and engaging with nursery rhymes) can be used in order to establish the components of literacy programmes for pupils with learning difficulties. These activities may then lead to the development of strategies (such as recognising the characteristic shapes of whole words; learning about phonic cues; and gaining support from contextual information) which would recognisably enable pupils with learning difficulties to engage with the objectives built into the *Framework for Teaching* for the National Literacy Strategy (DfEE, 1998b).

Many practitioners would argue that these possibilities remain, as yet, unproven as far as pupils with severe and profound and multiple learning difficulties are concerned. Practice, and the case study included in this chapter, indicate that the reality of literacy teaching for many pupils with learning difficulties is far more diverse, and encompasses the use of augmentative and alternative approaches to language, literacy and communication. It seems highly appropriate to continue to explore the potential of these approaches as we increasingly rely upon symbols, icons, alternatives to standard text and computer-assisted forms of communication in our everyday lives; to fail to do so would be less than inclusive. These approaches, however, while often enthusiastically championed by partisan commentators and adopted by pragmatic practitioners in their search for something that seems to work, tend to be under-researched.

Alternative and augmentative strategies

The role of information and communications technology (ICT) in supporting literacy for pupils with severe and profound and multiple learning difficulties, for instance, needs to be thoroughly evaluated. There has been little focused research to demonstrate the long-term efficacy of such approaches and some commentators (for example, Lewis, 1999) are cautious about the assumed positive impact of the use of ICT upon literacy skills for pupils with learning difficulties. School co-ordinators for English, literacy and ICT need a more secure basis, in theory and practice, for further collaboration.

We also need to investigate the relationships between augmentative and alternative approaches, and reading and writing in the traditional sense. Some commentators (Carpenter and Detheridge, 1994, for example) suggest that symbols can provide access to a literate world for pupils with learning difficulties. Other authors are less than fully convinced about this relationship. Even in 1991, van Oosterom was drawing upon research that suggested that pupils learn to recognise words more effectively without the use of pictorial cues and these complexities leave practitioners with a dilemma. It is clear that some adults with learning difficulties may need to use symbols as a long-term alternative to traditional literacy skills but practitioners need to be able to identify such learners at an early age in order to provide appropriate approaches. Other pupils with learning difficulties will ultimately gain traditional literacy skills and continue to refine them into adult life. They need to be identified at an early age in order that staff can provide appropriate approaches. At present, the research supports neither the identification of these contrasting groups of pupils nor the most effective means of teaching them.

Evaluating multi-modal approaches

The development of a 'multi-modal communication environment', with all modes in use from the early years, has been seen, in some schools, as a reasonable way of resolving the literacy dilemma. Again, this pragmatic and eclectic response has not been fully explored and evaluated and the simultaneous implementation of multi-modal approaches raises a number of questions for policy makers and practitioners alike. For example:

- if different pupils are taught through different modes, should they be taught communication and literacy skills in 'sets', grouping sign and symbol users together and readers and writers together, for example, or in mixed, multi-modal settings?
- should pupils with severe and profound and multiple learning difficulties and who have English as a second home language be taught using signs and/or symbols and should these signs and/or symbols be associated with their first language, with English, or with both?
- in any of these contexts, how useful are symbols which, in particular cases, may be pictorial but culturally laden ('dinner'); may require knowledge of traditional English orthography (names or questions); or demand some understanding of abstract symbols from other disciplines?

- do different modes of communication and literacy support one another or confuse pupils?
- are different modes of communication and literacy equally valid as outcomes for students with learning difficulties and equally useful in their adult lives?

FROM RESEARCH TO POLICY AND PRACTICE

There is, of course, a further question. Does learning to communicate lead towards literacy? Intuitively, it seems reasonable to assume that speaking and listening underpin reading and writing. Kemp (1996) challenges some of the assumed relationships in this area, however, and experience indicates that, for pupils with severe and profound and multiple learning difficulties, the connections are not necessarily causal or linear. The pupil who flicks through a set of symbols printed on cards in order to highlight 'Dean – go – dinner' is clearly communicating. It is not necessarily clear, however, whether Dean is using an alternative to speaking to get his message across or the proto-literacy skill of sequencing symbols. And when Narinder scans across her field of vision in order to eye-point the swimming towel as opposed to the horse-riding helmet, it is possible that she is deploying her established sense of directionality, a proto-literacy skill, in support of her emerging capacity to communicate. There is clearly a relationship between literacy and communication in these examples, but some pupils, and the case study of practice given here, may challenge our assumptions about the nature of this relationship. We argue, therefore, that school-based enquiry and research partnerships with practitioners should continue to explore these issues. The outcomes of such processes would provide effective support for the development of a purposeful, organised and structured response to the challenge of teaching literacy to pupils with severe and profound and multiple learning difficulties.

Staff working in specialist and inclusive contexts increasingly come from a range of backgrounds in terms of initial training and experience. At present, they are not sure whether pupils with learning difficulties should be taught literacy using:

- the range of alternative and augmentative methods which are widely used in specialist contexts;
- the objectives and methods proposed by the National Literacy Strategy;
- an eclectic mix of methods and approaches adjusted in response to individual requirements.

In order to achieve consistency, post-qualification, specialist professional development needs to reflect and to foster high-quality research into teaching and learning for pupils with severe and profound and multiple learning difficulties. At present, neither training for specialist teachers, nor the implementation programmes associated with initiatives like the Literacy Hour, are adequately based in such research. We contend that the development of a policy focused on progress towards a more inclusive education system needs to be driven by evidence of the effectiveness of the rapidly evolving and diverse range of strategies which characterise current practice.

REFERENCES

Ackerman, D. and Mount, H. (MEC Teacher Fellows) (1991) *Literacy for All: a 'Whole Language Approach' to the English National Curriculum for Pupils with Severe and Complex Learning Difficulties.* London: David Fulton Publishers.

Berger, A., Henderson, J. and Morris, D. (1999) *Implementing the Literacy Hour for Pupils with Learning Difficulties.* London: David Fulton Publishers.

Carpenter, B. and Detheridge, T. (1994) 'Writing with symbols', *Support for Learning*, 9 (1) 27–32.

Coupe O'Kane, J. and Goldbart, J. (1998) *Communication Before Speech: Development and Assessment.* London: David Fulton Publishers.

DfEE (1998a) *Meeting Special Educational Needs: a Programme of Action.* London: Department for Education and Employment.

DfEE (1998b) *The National Literacy Strategy Framework for Teaching.* London: Department for Education and Employment.

DfEE (1998c) 'Children with special educational needs', Supplementary guidance for *The National Literacy Strategy Framework for Teaching.* London: Department for Education and Employment.

Detheridge, T. and Detheridge, M. (1997) *Literacy through Symbols: Improving Access for Children and Adults.* London: David Fulton Publishers.

Devereux, K. and van Oosterom, J. (1984) *Learning with Rebuses: Read, Think and Do.* Stratford upon Avon: National Council for Special Education.

Fergusson, A. (1994) 'Planning for communication', in R. Rose, A. Fergusson, C. Coles, R. Byers and D. Banes (eds.) *Implementing the Whole Curriculum for Pupils with Learning Difficulties.* London: David Fulton Publishers.

Goldbart, J. (1994) 'Opening the communication curriculum to students with PMLDs' in J. Ware (ed.) *Educating Children with Profound and Multiple Learning Difficulties.* London: David Fulton Publishers.

Hassell, J. (1990) 'Resource pack, Part four: Reading', *Special Children*, 38 (April 1990) 1–12.

Kemp, C. (1996) 'Does teaching young children with disabilities to read facilitate their language development?: a critical review of current theory and empirical evidence', *International Journal of Disability: Development and Education*, 23 (2) 175–87.

Lewis, A. (1999) 'Integrated Learning Systems and pupils with low attainments in reading', *British Journal of Special Education*, 26 (3) 153–7.

NCC (1992) *Curriculum Guidance 9: The National Curriculum and Pupils with Severe Learning Difficulties.* York: National Curriculum Council.

QCA/DfEE (2001) *Planning, Teaching and Assessing the Curriculum for Pupils with Learning Difficulties.* London: Qualifications and Curriculum Authority/ Department for Education and Employment.

Staff of Blythe School (1986) *Working with Makaton at Blythe School.* Camberley: Makaton Development Project.

Staff of Rectory Paddock School (1981) *In Search of a Curriculum: Notes on the Education of Mentally Handicapped Children.* Sidcup: Robin Wren Publications.

van Oosterom, J. (1991) 'Aspects of English', in R. Ashdown, B. Carpenter and K. Bovair (eds.) *The Curriculum Challenge: Access to the National Curriculum for Pupils with Learning Difficulties.* London: The Falmer Press.

Part III

Policies and strategies

A consideration of the wider context

Chapter 10

Policies to support inclusion in the early years

Rob Ashdown

This chapter has two main aims. Firstly to provide information about current government initiatives and their implications for early years practitioners; and secondly to direct the reader to sources of practical advice on the creation of inclusive early years settings. The definition of 'early years' used throughout is from birth to five years. The term 'early years settings' means settings that receive nursery grant funding and schools with nursery- and reception-aged children. Therefore, early years settings can include local authority nurseries, nursery centres, playgroups, pre-schools, maintained schools, schools in the independent, private or voluntary sectors, and even accredited child-minders in approved child-minding networks.

It should not be necessary to remind readers that children with special educational needs (SEN) are children first or that each child is an individual. The provision of a label of special educational needs can at times obscure the necessity to look beyond stereotypes and assumptions about potential, and may inhibit the necessary focus upon learning which should be at the heart of any educational provision. The arguments that inclusion for all children is a human right and that the inclusion process has the power to cater for all children's needs and to establish positive attitudes towards people with disabilities has also been well rehearsed and will not be revisited in this chapter. These principles are well articulated for early years settings by Dickins and Denziloe (1998) and more generally by the National Association for Special Educational Needs (NASEN) in its two policy documents on early years and inclusion (NASEN, 1999a, 1999b). These publications have been produced with the specific intention of stimulating debate about provision; they argue the case for coherent planning and provision at this stage for children who have or who are likely to have SEN at school. Furthermore, they recognise that families of children with SEN should be regarded holistically and that there should be 'joined up' provision by different health, education and social care providers rather than a series of uncoordinated inputs. The NASEN policies also articulate a view on the relative responsibilities of central government, health services, social services departments, local education authorities (LEAs), schools, and voluntary and independent sector providers.

Dickins and Denziloe (1998) make the important and reassuring point that it is not necessary for early years practitioners to have in-depth knowledge of disabilities in order to include children with disabilities. Instead, they rightly argue that such knowledge is best acquired on a 'need to know' basis from the child's parents and they urge people to see beyond the disability and find ways of reaching the individual child.

NATIONAL DEVELOPMENTS

Mittler (2000) provides a historical account of provision for young children with SEN, setting this into the wider political and financial contexts. He characterises the past twenty years as being littered with disappointed hopes stemming from empty promises of a vast expansion in free state nursery education. In the Millennium Edition of the *Times Educational Supplement*, Northern (1999) comments on the reluctance of successive governments in the last century to commit themselves to the development of nursery education for all children. She suggests that progress towards nursery education has been inextricably linked with the progress of women's rights and that for too long there has been an attitude that the mother of a young child should play only that role and that she should not be seeking work outside the home. Northern reports data from the National Children's Bureau that indicate that in 1998 only 29 per cent of three and four year olds in England were in some form of state nursery education, usually part-time. The majority either stayed at home or were served by a fragmented system of playgroups, child-minders and private nurseries run by poorly paid women with a variety of qualifications or none. However, in recent years key members of the Labour Government of Prime Minister Tony Blair have stated that the expansion of early child-care opportunities is integral to the government's economic policy. This Government clearly believes that many women who have young children see the lack of affordable, accessible, quality child-care as a barrier to working and that the problem is particularly acute in less affluent areas of the country. Better opportunities for child-care are seen as a means of providing access to employment and training for parents, which in turn will reduce child poverty and increase the prosperity of individual families and the communities in which they live. Good-quality early years education will also give children a good start in life, which can bring long-term benefits for them and for the nation. Commentators like Northern (1999) are cautiously optimistic that at last central government is beginning to take positive action that could lead to a lasting improvement in early years education and child-care, although, as

Wolfendale (2000) cautions, good practice can be made safe from further political interference only if there is cross-party support and a long-term commitment to funding.

Certainly, the Government is proud of its achievements over the last few years. In the Green Paper, *Schools: Building on Success*, produced by the Department for Education and Employment (DfEE) there is a whole section which trumpets what was done in four years of office and sets out plans for a second term (DfEE, 2001a). This paper makes plain a preparedness to invest significantly in programmes that could have an impact from birth onwards and states an ambitious target of eliminating child poverty in twenty years. There is official recognition that a range of good early years services has been developed by education, health and social services as well as by voluntary organisations. The stated intention is to develop seamless, integrated provision for children and their families which builds on the best features of existing provision and is tailored to meet children's needs rather than to suit particular professional structures. One target is that there should be a free early education place for every three and four year old from September 2004 which entails a massive expansion of out-of-school child-care places. The government plan entails encouraging all early years settings to expand into new areas and extend their services.

The Sure Start programme is an innovative strategy that is intended to support families in disadvantaged areas from the beginning of a child's life in learning about parenting skills, nurturing and the development of babies and young children. Sure Start funding has been made available to reshape services and fill gaps, to provide better and more co-ordinated support, and to give better access to early education, health services and other family support services for those expecting a baby and for those with children up to the age of four. In 2001 the cross-party House of Commons Education and Employment Committee published a report on early years provision that recommended, among other things, that the best practice and learning from Sure Start should be widely shared (House of Commons, 2001a). In its response the Government made it plain that it hoped that Sure Start would have a wider impact beyond the disadvantaged areas in which the actual programmes operate (House of Commons, 2001b). The Sure Start programmes are supposed to offer models on integrated service delivery which can be replicated across the country and those elements of Sure Start that are shown to work are being disseminated through the Sure Start website (www.surestart.gov.uk) and a regular newsletter.

Sure Start funding has enabled a number of practical projects as evidenced in a Sure Start guide to good practice for planners which offers examples of how early identification and assessment services or support for children with complex needs might work in practice (DfEE, 1999a). These programmes include:

- befriending and social support from volunteer home visitors trained by 'Home-Start' schemes;

- workshops for expectant parents to prepare them for the emotional aspects of pregnancy, childbirth and infant care;
- courses on parenting skills covering normal child development, ways of making requests and setting boundaries, and ways of dealing with conflict and anger in the family;
- programmes for enabling parents to be their child's first teachers;
- neighbourhood family centres which can serve as 'one-stop shops' for a range of support services and play or child-care experiences;
- play schemes to develop children's linguistic, social and cognitive development;
- programmes that provide resources to encourage parents to share books with their children;
- support schemes for families under stress due to their child's disabilities or exceptional needs.

An 'Early Excellence Centre' (EEC) initiative was outlined in the White Paper *Excellence In Schools* (DfEE, 1997a). The intention was that EECs would demonstrate good practice in education, child-care and integrated services and that they would also provide training and disseminate good practice for early years practitioners. The work of one EEC, the Pen Green Centre in Corby, Northamptonshire, is described in a book edited by Whalley (2001). An evaluation of the work of all 29 EECs established by December 1999 has been published by the DfEE (Bertram and Pascal, 2001). Each of the EECs is different, but they are all making significant progress towards becoming one-stop shops offering integrated education, health and social care services. There is evidence of enhanced learning outcomes for children and good support for an average of 300 families per EEC. Perhaps as many as 5,000 parents are also accessing on-site training and group work activities each year in parenting skills, behaviour management, family literacy and nutrition, or pursuing courses leading to qualifications in basic skills, computing, child-care and so on. EECs are delivering courses to local early years practitioners and receiving many professional visitors each year. The Government also supports the development of EECs because they have been shown to be a highly cost-effective way of delivering multi-professional services when compared to more traditional service provision. Indeed, there are plans to increase the number of EECs to 100 by 2004.

The 2001 Green Paper also signals the Government's intention to establish 45,000 new nursery places in up to 900 'neighbourhood nursery centres' in disadvantaged areas by 2004. The intention is that many of these will bring together services for families and children through combined nursery education, child-care and family support. Also, 250 maintained nursery schools will be encouraged to develop a wider range of services by 2004 so as to serve their local community more broadly.

The Government has a response to concerns about the inconsistent quality of early years provision. One of its strategies is to rely on dissemination to early years settings of curriculum guidance produced by the DfEE and the Qualifications and Curriculum Authority (QCA) for the Foundation Stage which has been identified as a distinct early years phase covering children from the age of three years until the end of their Reception year in primary school. The guidance (DfEE and QCA, 2000) supports an earlier document on *Early Learning Goals* for the Foundation Stage (DfEE and QCA, 1999) that sets out what the majority of children should achieve by the end of their Reception year. There is some evidence in the report of a Parliamentary Select Committee (House of Commons, 2001a) of a debate about how best to strike a balance between the importance of play and discovery and formally teaching children the skills they need to cope with the demands of the National Curriculum and the Literacy and Numeracy Strategies at Key Stage 1. The Committee's view was that more structured learning should be introduced very gradually so that by the end of the Reception year children are learning through more formal whole-class activities for only a small proportion of the day. The particular significance of the curriculum guidance is that it is intended to apply to all early years settings that receive nursery grant funding as well as to schools with nursery- and reception-aged children.

Large sums of money have been made available by the current Labour Government for training and developing staff in early years settings, but it remains to be seen how adequate the funding is. The QCA has been asked to establish a comprehensive framework of early education, child-care and play-work qualifications, and a closer integration of qualifications for child-care and early years qualification is hinted at. Training of staff is the key to raising standards, but there are real difficulties. It is unrealistic to expect the same quality from a well-resourced nursery, where there are graduate staff, and from a setting where there are few resources or facilities and few qualified staff with possibly no qualified teachers. The Parliamentary Select Committee noted its concern that enhancing quality in all settings will be expensive, time consuming and labour intensive; certainly a few days of training will not suffice to reduce these massive gaps (House of Commons, 2001a).

Another catalyst for raising standards may come through the work of the Office for Standards in Education (Ofsted) which already inspects a range of nursery and primary school provision in the maintained sector according to a published framework (Ofsted, 1999). Ofsted will inspect child-care and early years provision through a new Early Years Directorate from September 2001. As for primary and nursery schools, it is expected that early years provision must show satisfactory or better standards and any that do not will have to put in place a clear improvement plan. Again, the Parliamentary Select Committee's report on early years recorded concerns about how Ofsted will operate in view of the levels of stress occasioned in many schools by the inspection process (House of Commons, 2001a).

All local government areas are now required to set up an Early Years Development and Childcare Partnership (EYDCP) in association with the local voluntary and independent organisations. One of the main issues for every EYDCP is that of ensuring quality in every setting that receives funding. The EYDCP has to draw up a plan that contains local strategic targets that replicate the national targets set by the government (DfEE, 2001b). Each EYDCP will be given its own budget for increasing the number of child-care places, recruiting workers for the expanding services, providing advisory support and training, setting up a child-minder network, improving information services for parents and better joint working. The EYDCP is required to work closely with other partners at a local level, particularly the Sure Start Partnership if one exists, and any other strategic partnerships such as the local Learning and Skills Council.

DEVELOPMENTS IN EARLY YEARS PROVISION FOR CHILDREN WITH SEN

These government initiatives present many opportunities and challenges for early years practitioners. This is a government that has decided not to invest only in maintained nursery schools and nurseries. It has chosen instead to increase the number of places and raise standards in the whole range of early years provision that exists across the country, including child-minders. Indeed, the government has articulated the view that the quality and appropriateness of the educational experience is far more important than the type of setting that the child attends and that the label of the setting will not matter once the Foundation Stage has become truly embedded (DfEE, 2001a; House of Commons, 2001b). (For some critical analyses of the government strategy see Mittler, 2000; NASEN, 2000; Russell, 2001; Wolfendale, 2000.) Now it is necessary to turn to what these developments in integrated provision in an increasingly diverse early years sector mean for children with SEN and those people who are concerned with developing inclusive practices and SEN expertise.

Early identification of children's needs and the development of inclusive provision is stated to be a key part of the current government's early years strategy in, most notably, its Green Paper *Excellence for All Children* (DfEE, 1997b), its SEN Action Programme (DfEE, 1998) and its Green Paper *Schools: Building on Success* (DfEE, 2001a). It is plainly looking to the EYDCPs to develop appropriate strategies in early years settings for children with SEN. By 2002, all settings must have identified and begun to train a settings-based SEN co-ordinator (SENCo) who is responsible for establishing and implementing the setting's own SEN policy. The government requirement is that each should receive three days of appropriate training by 2004, although this is hardly enough time to assimilate the knowledge, skills and understanding required for including children with a wide range of SEN. However, also by 2004, the EYDCP is expected to ensure that each early years setting will have access to a trained area SENCo who is a qualified teacher with relevant experience. The target is to have one area SENCo for every 20 providers and these SENCos will support the staff in the early years settings and make the necessary links to the LEA and other agencies. The government's expectation, as articulated in the 2001–2002 planning guidance for EYDCPs (DfEE, 2001b), is that this should result in better outcomes for the children themselves and in reducing the need for costly interventions later. Certainly, it offers a real opportunity for EYDCPs to develop a more proactive approach to planning and delivering services for young children with SEN across a range of provision in their area.

The *Code of Practice on the Identification and Assessment of Special Educational Needs* (DfE, 1994) contained a chapter on assessments and statements of children aged less than five years. The revised Code of Practice (DfES, 2001) further strengthens this important area. Dickins and Denziloe (1998) have explained its special significance for early years settings. The first set of planning guidance for EYDCPs required details of the arrangements for ensuring that settings could identify and provide for children with SEN and confirmation that they would have regard to the *Code* (DfEE, 1999b). The result in many areas was a flurry of training in SEN policy for representatives from a range of early years settings. The DfEE's consultation document on revisions to the SEN Code of Practice (DfEE, 2000) suggested that there would be significant changes in the chapter on identification, assessment and provision in early years settings to reflect the developments in early years provision, and this has proved to be the case. In its response to the consultation NASEN (no date) expresses concerns about the high levels of expectations on SENCos and the impact on small early years settings of the training, paperwork and general workload. Much depends upon the ability of each EYDCP to develop protocols so that early years settings have access to central services and advice.

The Government has repeatedly reaffirmed its commitment to developing a more inclusive system that is responsive enough to meet the needs of all children (DfEE, 1998, 2001a, 2001b). However, it is less than clear that there is general agreement about what constitutes inclusion and excellence in provision. Clearly, the curriculum guidance for the Foundation Stage could be influential and it does contain statements about planning to meet each child's individual learning requirements, including those children who need additional support or have particular needs or disabilities (DfEE and QCA, 2000). However, there are no practical guidelines about inclusive practices to be found here. Similarly, the training support package for the Foundation Stage for early years practitioners (DfEE, 2001c) is strong on ethos but offers little guidance about developing a truly inclusive curriculum. There is a growing literature on making the early years curriculum accessible to children with SEN: for instance, the works of Dickens and Denziloe (1998) and Wolfendale (2000) make particularly useful contributions. However, what many early years practitioners need is quality training and opportunities to view models of good practice and to get practical advice about specialist equipment, teaching materials and appropriate teaching methods from experienced SEN specialists. In this respect, staff in established SEN services, mainstream schools and special schools have much to offer. It is from such provision that area SENCos are likely to be recruited and everybody stands to gain a great deal from establishing close liaison both between clusters of mainstream schools and 'feeder' early years providers and also between specialist schools and services and all early years settings.

There are 125 Portage services across the country that provide a home-visiting service for families whose pre-school child (aged up to five) has disabilities and/or delays in development. Parents are supported by a home visitor to identify short-term teaching targets for their child and to select appropriate methods to address these. The Portage programme was highly innovative when it was first introduced in the mid-1970s: it recognised the potential of parents to be their child's first educators; it capitalised on the knowledge parents have about their children; and it provided a package for assessment and teaching which any early years practitioner, and the parents themselves, could quickly learn to use. As Mittler (2000) notes, the Portage model has many strengths, although he expresses some reservations including whether all parents feel comfortable with, or have the energy and time for, teaching and record keeping. However, where Portage workers and families work together well for the child they build up a productive relationship which can support parents throughout the process of transition to education in early years settings by helping them to approach providers and seek the information they need to make choices. Parry (2000) urges Portage services to look at ways in which they might promote the inclusion process through supporting the staff of early years settings through training about child development and learning styles, positive report writing about children, sharing ideas about ways of overcoming barriers to participation and learning, and reassuring them about their ability to include children with SEN. Mittler (2000) also suggests that in looking ahead to the next 25 years Portage services should consider extending their remit to include a wider range of children from poor and disadvantaged backgrounds and publicising their work.

Many local hospitals have a child development centre attached and staffed by a multi-disciplinary team of speech and language therapists, occupational therapists, physiotherapists, specialist nurses, clinical psychologists, and often a teacher and social worker, usually led by a paediatrician. This is an example of another service which has the power to influence practice and decision-makers as long as it is prepared to widen its remit beyond the rather narrow group of children with disabilities to include children without identified disabilities and milder developmental delays who are at risk of developing difficulties at school. The staff of a child development centre could well become the power house in an area for developing more effective screening for children with developmental delays and for improving the often criticised counselling processes for parents about the implications of the diagnosis of their child's difficulties and the range of appropriate services which are available.

In 2000 an interactive CD ROM, *Connecting Schools for Inclusion*, was launched, which was intended to show teachers first hand how others have tackled the challenges inclusion presents (DfEE/NASEN, 2000). The various modules demonstrate how stronger links between mainstream and special schools have benefited both sectors and pupils. The package could be used to promote discussions about how special schools with nurseries and reception classes could work with other early years settings to promote inclusion. This is not to deny that many special schools have a long history of promoting full-time and part-time inclusion and it is important to build on this wealth of experience (Tilstone, 1998).

Many areas will also have access to specialist support services for children with medical conditions, physical disabilities, sensory impairments, autism, emotional and behavioural difficulties and general learning difficulties. The child development centre, the Portage service and the children's information services set up by the EYDCP should be in a position to give parents and early years settings details about these services which can provide support and advice on the management of developmental and behavioural problems in early years settings and at home. They can also prepare children, parents and staff to facilitate transitions to and between settings and have open referral systems and well-developed informational and training packages for parents and practitioners which can be harnessed by the EYDCP.

Finally, it is necessary to consider what may be done to affirm the vital role of parents in the development and education of their children and to support them as educators of their children. One of the principles articulated in the curriculum guidance for the Foundation Stage and the associated training package is the importance of practitioners and parents working closely together (DfEE, 2001c; DfEE and QCA, 2000). Parental involvement is a key feature of the work of EECs (Bertram and Pascal, 2001). Hornby (2000) has written extensively on parental involvement and explains what practitioners can do to be genuinely helpful to parents. They should consider the impact of any intervention on the whole family and try to involve the whole family. They should also work hard to maintain two-way communication and as well as providing positive reviews of children's skills and progress, they should provide guidance about the development of the child and useful activities at home. Many parents will be looking for and should receive practical guidance about positive ways of managing problems. Practitioners should also be prepared to provide information about services, benefits and support services or to refer parents to somebody who has this specialist knowledge. Hornby also points out that it is not only what is said but the way they deal with families which is important, they should:

- use listening skills effectively and show empathy and patience;
- try to facilitate contacts with other families and networking;
- make home visits;

- seek information from parents and show that they value it;
- develop individual education plans, care plans and behaviour management plans in consultation with the parents.

Arnold (2001) looks closely at ways of adapting methods so that even the 'hard to reach' parents may be involved in their child's learning. Shah (1996) writes about families with children with a disability who experience the multiple problems of racism, poverty and common misunderstandings about the wishes and feelings of families in the Asian community.

It is salutary to conclude with a brief reminder of some of the difficulties experienced by many children with a disability and their families (Joseph Rowntree Foundation, 1999). As recently as 1999 it was stated that there is little evidence of co-ordinated approaches to family support. Many parents face relatively high costs in bringing up their child with a disability and many experience diminished employment opportunities because of the lack of suitable and affordable child-care. Often, they experience a lack of information about their entitlements to services and financial support. What helps is when children with a disability and their families experience professionals who genuinely listen to what they are saying, who provide information and advice, who have positive attitudes towards the children and their parents, and who do not lose sight of their human rights.

REFERENCES

Arnold, C. (2001) 'Persistence pays off: working with "hard to reach" parents', in M. Whalley (ed.) *Involving Parents: Children's Learning.* London: Paul Chapman.

Bertram, T. and Pascal, C. (2001) *Early Excellence Centre Pilot Programme: Annual Evaluation Report* (DfEE Research Publication RR258). London: DfEE.

DfE (1994) *Code of Practice on the Identification and Assessment of Special Educational Needs.* London: DfE.

DfEE (1997a) *Excellence in Schools* (Cm 3681). London: DfEE.

DfEE (1997b) *Excellence for all Children: Meeting Special Educational Needs* (Cm. 3785). London: DfEE.

DfEE (1998) *Meeting Special Educational Needs: A Programme of Action.* London: DfEE.

DfEE (1999a) *Sure Start: A Guide to Evidence-Based Practice* (updated December 1999). London: DfEE.

DfEE (1999b) *Early Years Development and Childcare Partnership: Planning Guidance.* London: DfEE.

DfEE (2000) *SEN Code of Practice on the Identification and Assessment of Special Educational Needs and SEN Thresholds: Good Practice Guidance on the Identification and Provision for Pupils with Special Educational Needs* (Consultation document). London: DfEE.

DfEE (2001a) *Schools: Building on Success.* (Cm. 5050). London: DfEE.

DfEE (2001b) *Early Years Development and Childcare Partnership: Planning Guidance 2001–2002.* London: DfEE.

DfEE (2001c) *A Training Support Framework for the Foundation Stage – Ensuring Sound Foundations: From Principles to Practice* (binder and video). London: DfEE.

DfEE and QCA (1999) *Early Learning Goals.* London: DfEE and QCA.

DfEE/NASEN (2000) *Connecting Schools for Inclusion*. London: DfEE.

DfEE and QCA (2000) *Curriculum Guidance for the Foundation Stage*. London: DfEE and QCA.

DfES (2001) *Special Educational Needs: Code of Practice*. London: DfES.

Dickens, M. and Denziloe, J. (1998) *All Together: How to Create Inclusive Services for Disabled Children and Their Families*. London: National Early Years Network.

Hornby, G. (2000) *Improving Parental Involvement*. London: Cassell Education.

House of Commons (2001a) *The Education and Employment Committee's First Report of Session 2000–01: Early Years* (House of Commons Paper HC33). London: House of Commons.

House of Commons (2001b) *The Government's Response to the Education and Employment Committee's First Report of Session 2000–01* (House of Commons Paper HC361). London: House of Commons.

Joseph Rowntree Foundation (1999) 'Supporting disabled children and their families', *Foundations*, November 1999.

Mittler, P. (2000) *Working Towards Inclusive Education: Social Contexts*. London: David Fulton.

NASEN (undated) *Membership Response to the Proposed Revision of the SEN Code of Practice and Accompanying Guidance on SEN Thresholds*. Tamworth: NASEN.

NASEN (1999a) *Policy Document on Early Years*. Tamworth: NASEN.

NASEN (1999b) *Policy Document on Inclusion*. Tamworth: NASEN.

NASEN (2000) *Early Years Development and Special Educational Needs*. Tamworth: NASEN.

Northern, S. (1999) 'Recognition of early years takes its time', *Times Educational Supplement*, 31 December 1999, p.15.

Ofsted (1999) *Handbook for Inspecting Primary and Nursery Schools with Guidance on Self-Evaluation*. London: Ofsted.

Parry, J. (2000) 'Becoming allies', *Portage Post*, 45 1–2.

Russell, P. (2001) 'Access to the system: the legislative interface', in B. Carpenter, R. Ashdown and K. Bovair (eds.) *Enabling Access: Effective Teaching and Learning for Pupils with Learning Difficulties* (2nd edition). London: David Fulton.

Shah, R. (1996) *The Silent Minority: Children with Disabilities in Asian Families* (2nd edition). London: National Children's Bureau.

Tilstone, C. (1998) 'Moving towards the mainstream: vision and reality', in C. Tilstone, L. Florian and R. Rose (eds.) *Promoting Inclusive Practice*. London: Routledge.

Whalley, M. (2001) (ed.) *Involving Parents: Children's Learning*. London: Paul Chapman.

Wolfendale, S. (2000) (ed.) *Special Needs in the Early Years: Snapshots of Practice*. London: Routledge.

Chapter 11

Education for an inclusive adult life

Policy for the 16 to 19 phase

Caroline Broomhead

The focus of this chapter is on the development of policies designed to promote and encourage inclusive practices during the 16 to 19 phase of education. As inclusive educational policies and practices develop within schools, it will become necessary to ensure that changes are made which enable students leaving school to become better equipped for life in a more inclusive society.

Every child, whatever their circumstances, requires an education that equips them for work and prepares them to succeed in the wider economy and society.

DfES, 2001

These words from Estelle Morris, Secretary of State for Education, express clearly the ultimate goal for education as viewed by the UK Government. For the teacher of pupils with special educational needs such a goal presents a challenge and during the post-16 phase it requires a focus upon the provision of a curriculum which will enable students to succeed in their post-school years. Consequently, in order to develop educational policies for effective inclusion it is necessary to look beyond the school years and to work closely with other agencies to ensure that all pupils participate fully in education, in employment, and in consumer and recreational activities that most of us take for granted (Inclusion International, 1996). For inclusion to succeed it is essential that a set of beliefs, values and principles are accepted by all the agencies responsible for supporting pupils towards the end of their years in formal education. Consultation is essential, therefore, with all stakeholders (staff, parents, students, governors, the careers service), who may be involved at the level of policy implementation. All must be determined to translate their collective beliefs into policies and their policies into practice.

POLICY DEVELOPMENT

Such policies, if they are to be effective, cannot be developed in isolation from the local, regional and national contexts. LEA policies and strategic plans for special educational needs and social inclusion will, for example, have an impact upon the extent to which a school's own policy on the inclusion of 16 to 19 year olds can be fully implemented. Some LEAs, for example, may have taken a decision to locate all educational provision for 16 to 19 year olds with learning difficulties in a tertiary or further education college or to provide specialist facilities for them in a separate location and, in devising their own policies, schools will need to take into account the environment for post-school provision, the nature of the curriculum on offer and the conditions required to accept students on specific courses.

The national profile of 16 to 19 education and training has changed radically as a result of the *Learning and Skills Act* (DfES, 2001a), and one of the aims of the newly established Learning and Skills Council (LSC) is to bring more coherence to all post-16 education and training. John Harwood, chief executive of the LSC, has stated that he aims to develop a strategy which will increase the number of people in learning, whether in school, college, the workplace or the local community and to ensure that the resources and teaching, in whatever environment, are of the highest quality. Nevertheless there can be a considerable overlap in educational provision for 16 to 19 year olds within a local education authority as education and training may be offered in schools, colleges or through adult training organisations, often with little collaboration to ensure a continuum or to address issues of quality. In the White Paper *Schools Achieving Success* (DfES, 2001b), the Government made a commitment to tackle the institutional and systemic barriers to the 14 to 19 phase of education (such as poor organisation and inadequate management of funding) by encouraging schools and colleges to co-operate more closely in providing a broader range of options more suited to the needs of individual pupils.

Governments have been active over the last decade in bringing about changes in society's attitudes towards people with disabilities (Tilstone, 2001). Legislation and guidance have been introduced which aim to ensure that young people with learning difficulties have an entitlement to mainstream educational opportunities and experiences, including *Meeting Special Educational Needs: a Programme of Action* (1998, DfEE) and the *Special Educational Needs: Code of Practice* (DfES, 2001). *Special Educational Needs and Disability Discrimination Act* (Disability Rights Commission, 2001) makes clear the Government's requirement that schools and other educational institutions should ensure that their organisational structures, admissions policies, programmes of study, resources and buildings are accessible to everyone. In the earlier *Disability Discrimination Act* (Disability Rights Commission, 1995) the Government persuaded providers of services and goods to review their practices and policies in relation to physical access and the provision of opportunities for social inclusion. Although it does not impose legal obligations, within the Disability Discrimination Act a *Code of Practice on Rights of Access to Goods, Facilities, Services and Premises* gives examples of where providers would be expected to make changes to their practices in order to promote social inclusion; in addition, the Disability Rights Task Force's report, *From Exclusion to Inclusion* (DfEE, 1999), sets out its recommendations in areas such as education, work, travel, housing, environment, local government, health and social services. Clearly, this wealth of legislation is intended to make a significant difference to the opportunities that young people with disabilities will have to help them lead full and active lives in their local communities.

It is important that schools have cognisance of all the legislation described above and undertake regular reviews of their own policies seeking to promote inclusion for students in the 16 to 19 phase. They will also need to take account of their own school policies related to equal opportunities, pastoral and medical care and health and safety. An audit of the school's principles and intentions pertaining to the post-16 phase should enable the development of a series of key policy objectives, which are likely to focus on:

- access to a full range of curriculum-related learning experiences appropriate to the age group;
- students' participation in a wide range of community-based learning experiences in order to provide first-hand, relevant contexts in which to develop appropriate knowledge and social/communication skills, self-esteem and self-confidence;
- the provision of structured opportunities for young people to participate in learning experiences, alongside their non-disabled peers and to reduce the effects and disadvantages of social isolation;
- the recognition of accredited and validated educational achievements which help young people with learning disabilities to make a successful transition into adult life and, possibly, employment;
- appropriate individual support for the pupil/student to participate fully in all age-appropriate educational, recreational and vocational activities;
- the professional development of all staff in order to provide an appropriate curriculum and a range of learning experiences for students;
- multi-disciplinary work for the benefit of individuals and groups of students.

POLICY IMPLEMENTATION

As the effective implementation of policies is usually dependent upon a well-structured plan of action within the school and upon the development of a policy for inclusive education at the post-16 stage, it is necessary to gain a consensus on the actions to be taken by all involved. Staff must have a clear vision of how they can translate the ideals of the policy into practice, and senior management and governing bodies must be responsible for providing direction, leadership and the management of funding. A shared set of principles and flexible management strategies are necessary if change is to take place, and it should be borne in mind that the implementation of policies may have significant implications for the structure of staffing, and for deployment and training. In addition, issues of health and safety, the welfare of staff and students and the financial support to implement new programmes will need to be taken into account. The following principles should be incorporated into the philosophy, policy making, planning, delivery and evaluation of the curriculum for pupils who experience difficulties in learning, including a commitment to:

- inclusion;
- independence;
- progression;
- curriculum relevance;
- interactive/experiential learning strategies;
- normalising, community-based learning, involving collaborative working between educational and other agencies;
- the provision of appropriate support;
- meaningful student involvement in setting targets, assessing personal progress, recording achievement and decision-making;
- access to a recognised national system of qualifications and accreditation.

Consequently, an appropriate curriculum to support students would include:

- communication/literacy;
- numeracy;
- personal, social and health education (PSHE);
- information communication technology (ICT);
- technology;
- creative arts;
- independence skills;
- independent study skills;
- sport and physical development;
- vocational education;
- work experience;
- placements;
- careers education and guidance;
- moral, spiritual and cultural education;
- residential experiences;
- leisure activities and community interests.

(See Broomhead, 1998 for a detailed analysis of how students with learning difficulties can be prepared for inclusion in the workplace.)

Providers of educational opportunities for post-16 students will need to be aware of the core literacy and numeracy curriculum, promoted through the Basic Skills Agency (2001a; 2001b) that builds upon the National Literacy and Numeracy Strategies and is designed to ensure continuity and progression beyond the statutory school years. The importance of rooting the curriculum in the realities of the world outside school cannot be overemphasised and, when seeking to promote independence skills through community-based activities, schools need to have policies on off-site visits and related health and safety issues. Any community-based learning activity that involves students with special educational needs is likely to be staff intensive, and a risk analysis needs to be taken to ensure that there is appropriate staffing (based on student need), fully appraised of potential hazards and safety procedures. Staff responsibilities must be clearly defined in annually reviewed job descriptions, and procedures for dealing with emergencies and the management of medication or other medical arrangements should be clearly articulated. New staff should be well supported by more experienced colleagues when off-site, and the responsibilities of off-site providers (such as employers) need to be discussed and agreed by all the parties concerned.

The value of such activities is considerable in helping young people to develop confidence, communication skills and social abilities. Nevertheless, many students with learning difficulties are vulnerable, and parents and carers need to be involved in decisions about such planned activities. Clear policies, guidance and procedures will allow staff, parents, students and people in the wider community to feel confident that students are being given adequate opportunities to participate fully and safely.

Resourcing inclusive practice requires careful management, and school policies will need to take into account the additional costs involved in the management of a 16 to 19 curriculum that supports students in community learning. Funding, for example, must be provided to enable students to participate in college links and, as the approach requires adequate staff time and may incur considerable transport costs, inadequate support may be a disincentive for students or schools to become fully involved in the important process of transition. In extreme cases, some pupils may require additional staffing in order to make a successful transition from the relatively sheltered existence of a school into the larger community of a college or the workplace. Although the benefits to be gained through a well co-ordinated, secure and structured transition to a more adult environment are considerable, the logistics of managing such initiatives may be demanding and the financial implications considerable.

In addition, the relatively high costs of accreditation need to be taken into account as prospective employers have recently become aware of the wide range of accreditation opportunities available through schools and colleges. Students must be provided with a chance to gain qualifications if they are not to be disadvantaged when they seek employment and the *National Standards Framework* (QCA, 2000) stresses that an emphasis upon vocational and general qualifications will continue to provide a focus in the post-16 years. Schools must not only have cognisance of the wide range of qualifications available, but must ensure that their policies provide opportunities for students with disabilities and learning difficulties to gain access to education and employment alongside their peers.

From April 2002 all school provision for students aged 16 to 19 will be funded through the Learning and Skills Council, but although it is not yet clear what implications this may have for school budgets, the Government is firmly committed to greater flexibility in the location of provision and in funding opportunities (DfES, 2001a).

MONITORING AND EVALUATION

How do schools know that they are providing high-quality learning experiences for pupils with special educational needs? Their starting point must be a clear statement of aims and objectives for post-16 provision, including a focus upon the individual needs of students and on systems for monitoring and evaluating the success of policies and practices using:

- the analysis of performance on accredited courses;
- the observation of student development in terms of social competencies;
- the assessment of performance during work experience or in newly provided learning environments (for example, placement on a college course).

Some schools have established *standards* or *performance indicators*, which often comprise a range of statements such as, each student:

- takes part in a college link programme;
- takes part in work experience placements;
- achieves targets through accredited pathways for communication skills;
- makes progress in relation to the targets set in Individual Education Plans;
- takes part in careers guidance;
- takes part in a vocational education programme;
- learns to prepare simple meals;
- has an opportunity to learn to travel independently;
- has a transition plan for post-school life;
- is enabled to assess his or her own strengths, needs and successes.

In addition:

- parents are actively involved in planning and reviewing post-16 programmes;
- students' and parents' views on future education and/or employment are sought and acted upon;

- employers' perspectives on the opportunities available are taken into account;
- staff evaluate their own contributions to post-16 programmes and provision;
- all staff participate in professional development geared to the needs of 16 to 19 year old students with learning difficulties;
- the school development plan identifies continuing professional development priorities and sets targets;
- staff, within and outside the institution, contribute to the annual review procedures;
- individual student transition plans, with clearly stated targets, are prepared jointly.

These examples of performance indicators, from school documentation, assist in the measurement of a school's effectiveness; individual schools will need to identify others according to specific needs and the potential local provision. Whatever the means used for the evaluation of performance, it will be necessary for schools to monitor and to modify them on a regular basis. It is likely that they will make use of a wide range of evidence from teacher records (including video and photographic materials), student self-assessments, information from parents and employers and critical comments from the outside agencies closely involved. Nevertheless, none of this material is of value unless clearly defined criteria are established which enable schools to measure their own performance and to set targets for continued improvement. In addition, programmes will need to be changed in order to meet student needs, to respond to new national and local initiatives or to introduce new opportunities for accreditation or training.

ROLES AND INVOLVEMENT

A co-ordinated team approach is vital to the successful implementation of 16 to 19 inclusion policies, and the following example may prove useful to those embarking on a modification or a development of their own post-16 management practices.

Responsibilities

Students

Planning; self-assessment; assessment of provision; ownership of individual education plans, career plans and targets; reports for annual reviews; decisions regarding subject options, work experience placements and leisure activities.

Parents/carers

Working alongside staff; an understanding of student needs; attendance at meetings and annual reviews; liaison with the connexions service; work on

IEPs at home; help with preparation for interviews; encouraging choice and decision-making; preliminary visits to colleges or the workplaces.

Teaching

Post-16

Planning the curriculum and a range of learning experiences; community liaison; monitoring progress and writing reports; the planning of visits and the preparation of resources; the matching of teaching styles to the preferred learning styles of students; annual reviews of planning to reflect the views and needs of student cohorts; pastoral care mechanisms; liaison with parents; awareness of current developments, including accreditation.

Pre-16

Liaison with post-16 staff to ensure good transition and effective management of student records; the management of visits to post-16 provision; up-to-date documentation, including records of achievement and transition plans; attendance at pre-admission planning meetings and discussions on individual student needs with the receiving teacher.

Post-19 in colleges

Liaison with the school on admissions; attendance at 19+ transition meetings and parents' evenings; the planning of link programmes in partnership with the school; the provision of opportunities for social activities alongside peers; ensuring that college courses build upon previous experiences and do not unnecessarily repeat previous work; building upon previously achieved accreditation; acting as advisers to parents on leisure opportunities, on careers and the broadening of experiences.

Support staff

Flexibility in work with individual students or small groups; assessment of student progress; documentation for accreditation; resources; attendance at meetings and reviews; contributions to the school's processes of evaluation; involvement in continuing professional development.

Connexions services

Personal advisers will work alongside teachers to offer advice to post-13 students on post-school placements and careers, a service which will continue throughout the final years of school, into college life and the early years of adulthood; work to achieve a 'seamless link' with post-19 services.

Social services and transition support teams

Liaison with students and their families; planning for transition into adult services and providing the necessary support; advising schools on family issues and the possible options at 19, where necessary providing personal support to students during transition.

Employers

Opportunities for vocational development including visits to schools and return visits to the workplaces; practice interviews; the provision of a clear breakdown of skills and competence expectations; the assessment of students in the workplace; advising schools on vocational education programmes; assistance to schools in the assessment of the suitability of individual students for specific post-school opportunities; involvement in mini enterprise projects; carefully monitored and managed work-based learning experiences; reports to schools on the performance of students; identifying strengths and possible areas for development.

Health services

Visits to schools as part of health education programmes; visits to services; work with other professionals to ensure that the health and welfare needs of young people are understood and managed.

Local Education Authorities

The provision of advice on the development and continuity of provision for post-16 students; a considered approach to the funding of schools including the provision of off-site working; the monitoring of annual reviews and transition procedures; the articulation of a clear vision for inclusion and the consequent development of a well-integrated range of services; close liaison with all providers to monitor the effectiveness of provision as required by the Disability Discrimination Act (DRC, 2001).

CONCLUSION

This chapter has sought to provide some guidance on developing policy and procedures to promote inclusion for post-16 students with learning difficulties. The 16 to 19 phase of education is crucial for all students and has, on occasion, been an area in which services and provision have failed students with special educational needs. It is the crucial stage in young people's lives in which they should be enabled to build upon previous learning, and to develop self-confidence, maturity, independence and the ability to make choices. Tomlinson (1996) went further and emphasised that the aim of all learning must be inclusion into our communities. Too many students (and their parents) have experienced frustration in the post-school years when there has been a lack of support or educational opportunities. The UK Government is clearly seeking, through a variety of legislation, to promote practices which will bring about a more inclusive society. The Disability Rights Task Force made a number of wide ranging recommendations included in the *Special Educational Needs and Disability Discrimination Act* (DRC, 2001). Legislation alone, however, will not fulfil Morris's requirement that pupils need an 'education that equips them for work and prepares them to succeed in the wider economy and society' (DfES, 2001b). The starting point for an inclusive life for those with learning difficulties must be carefully planned and structured learning opportunities which address their needs throughout their education and, in addition, the development and implementation of robust school policies leading to a range of exciting and meaningful experiences for post-16 students.

REFERENCES

Basic Skills Agency (2001a) *Adult Literacy Core Curriculum*. London: BSA.

Basic Skills Agency (2001b) *Adult Numeracy Core Curriculum*. London: BSA.

Broomhead, C. (1998) 'Planned transition from education to employment for young people with severe learning difficulties', in C. Tilstone, L. Florian and R. Rose (eds.) *Promoting Inclusive Practice*. London: Routledge.

Department for Education and Employment (1998) *Meeting Special Educational Needs: a Programme of Action*. London: DfEE.

Department for Education and Employment (1999) *From Exclusion to Inclusion: Report of the Disability Rights Task Force on Achieving Civil Rights for Disabled People*. London: DFEE.

Department for Education and Skills (2001) *Special Educational Needs: Code of Practice*. London: DfES.

Department for Education and Skills (2001a) *Learning and Skills Act*. London: DfES.

Department for Education and Skills (2001b) *Schools Achieving Success*. London: Department for Education and Skills.

Disability Rights Commission (1995) *Disability Discrimination Act*. London: HMSO.

Disability Rights Commission (2001) *Special Educational Needs and the Disability Discrimination Act*. London: The Stationery Office.

Inclusion International (1996) *Inclusion: News from Inclusion International*. Brussels: Inclusion International.

Qualifications and Curriculum Authority (2000) *National Standards for Adult Literacy and Numeracy*. London: QCA.

Tilstone, C. (2001) 'Changing public attitudes', in B. Carpenter, R. Ashdown and K. Bovair (eds.) *Enabling Access: Effective Teaching and Learning for Pupils with Learning Difficulties* (2nd edition). London: David Fulton.

Tomlinson, J. (1996) *Inclusive Learning: Report of the Learning Difficulties and Disabilities Committee*. London: Further Education Funding Council.

Chapter 12

The role of LEAs in promoting inclusion

Sue Fagg

In this chapter Sue Fagg considers the role of Local Education Authorities in ensuring that inclusive education opportunities are available for all pupils and the consequent present and future challenges. Her ideas will stimulate imaginative responses to school and LEA policies for inclusion.

The role and the future of Local Education Authorities (LEAs) has been an area of significant political debate during the last decade. Tension exists between the need for local interpretations of legislation and the DfES guidance to meet the educational needs of the community, and a desire to control provision from central government. The LEA can be seen as having an unenviable task in delivering educational provision within a centrally controlled legislative framework through differing local resources. There are few areas more emotive and demanding for individual pupils than inclusion, and consequently the inclusion agenda for the LEA can easily become politically charged.

Change and the modernisation of local government has become central to recent national policies and have been foremost in the minds of LEA staff, who have watched their powers diminish with the increased delegation of responsibilities to schools. The LEA can be seen as a facilitator for central and local policies with resources increasingly within the control of others. Efficient and effective practice is essential if the remaining LEA resources are adequately to meet the challenging inclusion agenda.

NATIONAL EXPECTATIONS IN RELATION TO INCLUSION

Inclusion can be seen as having two key strands: social inclusion and inclusion for pupils with special educational needs (SEN). Whilst there is an obvious association between the two, it is helpful to clarify specific points from the national agenda. The Secretary of State imposes, through DfES circulars or letters, duties on LEAs without legal foundation.

> Perhaps the area where most 'de facto legislating' occurs is in respect of the LEA functions which broadly fall within the ambit of the term 'inclusion'.
> Whitbourn, Mitchell and Roberts, 2000, p.165

Such statements can be specifically related to social inclusion, and LEAs, which like schools are now subject to Ofsted inspections, take such guidance seriously. In the management of special educational needs, LEAs must have regard to a statutory *Code of Practice* issued by the Secretary of State under Section 313 of the 1996 Act. The LEA is required to involve parents and voluntary organisations in the development of the SEN policy and associated practices, and needs to provide parents with relevant information and to make them aware of the legal duty for all maintained schools to publish their SEN policy (DfEE, 2000a). Delays in government guidance and legislation prove challenging to LEAs as the expectations placed upon them do not change if there is a 'central' delay. The LEA can also be placed in the unenviable position of apparently being reluctant or ineffective by not producing 'by default' documents for parents, schools and other stakeholders.

As stated in Section 316 of the 1996 Act, the LEA has a duty to educate a child with SEN in a mainstream school, not a special school, unless such a placement is incompatible with parental wishes or subject to certain conditions. The conditions are that educating a child in a mainstream school would not be compatible with:

- receiving the special educational provision which the learning difficulty calls for;
- providing efficient education for other children;
- the efficient use of resources.

Inevitably the interpretation of the above conditions varies between LEAs, schools, pupils and families.

LEAs are required to have an inclusion strategy, the implementation of which must take into account the Human Rights Act 1998, introduced in October 2000. Through this Act, the principle is established that the LEA has to act in a manner compatible with the European Convention on Human Rights and, in relation to inclusion, it is a powerful piece of legislation that could result in legal challenges if due care is not taken. An LEA needs to identify which members of its community are at risk of exclusion and therefore whom the strategy should incorporate. This group extends far beyond the definition provided by Inclusion International (1996):

Inclusion refers to the opportunity for persons with a disability to participate fully in all of the educational, employment, consumer, recreational, community, and domestic activities that typify everyday society.

Inclusion International, 1996

Inclusion, historically, has been associated with pupils with special educational needs, and the statutory definition is included in the *Education Act 1996*, Section 312:

A child has 'special educational needs' for the purposes of this Act if he has a learning difficulty which calls for special educational provision to be made for him.

A child has a learning difficulty for the purposes of this Act if:

(a)   he has significantly greater difficulty in learning than the majority of children of his age;

(b)   he has a disability which either prevents or hinders him from making use of educational facilities of a kind generally provided for children of his age in schools within the area of the local education authority, or

(c)   he is under the age of five and is, or would be if special educational provision were not made for him, likely to fall within paragraph (a) or (b) when of or over that age.

HMSO,1996, p.177

During the late 1990s social inclusion was recognised as an area needing greater consideration. DfEE (1999a) Circular 10/99 *Social Inclusion: Pupil Support*, identifies groups at risk and acknowledges that unidentified SEN can result in behavioural difficulties as well as being a link between disaffection and criminal activities. Circular 11/99, *Social Inclusion: the LEA Role in Pupil Support* (DfEE, 1999b), reinforces the law in relation to the LEA's responsibility to ensure school attendance and for educating and reintegrating excluded pupils.

These recent guidance documents adopt a more realistic stance towards the broader inclusion agenda which LEAs are expected to manage. The Warnock Report (DES, 1978) did not fully consider those pupils who were failing to succeed owing to social difficulties, but an LEA has a duty to ensure that all pupils have access to appropriate learning opportunities. Unfortunately such access has yet to be achieved for a significant number of pupils.

WHAT IS EDUCATION FOR?

Since the implementation of the National Curriculum in the 1990s, academic attainment has, on occasions, appeared to be the sole focus of education. Accountability has been measured by pupil attainment and is a significant feature of the judgements made about schools or LEAs through the process of Ofsted inspections. The publication of data, recording the performance of individual schools and LEAs, has created a competitive ethos which many have interpreted as detrimental to inclusion (Booth, Ainscow and Dyson, 1997; Rose, 2001; Rose and Howley, 2001). The annual publication of test results (with bench marks of Level 4 at the end of Key Stage 2 and GCSEs at grades A–C becoming recognised targets) understandably resulted in some schools becoming concerned about the inclusion of pupils who were unlikely to attain these levels and reluctant to accept pupils with more complex needs than they had traditionally been expected to address. An ethos of inter-school competition is not conducive to inclusion, as comparisons between schools have often been made in relation to pupil attainment with no value-added considerations. Ofsted inspections for schools and LEAs allowed and, on occasions encouraged, the media to 'name and shame', adding to the anxieties of teachers as those pupils who were seen to be achieving below age-related expectation could unduly influence the school's perceived standing. In this climate, it is not surprising that, in some LEAs, the needs of the minority were temporarily overlooked, while the desire to attain appropriate results for the majority became the obvious focus. Target setting, for individual schools, is now part of the annual cycle of school life, but teachers are aware that even with excellent teaching some pupils struggle to attain average grades.

The Ofsted framework and the National Curriculum now encompass the expectation that schools will be inclusive, as LEAs have targets to reduce exclusion and value-added criteria are being incorporated into pupil attainment. The drive to enhance inclusive practices has been accelerated as a direct consequence of school inspections and the annual publication of results. Nevertheless the opportunities provided during the mid-1990s by many mainstream schools can be seen to have increased primarily as a result of the dedication of schools and local communities, and their desire to establish a truly inclusive society. It is now acknowledged that some pupils enter education in a position of greater advantage as:

> ... most children who are underachieving or academically less able are also living in areas of social and economic disadvantage.
>
> Mittler, 2000, p.2

It is essential that we question whether these pupils are actively and successfully included in the education system and a closer examination may well reveal that the group is disproportionately represented in pupils who are not accessing full-time educational provision owing to exclusion, teenage pregnancy, lack of mobility or the responsibility of caring for dependent relatives.

IS INCLUSION A REALITY?

An LEA's inclusion policy should apply to pupils who traditionally have SEN, as well as those who more recently have been referred to as 'socially excluded'. The Qualifications and Assessment Authority (QCA) in revising the National Curriculum sought to increase inclusion:

> The National Curriculum secures for all pupils, irrespective of social background, culture, race, gender, differences in ability and disabilities, an entitlement to a number of areas of learning and to develop knowledge, understanding, skills and attitudes necessary for their self fulfilment and development as active and responsible citizens.
>
> QCA/DfEE, 1999, p.12

This curricular access allows the LEA to provide education in a range of settings, including mainstream and special schools, pupil referral units or by facilitating access to college placements and extended work experience. The LEA should ensure equity of provision for pupils with similar needs which, if it is to be a reality for all involved, must be clear on which individuals and groups of pupils may require support through an inclusive policy. Equity may not be easily attainable from the resources available and the provision of education through selection causes significant challenges to inclusion. Selection can occur for a variety of reasons, including faith, academic attainment or aptitude and the recent extension of faith and specialist schools may cause further challenges to the inclusive approach. For many parents inclusion is interpreted as their child attending their local mainstream school, for others it may mean travelling to a school that supports their faith. There has been surprisingly little debate in relation to the exclusion of pupils from schools on the grounds of faith or attainment. Dawkins questions the extension of a sectarian division:

> The idea that primary schoolchildren could be labelled 'Protestant children' or 'Catholic children' is as absurd as 'Tory children', 'Labour children' or 'Liberal children' would be.'
>
> Dawkins, 2001, p.17

It appears that, as a move away from labelling pupils as 'special' develops, other non-inclusive provision is made. The argument about pupils with differing needs and abilities sharing experiences in order to enhance genuine inclusion does not automatically include faith. Inclusion is an ideal supported by some, who exclude themselves from the reality, by paying for their own children to attend independent schools and, therefore, public schools may be seen as the most socially exclusive of all. Is it only the LEA non-selective schools that are expected to be truly inclusive?

WHICH PUPILS REQUIRE SUPPORT FROM AN INCLUSIVE POLICY?

An LEA needs to identify specific groups, but it should bear in mind that their needs, and the issues raised, vary. Groups are not mutually exclusive: for example, pupils from a socially excluded group may also have SEN. The definitions given in *Evaluating Educational Inclusion, Guidance for Inspectors and Schools* (Ofsted, 2000) need to be adopted by both LEAs and schools:

> Educational inclusion is more than a concern about any one group of pupils such as those pupils who have been or are likely to be excluded from school. Its scope is broad. It is about equal opportunities for all pupils, whatever their age, gender, ethnicity, attainment and background. It pays particular attention to the provision made for and the achievement of different groups of pupils within a school.
>
> * girls and boys;
> * minority ethnic and faith groups, Travellers, asylum seekers and refugees;
> * pupils who need support to learn English as an additional language (EAL);
> * pupils with special educational needs;
> * gifted and talented pupils;
> * children 'looked after' by the local authority;
> * other children, such as sick children, young carers, those children from families under stress, pregnant school girls and teenage mothers;
> * any pupils who are at risk of disaffection and social exclusion.
>
> Ofsted, 2000, p.4

This definition illustrates that all pupils may, at some time, require positive support to access inclusive schooling, a possibility initially highlighted in the Warnock Report (DES, 1978).

Some of the consequent challenges, which need to be addressed by LEAs and schools, include the intolerance of some pupils and a desire by others not to be included. For example, the 'traveller' population includes disparate groups and 'new age travellers' are not always accepted by traditional groups such as 'Irish travellers'. Some travellers value primary schools and their ability to teach children to read, but inclusion within a secondary school is seen by some parents as having a negative influence on their children. In contrast, asylum seekers, as Fursland (2001) states, may actively seek education but find access difficult owing to their placement in temporary accommodation.

Statistical data produced by the DfEE (2000a) allow an easy comparison of LEA's statemented pupil populations. A high percentage of statements in statistically comparative neighbouring authorities are viewed as inappropriate, although the lack of a national definition of SEN does not assist in the development of an equitable system. LEAs may statement a higher number of pupils for a number of reasons, including pressure from parents and from lobby groups.

A successful parental challenge at tribunal may undermine an LEA's ability to reduce the number of statements. As legislated in the 1996 Education Act, SEN tribunals should have brought consistency, but if national criteria are not available they will lack the basis on which to make judgements. The DfEE (2000b) and the DfES (2201) *Code of Practice* has begun to address common definitions but it remains unclear if responses are challenging national definitions. Such definitions, which are politically sensitive to parents, schools and LEAs, are being used to produce SEN policies and Behavioural Support Plans; both need careful integration into Educational Development Plans (EDP). These documents, which have to be scrutinised and agreed at national level, are crucial in the active promotion of inclusion through the identification of groups of children and of the available resources.

A CONTINUUM OF PROVISION TO FACILITATE INCLUSION

Ideological advocates of inclusion seek mainstream placements for all pupils and Figure 12.1 illustrates one model of provision, in which the LEA has responsibility for admissions, planning and provision for all pupils. Pupils and pre-school children are educated and assessed within a continuum of provision, including special schools, pupil referral units, mainstream schools, playgroups and child development centres. Mainstream provision meets the needs of the majority and the consequent additional resources provide opportunities for pupils requiring a more specialised provision. Although primary and secondary schools have been resourced for sensory, physical and communication difficulties since the 1980s, Learning Support Units have only recently been developed, through the Standards Fund (1999–2002), to assist pupils who are disaffected or display behavioural problems as identified in Circular 10/99 (DfEE, 1999a).

LEAs have a duty to foster a flexible approach to inclusion and new schools should be 'barrier free' to facilitate access for pupils with mobility difficulties. As Robertson (1998) argues, flexibility is required to meet diverse learning needs and co-location developments in mainstream and special schools facilitate inclusion whilst retaining specialist resources at a central base.

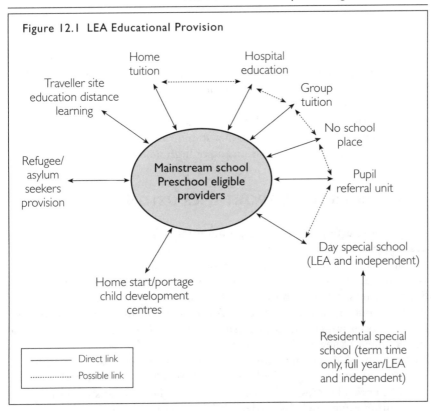

Figure 12.1 LEA Educational Provision

Inclusive mainstream schools may be concerned that they will not be as attractive to parents as examination grades may not be as high as those in neighbouring schools and, consequently, parents may express concerns over the potentially disruptive nature of some pupils with special educational needs. Research, however, indicates that four out of five parents were not influenced by league tables (*Education Guardian*, 29 February 2000), and the majority of parents want their children to be happy at school. Thus schools which are able to assist individual pupils to succeed are often those where pupils are happy and have high self-esteem.

Special schools continue to provide for a pupil population which varies significantly between LEAs (DfEE, 2000a). Those LEAs working in close liaison with mainstream schools can support alternative and more inclusive provision, although this ideal is not sought by all.

Some new schools for children with emotional and behavioural difficulties have been created in response to inexorable demands for alternatives to mainstream schools.

Mittler, 2000, p.187

Parents of pupils with medical needs prefer, on occasions, the safety of a smaller special school and pupils who have SEN and have been bullied may thrive in its more 'protective environment'. There has also been a growth in the number of pupil referral units in the last decade and inclusion is most challenging in the area of social and behavioural difficulties. While increasingly physical, learning or sensory needs can be met in mainstream schools, disaffection, social and behavioural difficulties may be more inhibiting. Such pupils do not usually have the protection of a statement and are more highly represented in areas of social deprivation and of high mobility.

RESOURCES TO SUPPORT INCLUSION

An LEA has a responsibility to promote inclusion, and central funding is available to facilitate access, including access to buildings, and a more proactive approach has been taken towards social inclusion. Standards Funding has been increased and consequently has enabled the development of Learning Support Units in line with the DfEE Circular 10/99 (1999a). Such funding is welcome, but its present short-term nature can result in *ad hoc* initiatives that have not been integrated in successful practice. As readers will be aware the development of new projects takes time.

A specific challenge for LEAs rests in the targets established in 1999 and supported through the Standards Funds in 1999–2000 (DfEE, 1998b, Circular 13/98) to provide access for all excluded pupils. Funding to support building and staffing is now available to develop the provision for pupils who have been excluded from school. In 2000–2001 the Standards Fund became the Pupil Retention Grant (DfEE, 2000c), which had to be delegated to secondary schools to promote support and inclusion for disaffected pupils and those at risk of exclusion. Both areas required development; both are laudable, but changing the proposals, after such a brief period for LEAs, could be viewed as unreasonable and the first year of the Pupil Retention Grant has not seen a national reduction in exclusions. The additional funding, plus the increased flexibility of the curriculum at Key Stage 4, was viewed as a potential turning point. In addition, multi-disciplinary Youth Offending Teams were established in line with Circular 11/99 (DfEE, 1999b) incorporating aspects of LEA support work with pupils who 'offend', aiming to facilitate early reintegration.

The Standards Fund has now identified some of the challenges for schools and LEAs, and an attempt has been made to simplify the funding which, for the first time, can now be carried forward until the end of the school year. Recent national initiatives, such as Excellence in Cities, Sure Start, the Children's Fund and Connexions, have been incorporated into the Neighbourhood Renewal Unit enabling schools to bid for additional funding. The Prime Minister, Tony Blair, in the Foreword to the *National Strategy for Neighbourhood Renewal* outlines his vision:

My vision is of a nation where no-one is seriously disadvantaged by where they live, where power, wealth and opportunity are in the hands of the many not the few. The Action Plan is a crucial step in creating one nation, not separated by class, race or where people live.

Social Exclusion Unit, 2001, p.5

This co-ordinated approach must be welcomed as it acknowledges the need to work co-operatively. The initial implementation may, however, rest with LEAs to find the adequate personnel resources able to draw up bids for funding when, as resources become more limited, the challenges increase. External recognition such as 'Beacon Council Status' encourages LEAs to work in close partnership with other local authority departments. In 2000, bids were made for underachieving groups and, in 2001, they were sought for life-long learning, both of which supported the inclusion agenda. Positive outcomes such as the development of Sure Start should, in future, enhance attainment for more disadvantaged groups.

'Looked after' children, for whom an LEA has a statutory duty to work in close liaison with social services to ensure that they receive adequate 'parenting', have been recognised as a seriously underachieving group. Schools need to identify them and, if they are new to an LEA, they should be found a school placement or offered out-of-school provision immediately. Standards Fund 2001–2002 (DfEE, 2000c) supports initiatives to appoint personnel specifically to enhance educational opportunities. A dilemma arises when 'looked after' pupils are well established in foster care and have no desire to be identified as 'different', a situation in which identification could prove counterproductive.

LEAs working with schools

The interface between LEAs and schools remains crucial to the identification of pupils who need support to access an inclusive education and resources, and one of the most sensitive issues is exclusion or the threat of exclusion. LEAs are allowed to reduce the Pupil Retention Grant which can be passed on to facilitate a fresh start if a new school can be found. Nevertheless, few schools are willing to accept previously excluded pupils and their inclusion may also be delayed owing to a history of teacher action over assaults on staff. LEAS were supported in appointing reintegration officers (DfEE, 1999c) but their impact has yet to be measured. Some schools avoid exclusion and associated costs by suggesting that pupils move on and, although this practice is inappropriate, many parents do not wish their children to remain in schools where they are not wanted.

The range and location of schools within LEAs mean that comparisons of what parents may reasonably expect is unlikely. One of the most difficult roles for LEAs, in liaison with schools, is to ensure equity of provision, as individuals, who believe that their children's educational needs are not being adequately met, are increasingly suing them. In future, schools themselves may also become involved in comparable litigation at a time when LEAs must delegate increasing funding to them.

Under Fair Funding, 85% of the Local Schools budget has to be delegated to schools from April 2001 with a possible increase to 90% by April 2004. LEAs have often retained funding associated with inclusion (Gray, 2001) in the form of support services, but in future these monies will be included in the budgets of the schools themselves, which will be able to determine their use: to purchase specialist support from the LEA or from other agencies. Although LEAs have a duty to monitor and evaluate the work of schools, self-evaluation is on the increase and governing bodies now have greater responsibilities as highlighted in *A Guide to the Law for School Governors* (DfEE, 2000d). LEAs will need to consider the use of their remaining resources carefully as they must now incorporate the following:

- statutory assessment for pupils with SEN;
- admissions;
- statutory duties in relation to attendance;
- educational provision for excluded pupils.

Best Value encourages LEAs to consider whether they should be the providers of services, and independent bodies such as the Royal National Institute for the Blind (RNIB), and not the LEA, may provide additional services, such as 'behavioural support' as a consequence of delegated funding.

LEAs working with others to enhance inclusion

For inclusion to be successful, LEAs must work proactively with other agencies, including health authorities and social services:

> The (*Excellence for all Children*) Green Paper drew attention to the difficulties in securing therapy services for children with SEN, which partly results from different statutory responsibilities and priorities of health authorities and LEAs, and lack of clarity over funding. The difficulties are most pronounced in the area of speech and language therapy but similar issues apply to occupational therapy and physiotherapy. There was clear agreement on the nature of the problem; but not on possible solutions.
>
> *SEN Programme of Action*, DfEE, 1998, p.34

A working group was formed in 1998 to consider speech and language therapy and one of its recommendations was:

The Department of Health should arrange for educational interests to be represented on NHS consortia.

DfEE, 2000d, p.12

While it may be surprising that in an era of 'joined-up thinking' this statement needs to be made, it has to be seen as a welcome recommendation. If children's needs are to be met, services working with individual children must effectively co-ordinate their resources. At a national level, developments have occurred that encourage LEAs to liaise with other agencies. In the provision of health services, a shire authority may liaise with several health authorities with very different policies on, and practices in, provision, and changes may be needed to the 'where' and 'how' of provision in order to enhance inclusion. Liaison with social services over 'looked after pupils' is vital.

THE FUTURE

With the increasing delegation of specialist support for inclusion to schools, it is anticipated that the LEA's role, in association with support services, is expected to increase the confidence of schools in dealing with the consequent challenges. Although it is accepted that greater national diversity would result from the incorporation of local needs, such comment does little to indicate an LEA's role in future developments.

Equity and inclusion will continue to remain a major challenge as life-long learning access for inclusive practice for children under five is increasing. The extension of provision for three and four year olds is ensuring greater equity of access and inclusion during the early years of education. For example, Sure Start is likely to make a significant difference in some communities. The Children's Fund and New Opportunity Funding are both now available to assist groups of pupils and Excellence in Cities assists the low and high achievers and encourages schools to accept a full range of ability.

Change is now part of daily life in LEAs and they no longer have the flexibility to 'ease' the inclusive route for individual pupils through the provision of additional resources. Now their role has to be that of facilitators and partners leading to a shared vision of an inclusive, equitable future.

REFERENCES

Booth, T., Ainscow, M. and Dyson, A. (1997) 'Understanding inclusion and exclusion in the English competitive education system', *International Journal of Inclusive Education*, 1 (4) 337–55.

Dawkins, R. (2001) 'No faith in the absurd', *Times Educational Supplement*, 23.

DES (1978) *Special Educational Needs: Report of the Committee of Enquiry into the Education of Handicapped Children and Young People* (The Warnock Report). London: HMSO.

DfEE (1994) *Code of Practice on the Identification and Assessment of Special Educational Needs*. London: HMSO.

DfEE (1998a) *Meeting SEN: a Programme of Action*. London: DfEE.

DfEE (1998b) Circular 13/98: *The Standards Fund 1999–2000*. London: DfEE.

DfEE (1999a) Circular 10/99: *Social Inclusion: Pupil Support*. London: DfEE.

DfEE (1999b) Circular 11/99: *Social Inclusion: the LEA role in Pupil Support*. London: DfEE.

DfEE (1999c) Circular 16/99: *The Standards Fund 2000–2001*. London: DfEE.

DfEE (2000a) *Statistics of Education Special Educational Needs: January 2000*. London: HMSO.

DfEE (2000b) *SEN Code of Practice on the Identification and Assessment of Pupils with Special Educational Needs and SEN Thresholds: Good Practice on Guidance on Identification and Provision for Pupils with Special Educational Needs*. London: DfEE.

DfEE (2000c) *The Standards Fund 2001–2002*. London: DfEE.

DfEE (2000d) *A Guide to the Law for School Governors*. London: DfEE.

DfEE (2000e) *Provision of Speech and Language Therapy: Services to Children with Special Educational Needs (England)*. London: DfEE.

DfES (2001) *Special Educational Needs: Code of Practice*. London: DfES.

Fursland, E. (2001) 'School's Out', *The Guardian*.

Gray, P. (2001) *Developing Support for More Inclusive Schooling: A review of the role of support services for special educational needs in English Local Education Authorities*. London: DfEE/NASEN.

HMSO (1996) *Education Act 1996*. London: HMSO.

Inclusion International (1996, April) *Inclusion: News from Inclusion International*. Brussels: Inclusion International.

Mittler, P. (2000) *Working Towards Inclusive Education: Social Contexts*. London: David Fulton.

Ofsted (2000) *Evaluating Educational Inclusion: Guidance for Inspectors and Schools*. London: Ofsted.

QCA and DfEE (1999) *The National Curriculum*. London: HMSO.

Robertson, C. (1998) 'Quality of life as a consideration in the development of inclusive education for pupils and students with learning difficulties', in C. Tilstone, L. Florian and R. Rose *Promoting Inclusive Practice*. London: Routledge.

Rose, R. (2001) 'Primary school teacher perceptions of the conditions required to include pupils with special educational needs', *Educational Review*, 53 (2) 147–56.

Rose, R. and Howley, M. (2001) 'Entitlement or denial: The curriculum and its influence upon inclusion processes', in T. O'Brien (ed.) *Enabling Inclusion: Blue Skies ... Dark Clouds*. Norwich: The Stationery Office.

Social Exclusion Unit (2001) *A New Commitment to Neighbourhood Renewal: National Strategy Action Team*. London: Cabinet Office.

Whitborn, S., Mitchell, K. and Morris, R. (2000) *What is the LEA for?* Slough: EMIE/NFER.

Chapter 13

'The tide has turned'

A case study of one inner city LEA moving towards inclusion.

Jim Wolger

This chapter describes the planning and development of the inclusion policy of an inner London Local Education Authority (LEA). It considers work with pupils with special educational needs at a time when the roles of LEAs are being seriously weakened, but also when they are being asked to play a major part in carrying forward the principles of inclusive practice.

During the past decade, the roles and responsibilities of local education authorities have become reduced and have changed direction in many areas (see the chapter by Sue Fagg), although they still retain a significant responsibility for pupils with special educational needs (SEN). The extent of their responsibilities is surprising as SEN has, according to 100 Ofsted inspections between 1996 and 2000, consistently been one of its less successful areas of work (Ofsted, 2001b). Nevertheless, despite the moves towards the self-management and self-evaluation of individual schools (MacGilchrist, Mortimore, Savage and Beresford, 1995; MacGilchrist, Myers and Reed, 1997; Caldwell and Spinks, 1988) it would be unfortunate if the local knowledge and expertise that LEAs have built up in supporting children with special educational needs was lost (Mittler, 2000; Ainscow, Farrell, Tweddle and Malkie, 1999; Johnstone and Warwick, 1999).

This chapter discusses the proposals for a practical inclusion policy of one inner city LEA which, alongside a number of other similar authorities, was originally considered by Ofsted to have some major problems in its management and organisation, but which solved a difficult problem and produced positive policies for pupils with special educational needs.

CASE STUDY

In May 1999, Islington Local Education Authority, in north London, received a critical Ofsted report (Ofsted, 1999) and, in April 2000, most of the LEA's statutory functions were transferred to Cambridge Education Associates (known as CEA@Islington). In the report, Islington's Special Education Department, although given a 'satisfactory' rating, was described as having:

> ... shortcomings in almost every aspect of provision, notwithstanding pockets of good practice,

a criticism which was overwhelmingly due to the absence of a:

> ... clear and comprehensive strategy for special needs and the lack of translation of such a strategy into operational plans implemented to good effect ...

> Ofsted, 1999, para. 141

In general, the LEA's work was described as having 'few strengths but many weaknesses' (Ofsted, 1999, para. 6) and, consequently, it was concluded that it was failing in its primary duty of supporting school improvement in order to secure a suitable and effective education for the pupils in its care. The development of a more inclusive approach to the education of pupils with special educational needs and the provision of higher-quality facilities for those pupils were identified as priority areas for action (Ofsted, 1999, paras. A (iii), 22 and 52).

Some years from those damning comments the picture is very different, and a second Ofsted report, in March 2001, stated that:

> The tide has turned in Islington. Strong foundations have been laid ... There is a forward momentum which is engendering the confidence needed to raise expectations on all fronts ...

> Ofsted, 2001a, para 10

This report describes the work of the Special Education Department as 'impressive' (para. 142) and specifically praises its work on inclusion. The comments are quoted in full as they provide a succinct critique of collaboration between special and mainstream schools:

> Islington's inclusion policy contains a clear and realistic vision, and set of principles that are well conceived. These principles have guided the development of a strategy that over time should bring measurable improvements in provision and in pupil related outcomes. This strategy, which is at an early stage, is based on the notion that all schools have a role to play in developing inclusive education, but some, supported by their local special school, are better placed to introduce specialist provision to meet particular types of need. Every school is linked to one of four service areas and thus to Islington's special schools. Each area is supported in the

development of a particular range of expertise that will be available to the whole borough and, in time, resources will be devolved to area level. The provision developed at area level will include within its range, the needs of a significant proportion of children currently educated outside the borough. This should help vulnerable pupils to secure closer links with their families and at the same time reduce expenditure. The strategy is backed up by the 'SEN Framework for Action' the activities within which are clear, well matched to strategic aims and linked well with other activities, although more emphasis on success criteria and measurable outcomes would strengthen the monitoring of impact, an essential ingredient of future success.

Ofsted, 2001a, para. 143

According to the Ofsted grading system, such an endorsement places Islington in the top 5% of LEAs in supporting pupils with SEN (Ofsted, 2001b), a situation which has inevitably been influenced by the progress on inclusive practice in the UK in general.

THE PROGRESS OF INCLUSION IN THE UK

Mittler (2000) contends that the move towards inclusion is a 'journey without end', and if this is true then the speed by which the traveller has journeyed has certainly increased over the past five years in the UK. Books and journals dealing with the many aspects of inclusion have reflected the tensions and challenges to be found on the 'journey': some couched in terms of 'the ideal versus the pragmatic' (Croll and Moses, 2000); some carrying heated exchanges reflecting the strong feeling for and against the practicalities of inclusion (Wilson, 2000; Barrow, 2000; Thomas, 2000; Vislie, 2000); others providing an overview of current practice (Mittler, 2000; Ainscow et al., 1999). There have been frequent discussions on 'definitions' and 'ideology' (see, for example, Wilson, 1999; Norwich, 1996); and descriptions of specific practices in the UK (Bannister, Sharland, Thomas, Upton and Walker, 1999; Johnstone and Warwick, 1999; Knight, 1999; Richards, 1999; Florian, 1998; Jacklin and Lacey, 1993) and abroad (Meijer and Stevens, 1997; Zigmond and Baker 1997; LeRoy and Simpson, 1996).

The debates about *how* and *why* inclusion might be achieved have mainly focused upon the moral principles of 'human' and 'equal' rights and 'equality of opportunity' (Mittler, 2000; Wilson, 1999; 2000) and, less commonly, upon the financial arguments on the 'efficient' and 'effective' use of resources (Rubain, 2001). Interestingly, both arguments have been used 'for' and 'against' the inclusion of pupils with special educational needs into mainstream provision. The trend in the UK has been towards the *gradual* inclusion of pupils with special educational needs into mainstream schools, unlike in some other countries where special schools have closed almost overnight, and mainstream schools have been expected to cope with an influx of pupils with complex needs (Abbring and Meijer, 1994). Such a 'gentle' approach has meant that special and mainstream schools are still functioning alongside each other, although there have been some exceptions such as the developments in the London Borough of Newham (Burke, 1999), but even in such a vanguard authority, a special school is still in existence to meet particular complex needs, and other pupils with such needs are placed in specialist provision outside the borough.

Although gradual, the move towards inclusion in the UK has had some notable landmarks over the years. In the 1970s, for example, children with severe mental handicaps who were previously considered to be 'ineducable' were brought into the educational framework for the first time and, from the 1990s onwards, a whole raft of government documents and legislation has set out an educational vision in which the inclusion of children with special educational needs is seen as a major part of the future development of educational provision in this country, and the rights of children to that provision have been legally established (DfEE, 1997; 1998; DfES, 2001). Such initiatives have had at least three important effects:

1. Attention has been drawn to the wide continuum of need within the term 'special educational needs' which has fuelled a continuing debate on the categorisation of children with such needs. At one end of the continuum are those pupils who have profound and multiple disabilities and who are likely to need specialised education throughout their lives; at the other are those whose disabilities are transitory and can be met by prompt and effective action in the form of particular educational strategies and management.

2. The debate about assessment and the curriculum has moved from a deficit ('can't do') model, which describes the problem as being mainly 'within the child', to a positive ('can do') model, which focuses attention upon what the child is capable of achieving, and uses it as a starting point to make appropriate provision to meet his or her needs (see the chapter by Sue Sanderson). Consequently, schools have been encouraged to consider what they are able to offer pupils with special educational needs in terms of appropriate teaching strategies and environmental changes, rather than rejecting them because they do not *fit* the needs of the institution.

3. The rights of all children to equality of educational opportunity has been highlighted and, importantly, attention has focused on the basic right of any child to an education that is best suited to meeting his or her individual needs. Flexible patterns of inclusion have emerged which offer a variety of mainstream and special school experiences.

David Blunkett, until recently Secretary of State for Education, summed up the importance of focusing upon those with special educational needs:

The education of children with special educational needs is a key challenge for the nation ... It is vital to the creation of a fully inclusive society in which all members see themselves as valued for the contribution they make. We owe all our children – whatever their particular needs and circumstances – the opportunity to develop to their full potential, to contribute economically, and to play a full part as active citizens.

DfEE, 1998, p.2

Despite such statements, Feiler and Gibson (1999) are critical of the lack of practical support from the Government and give a number of reasons why inclusive practice in the UK has not moved on at the same pace as some other European countries. They include:

- the competitive atmosphere engendered in schools by the 1988 Education Act;
- the vested interests on the part of educationalists and researchers who are seen as coming either from the 'segregationist' or 'inclusionist' camps;
- confusion about terminology (for example, what is meant by 'inclusion/integration' or 'special educational needs');
- the lack of empirical data on the benefits (or disadvantages) of inclusion either for pupils or for schools;
- 'internal exclusions' created by intentional streaming;
- highly structured and prescriptive organisational requirements stemming from curriculum initiatives such as the national literacy and numeracy strategies;
- the preference of some schools for using a deficit model, rather than the more positive 'can do' model to protect their academic status;
- the use of 'popular' diagnoses such as dyslexia, ADHD and autism by both professionals and parents alike, to protect, or gain, scarce resources.

Lorenz (1995), in a similar list drawn up some years earlier, includes the introduction of Local Management of Schools; the National Curriculum; the use of standard assessment tasks (SATs); and the publication of league tables as being additional stumbling blocks to inclusion. She maintained that the reluctance or inability of schools to take on board some of these challenges was the reason why inclusion, in her own and similar LEAs, was driven by local 'political' imperatives rather than other motives such as a response to parental concerns.

Index for inclusion

Recently, however, schools have had some practical help in overcoming the barriers to inclusion.

The *Index for Inclusion* published by the Centre for Studies on Inclusive Education (CSIE, 2000) was sent to all schools by the (then) DfEE and provides a set of materials to support institutions in the process of inclusive school development. The materials aim to help schools restructure their cultures, policies and practices and to enable *all* those pupils vulnerable to 'exclusionary pressures' (including those with special educational needs) to increase their participation in the life of the school and in their local communities. Schools are encouraged to engage in challenging explorations of their practices through a consideration of indicators and questions. Within the *Index,* the concept of special educational needs is replaced by the term 'barriers to learning and participation', and the emphasis is on the capacity of the school to include students with diverse needs (see the chapter by Liz Gerschel for a further discussion on the materials).

Although the DfEE was responsible for distributing the *Index*, and therefore endorsed it, Mittler (2000) emphasises that the Government seems to be unclear on whether segregated provision should exist. The closing of all segregated provision is not a view to which all educators subscribe and Croll and Moses (2000) report the views of thirty-eight LEA officers and headteachers (of special and mainstream primary schools) across eleven LEAs who, although supporting the 'ideal' of full inclusion in principle, hold a more pragmatic view on its implementation. They saw it as an 'unrealistic' or 'Utopian' ideal' for some children with severe and complex needs and with emotional and behavioural difficulties, and suggested that these children would always require separate provision as their 'overriding right' to an educational environment that best served their needs. Norwich (1996), in discussing the 'dilemmas and tensions' of inclusion, sees the special school perspective as a useful reminder to mainstream colleagues of the diversity of values, assumptions and methods of education required for a minority.

The Government has certainly suggested ways in which special schools can take a more central role in the development of inclusive practices, including:

- building on their strengths to ensure that they become an integral part of an inclusive education system;
- allowing more flexibility on admitting pupils (for example, taking them for shorter lengths of time to meet specific short-term needs);
- encouraging their staff to work with mainstream schools in order to plan support for pupils who may benefit from a mainstream setting;
- acting as a source of expertise, advice and professional development for mainstream colleagues;
- providing staff to work in resourced schools, and units in mainstream schools;
- amalgamating small special schools and encouraging them to work as a large part of a mainstream campus;

- giving their teachers an explicit remit to provide support and training for mainstream colleagues;
- sharing facilities and resources, including teaching and non-teaching expertise;
- providing support for pupils who move between special and mainstream schools;
- becoming part of 'cluster' arrangements with mainstream primary and secondary schools.

Many writers, whilst acknowledging that special schools can be barriers to the inclusion process, agree that such schools must have a positive role in the move towards inclusive practices (for example, Ainscow et al., 1999; Knight, 1999; Mittler, 2000). They consider that the principles of inclusion must be 'infused' rather than 'imposed', and Letch (2000), commenting particularly on the role that special school staff should play in preparing their mainstream colleagues for the task of including pupils with special educational needs, sees the work as extremely challenging for both:

> It will mean a reappraisal of the skills and competences of staff in specialist schools to see how far these can be applied in mainstream situations. It will also mean planning appropriate ways for these teachers to teach other adults since most teachers are used to teaching children but not their peers. Maybe most of all, it will entail mainstream teachers being ready to change time-honoured practices. (p.117)

LEAs have a responsibility to support such tasks and, in a wide-ranging report on inclusive practice in Norway, Spain, Italy, Denmark and the UK, Johnstone and Warwick (1999) lay down some 'action points' for LEAs who are intending to support the process in a planned and proactive way. These include:

- regular staff discussions on the principles and values at the heart of inclusion policies;
- the encouragement of positive attitudes towards inclusion;
- the establishment of a realistic agenda towards inclusive practices; teachers and LEA officers must be empowered to use a clear set of guidelines;
- the regular revision of the policies;
- a strong commitment to a supportive framework for continuing, professional development for teachers and support staff;
- a high-quality, broad-based, and responsive framework of support aimed at achieving inclusion must be in place within the LEA to ensure that all of the above can be carried through.

CEA@Islington has responded to these action points and has produced its own document for the future of its special needs provision, which takes into account many of the suggestions made by Johnstone and Warwick. A strong emphasis within this 'framework' document is the Government's vision of the creation of a new role for special schools.

CEA@ISLINGTON'S SEN FRAMEWORK FOR ACTION

Over the last five years Islington LEA has been engaged in discussions on inclusive education, which have resulted in what could best be described as 'expressions of good intentions'. However, the launch of the first Annual SEN Conference in 1999 fuelled the debate, and as a consequence of the inception of CEA in April 2000, positive action has resulted. Widespread discussions have taken place at a variety of levels on CEA@Islington's new publication *Special Educational Needs Framework for Action 2000–2003* and included:

- officers of the Special Education Department and other senior officers from CEA@Islington;
- the heads and chairs of the governing bodies of the four special schools in the LEA (through a series of meetings and presentations);
- three annual SEN conferences involving borough officers and councillors, heads, deputies, governors and SENCos from all the mainstream and special schools in the borough;
- representatives from various professional teams including early years; learning support; educational psychology; social services and educational welfare; youth; play and community.

In addition to these discussions, a video was produced and widely circulated, and a series of public 'focus' meetings was held across the borough with governors, schools, pupil referral units and early years centres, parents, representatives from the trade unions and voluntary organisations. It was the biggest and most wide-ranging consultation ever to take place in the borough and written responses to the document highlighted the following key issues:

- the borough should be moving towards inclusive education (84%);
- children have the right to attend a mainstream school (66%);
- special schools should play a central role in developing inclusive practice (81%).

The document

It is understood and accepted by the LEA that there must be a clear policy framework backed by an achievable action plan and that the good practice of wide consultation should continue with the involvement of all key players at all stages in order to promote a shared vision and a culture of inclusion. It was also recognised that proper support systems for mainstream schools would need to be in place, together with the development of ways of measuring progress in order that potential barriers to inclusive practice (such as test/examination results and league tables) could be monitored and nullified as far as possible. The framework document should build upon the strengths of practice identified by the Ofsted reports, mentioned above, which include: strong partnerships with the early years service; effective collaboration with Health and Social Services; good regional developments with other London boroughs in the areas of language and communication and dual sensory impairment; high-quality special schools; and a comprehensive network of advice and support for parents.

Aims and principles of the new policy

The main principle, which governs the 'framework', is the improvement of the quality and co-ordination of services for children and families. It brings together placement and service planning and involves education, health and social service professionals. Consequently the overall needs of the child (during the school day, after school, at week-ends and during holidays) can be comprehensively provided for, whilst at the same time respite care and support for parents can be more readily available.

The aim of CEA@Islington's strategy for inclusion is that through supported teaching and learning over the next five years, all children with SEN will have their needs met within local educational provision and that inclusive education will form an integral part of the vision for improving standards and raising achievement for all schools. A main task for the LEA is, therefore, how best to support schools to increase their ability to meet a wider range of special educational needs cost effectively and, at the same time, take into account the current profile of provision. Eight general principles have been identified which provide a useful checklist for the initial monitoring of the involvement of the LEA, to:

1. give greater flexibility and more power to the schools;
2. focus support in order to improve the schools' capabilities to meet the needs of a wide range of pupils;
3. create a transparent and equitable system of resourcing;
4. reallocate existing resources;
5. measure the impact of the additional support provided;
6. develop partnerships with parents and pupils;
7. ensure that *all* teachers are teachers of children with special educational needs;
8. enhance the skills and knowledge of the staff of schools and enable them to move confidently towards inclusion.

Headings from the research of Ainscow et al. (1999) into the role of twelve LEAs in developing inclusive policies and practices have been used to identify strategies needed to implement the 'framework'. These are: policy development; funding strategies; processes and structures; management of change; partnerships and external influences. The main tasks under each heading are discussed below.

Policy development

All schools and services will have a SEN policy which reflects the principles and aims of the framework.

Funding strategies

In the light of the consultation process it was decided that schools were best placed to assess the day-to-day needs of pupils with SEN and therefore funds for pupils, with and without Statements, will be delegated to schools on a 'whole-school basis' within one overall SEN budget. The duty of schools and governing bodies to ensure that provision is made for all pupils with SEN and additional educational needs (AEN) within their schools will be monitored by the LEA (which still has overall responsibility for children with Statements). By delegating funds in such a way it will be possible to:

- enable schools to identify and meet SEN at the earliest possible stage;
- provide schools with more stability and flexibility;
- encourage the development of permanent specialist SEN teams;
- reduce bureaucracy;
- lessen the need for statements of need to be seen as the 'gateway' to SEN funding.

In addition, funding for pupils with low-incidence disabilities (visual impairment, hearing impairment, autism, physical disabilities, severe and profound and multiple learning difficulties) of such a severity that they would normally require a statement, should continue to be devolved to schools following an individual assessment. Funding will also continue to be retained for pupils with severe and complex and emotional and behavioural difficulties whose needs cannot be met in mainstream settings.

A substantial number of Islington pupils with SEN attend mainstream schools (maintained and independent) outside the borough and at a considerable cost. It is intended that the quality of local provision will be developed to such an extent that parents will be more likely in future to choose local schools for their children rather than sending them out of the borough.

Processes and structures

A new facilitative role for special schools will be developed, with less emphasis on the delivery of direct provision for individual pupils and more on a focused move towards inclusion. These schools will provide an education for their own pupils and also services for mainstream colleagues including:

- advice, support and information;
- help with the identification and assessment of need;
- the moderation of the levels of support required;
- curriculum and resource development;
- examples of evidence-based practice;
- shared professional development;
- time limited placements in special provision for some pupils.

Four service areas will be developed from the existing special schools, based upon the areas of disability identified in the *Draft Code of Practice* (DfEE, 2000): learning and cognition; emotional, social and behavioural difficulties; communication and interaction; physical and/or sensory. These service areas will be responsible for developing a continuum of provision in order to facilitate the maximum level of inclusion for pupils with special needs in mainstream schools and will offer varied patterns of support which may include:

- total inclusion within a mainstream class;
- separate provision for a limited time;
- part-time or short-term placements;
- specific in-class support;
- learning support bases for withdrawal teaching.

It is envisaged that such a move will increase the ability of mainstream schools to provide for a range of pupils with SEN and to improve the links between special and mainstream schools. All four service-areas will provide targeted support for high-incidence disability directly to mainstream schools. Mainstream schools will be encouraged to identify a low-incidence disability in which they are interested in developing further skills (for example, hearing impairment, visual impairment, physical disability, autism, severe and profound and multiple learning difficulties). Working in clusters, they will be supported by the appropriate service area. It is likely that in future they will become 'additionally resourced' schools, which will have developed expertise in a certain area of SEN and will consequently receive additional funding. Schools will determine the way in which their own provision develops and could vary from a discrete unit base to total inclusion. An example of such a model is provided below.

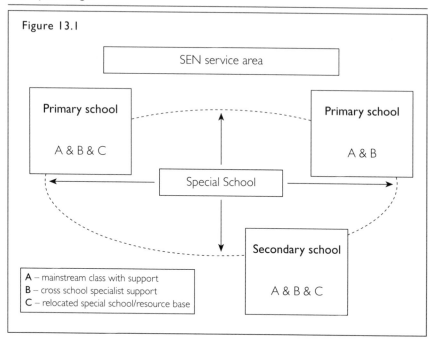

Figure 13.1

Management of change

It is acknowledged that staff and parents will feel insecure as the SEN 'framework' is put into practice and strategies will need to be devised to ensure that current expertise is recognised and a full package of training is offered and developed for teachers, support staff, governors and parents. Islington's special education department will be responsible for developing work in a number of key areas:

- an agreed policy for placement in non-mainstream provision;
- developing links with the Connexions Service for children aged thirteen plus;
- conciliation arrangements with an independent element to help to resolve disputes;
- rigorous accountability for resources.

In addition, improvements are planned in the arrangements for admission to schools and transfer between phases for children with statements of SEN. One of Islington's special schools already has established a training unit, which is offering training to teaching assistants in the LEA and a number of other London boroughs (Imray and Wolger, 1999). It is intended to develop this resource to form a training facility, capable of offering nationally accredited courses for teaching assistants and teachers and to support the work within Islington's service areas.

Partnerships

Parents must feel confident that the needs of their children will be met in the move towards inclusive education. The following concerns were expressed by some parents during the consultation process:

- the practical realities of inclusive education;
- unsuccessful experiences in mainstream schools;
- health and safety issues and bullying in mainstream schools;
- funding and resources (some parents did not trust schools to spend money devolved to them for SEN for the intended purpose);
- transition from one phase of education to another (primary to secondary, for example).

Parents did, however, have some suggestions on how to make the process more comfortable for them. In the main these centred on improved communication and information between parents and professionals. For example, proper support networks should be in place before the child's problems become critical, together with clearer guidance, in plain English. Parents also felt strongly that school staff needed to be better trained and more knowledgeable in SEN and that it was important for the whole child to be considered and not just his or her disability.

External influences

It is important that the move towards inclusive education will be reflected in, and facilitated by, all educational initiatives in order to assist, rather than to obstruct, the process. Such initiatives will ensure that:

- inclusive education is the central theme of the LEA's Education Development Plan;
- the national literacy and numeracy strategies focus on raising the standards of *all* children including those with special educational needs;
- the LEA's School Organisation Plan provides opportunities for the development of resource bases and the relocation of current specialist provision;
- the needs of pupils with emotional, social and behavioural difficulties are a particular focus of the LEA's Social Inclusion Strategies and Behaviour Support Plan;
- early identification and preventative work will be the core of the Early Years Development Plan;
- the LEA's responsibilities for 'children in need' and 'looked after children' will be reflected in the Children's Services Plan and the Quality Protection Management Action Plan.

CONCLUSION

In this chapter CEA@Islington's Framework for Action has been discussed with reference to the national initiatives on inclusive education and insights have been given into how parents and professionals within the borough view the proposals. Although it is impossible to discuss its effectiveness at this early stage, it can be reported that progress has been made on the planning, development and implementation of the four service areas and the heads of the special schools have been appointed as the heads of these services. Funding for mainstream schools in relation to the management of pupils with high-incidence disabilities is now in place, and further consultation with mainstream and special schools on the strategy for funding pupils with low-incidence disabilities has already started. The 'action points' identified in Johnstone and Warwick's research (1999) will ultimately be used to determine the success of the inclusion policy being promoted by CEA@Islington, but the recent Ofsted inspection reveals that the team consider the framework to provide:

> ... a well-conceived, positive, clear and realistic vision that should bring benefits over the next three to five years.
>
> Ofsted, 2001, para. 143

The Inspection Team report that

> ... there is still a long way to go before all school staff are convinced about the merits of inclusion, but improved advice, training and support at all levels for teaching and non-teaching staff are beginning to improve confidence and expertise in schools.
>
> Ofsted, 2001, para. 149

It would seem that the tide has turned and that many of the correct strategies are in place for this policy on inclusion to become a reality.

REFERENCES

Abbring, I. and Meijer, C.W.J. (1994) 'Italy', in C.W.J. Meijer et al. (eds.) *New Perspectives in Special Education: A Six Country Study of Integration.* London: Routledge.

Ainscow, M., Farrell, P., Tweddle, D. and Malkie, G. (1999) 'The role of the LEA in developing inclusive policies and practices', *British Journal of Special Education*, 26 (3) 136–40.

Bannister, C., Sharland, V., Thomas, G., Upton, V. and Walker, P. (1999) 'Changing from a special school to an inclusion service', *British Journal of Special Education*, 25 (2) 65–9.

Barrow, R. (2000) 'Include me out: a response to John Wilson', *European Journal of*

Special Needs Education, 15 (3) 305–13.

Burke, B. (1999) 'LEA Support Services: a Newham Perspective', in B. Norwich (ed.) *Rethinking Support for More Inclusive Schooling*. Tamworth: NASEN.

Caldwell, B.J. and Spinks, J.M. (1988) *The Self-managing School*. London: The Falmer Press.

Croll, P. and Moses, D. (2000) 'Ideologies and Utopias: education professionals' views of inclusion', *European Journal of Special Needs Education*, 15 (1) 1–12.

CSIE (2000) *Index for Inclusion: Developing Learning and Participation in Schools*. Bristol: CSEI and London: DfEE.

DfEE (1997) *Excellence for All Children: Meeting Special Educational Needs*. London: The Stationery Office.

DfEE (1998) *Meeting Special Educational Needs: a Programme for Action*. London: DfEE.

DfEE (2000) Draft *Code of Practice on the Identification and Assessment of Pupils with Special Educational needs and SEN Thresholds*. London: DfEE.

DfES (2001) *Inclusive Schooling: Children with Special Educational Needs*. London: DfES.

Feiler, A. and Gibson, H. (1999) 'Threats to the inclusion movement', *British Journal of Special Education*, 26 (3) 147–51.

Florian, L. (1998) 'An examination of the practical problems associated with the implementation of inclusive education policies', *Support for Learning*, 13 (3) 105–8.

Gerschel, L. (1998) 'Equal opportunities and special educational needs: equity and inclusion', in C. Tilstone, L. Florian and R. Rose (eds.) *Promoting Inclusive Practice*. London: Routledge.

Hegarty, S. (1993) 'Reviewing the literature on integration', *European Journal of Special Needs Education*, 8 (3) 194–200.

Imray, P. and Wolger, J. (1999) 'A home-grown answer to the problem of support staff training', *SLD Experience*, 25 (Autumn) 2–4.

Jacklin, A. and Lacey, J. (1993) 'The integration process: a developmental model', *Support for Learning*, 8 (2) 51–7.

Johnstone, D. and Warwick, C. (1999) 'Community solutions to inclusion: some observations on practice in Europe and the United Kingdom', *Support for Learning*, 14 (1) 8–12.

Knight, B.A. (1999) 'Towards inclusion for students with special educational needs in the regular classroom', *Support for Learning*, 14 (1) 3–7.

LeRoy, B. and Simpson, C. (1996) 'Improving student outcomes through inclusive education', *Support for Learning*, 11 (1) 32–6.

Letch, R. (2000) 'Special educational needs and inclusion', in J. Docking (ed.) *New Labour's Policies for Schools: Raising the Standard?* London: David Fulton, in association with Roehampton Institute, London.

Lorenz, S. (1995) 'The placement of pupils with Down's Syndrome: a survey of one northern LEA', *British Journal of Special Education*, 22 (1) 16–19.

MacGilchrist, B., Mortimore, P., Savage, J. and Beresford, C. (1995) *Planning Matters: The Impact of Development Planning in Primary Schools*. London: Paul Chapman Publishing.

MacGilchrist, B., Myers, K. and Reed, J. (1997) *The Intelligent School*. London: Paul Chapman Publishing Ltd.

Meijer, C.J.W. and Stevens, L.M. (1997) 'Restructuring special education provision', in S.J. Pijl, C.J.W. Meijer and S. Hegarty *Inclusive Education: a Global Agenda*. London: Routledge.

Mittler, P. (2000) *Working Towards Inclusive Education: Social Contexts*. London: David Fulton.

Norwich, B. (1996) 'Special needs in education for all: connective specialisation and ideological impurity', *British Journal of Special Education*, 23 (3) 100–4.

Ofsted (1999) *Inspection of Islington Local Education Authority*. London: Office of Her Majesty's Chief Inspector of Schools in conjunction with the Audit Commission.

Ofsted (2001a) *Inspection of Islington Local Education Authority*. London: Office of Her Majesty's Chief Inspector of Schools in conjunction with the Audit Commission.

Ofsted and Audit Commission (2001b) *Local Education Authority Support for School Improvement*. London: The Stationery Office.

Richards, I. (1999) 'Inclusive schools for pupils with emotional and behavioural difficulties', *Support for Learning*, 14 (3) 99–103.

Rubain, D. (2001) 'Transforming legislation', in *The Times Educational Supplement* (Curriculum Special, 6 April), 4.

Thomas, G. (2000) 'Doing injustice to inclusion: A response to John Wilson', *European Journal of Special Needs Education*, 15 (3) 307–10.

Vislie, L. (2000) 'Doing justice to inclusion: A response to John Wilson', *European Journal of Special Needs Education*, 15 (3) 311–13.

Wilson, J. (1999) 'Some conceptual difficulties about inclusion', *Support for Learning*, 14 (3) 110–12.

Wilson, J. (2000) 'Doing justice to inclusion', *European Journal of Special Needs Education*, 15 (3) 297–304.

Zigmond, N. and Baker, J.M. (1997) 'Inclusion of pupils with learning disabilities in general education settings', in S.J. Pijl, C.J.W. Meijer and S. Hegarty (eds.) *Inclusive Education: a Global Agenda*. London: Routledge.

Chapter 14

The role of the educational psychologist in the inclusive process

Sue Sanderson

This chapter aims to explore how psychologists can use their skills to assist schools in the development and implementation of policies to promote inclusion. These skills and this knowledge include: an in-depth appreciation of how children and adults think and learn; an understanding of dynamic approaches to assessment; and an appreciation of approaches to teaching and learning.

Educational psychologists have traditionally been viewed as professionals employed by a local education authority (LEA) to assess whether pupils *need* additional support in mainstream schools or if they would be better placed in a specialist educational provision. Although current government advice (DfEE, 1994; DfEE, 2000a; DfES, 2001) suggests that more responsibility for the initial identification of children with special educational needs should be transferred to teachers, education services continue to demand that the identification and subsequent assessment of these pupils is verified by educational psychologists, certainly where there are financial implications (Beaver, 1998).

Increasingly many educational psychologists are frustrated by the matching of pupils against processes and criteria, and by the monitoring of the use of funds through the allocation of Statements. Fortunately, shifts in LEA policy (Ainscow, Farrell, Tweddle and Malki, 1999) together with subtle changes in legislation (DfEE 1997; DfEE 1998) have meant that there is an increase in the delegation of special needs resources to schools. As Beaver (1998) points out, this increase has encouraged educational psychologists to demonstrate their effectiveness in other ways, particularly in 'case work' where the opportunity to revive the focus on psychological skills is seen by many as a welcome move. The professional training and work of psychologists is diverse and varied, and is consistently undergoing change in the light of formal and informal demands. The fundamental basis of this work remains a combination of theory and practice in the key areas of psychology and education. Consequently one of the major contributions of educational psychologists to education has been their ability to combine information from theories of child development with an understanding of educational processes in order to develop assessment and intervention tools. As most educational psychologists are employed by the 'special needs arm' of LEAs and are expected to focus on those children whose learning is considered 'deviant' or 'problematic', it is often forgotten that they have much to offer in the enhancement of the learning of *all* pupils.

THE ROLE OF PSYCHOLOGISTS IN THE ASSESSMENT OF LEARNING

The stereotypical view of the educational psychologist is one where he or she, armed with IQ tests, removes a child from the classroom environment in order to determine his or her intelligence, encouraging the belief that an IQ is fixed and immutable. Such practices played a significant part in ensuring that special education was predominantly concerned with segregated provision and therefore tests were designed which were specifically created to:

> ... pick out in advance those children who were not likely to learn much from the curriculum of ordinary schools.
>
> Kamin, in Eysenck and Kamin, 1981, p.80

These children were then placed in special schools or, before 1971 in the case of children with severe and profound learning difficulties, outside education in junior training centres run by local health authorities. The use of IQ tests brought about the adoption of a medical 'diagnostic' model of assessment where 'deficit' information about what a child could *not* do (rather than where his or her abilities lay) was sought. As a consequence, the tests largely served to compare one child in numerical terms with his or her peers. Unfortunately the terminology surrounding IQ testing is still prevalent and Solity (1991), cited in Lunt (1993), states:

> The way educationalists refer to children's 'ability' is a potentially insidi-ous form of discrimination. So although we may no longer support the use of intelligence tests to ascertain children's ability and learning potential, the language of the intelligence test still abounds. This may, in the most negative instances, lead to children being quite arbitrarily identified as lacking in intelligence or ability, with the inevitable consequence that expectations for their future learning are low. (pp.148–9)

In defence of their use it can be argued that IQ tests offer experienced profes-sionals structured opportunities to observe a child's thinking processes, attitudes and behaviours over a set period, whilst completing a range of struc-tured activities. Kaufman (1979) considered that they could help to identify specific learning styles, strengths and weaknesses, which will aid teachers to plan specific teaching programmes. Although many people currently believe that IQ testing is of limited value, even those advocating more constructive ways of working (see following section) do continue to see some merits. Lunt (1993), for example, refers to using the traditional IQ tests dynamically and believes that this, 'has yielded rich diagnostic information'.

THE ROLE OF THE EDUCATIONAL PSYCHOLOGIST IN USING THEORIES ABOUT LEARNING AND ASSESSMENT

The psychological theories of the early part of the twentieth century dwelt on the behaviourist notion that learning could be broken down into discrete skills, which could be combined later in order to develop more complex ones (Gipps, 1994). This inevitably led to the idea that learning was sequential and that complex understanding only happens when previous skills have been mastered. Despite criticism of the early work of Skinner, he did raise the awareness of the need to employ 'schedules of reinforcement' in the classroom, and criticised lessons and examinations which were designed to reveal what pupils *do not know* and *cannot do*, rather than to expose and build upon what they *do know* and are *able to learn* (Wood, 1999). Although this linear theory of learning persisted (and still does to some degree), it can be criticised for its insistence on the observable, and its refusal to take account of such internal drives as motivation and interest. In contrast, theories of learning developed by psychologists such as Piaget:

> ... placed action and self-directed problem-solving at the heart of learning and development. By acting on the world, the learner comes to discover how to control it.
>
> Wood, 1999, p.5

Piaget was not interested in what children *could not do*, but what they *could do* at certain stages of development, and postulated that the nature of intelligence changed considerably over their development; something which has a profound effect on many educational psychologists' thinking. Although Piaget was interested in the structure of thinking and learning, it was Bruner (an American psychologist working at about the same time) who became concerned with the processes which affected thinking and learning. Both agreed, however, that action and problem solving were important and that abstract thinking grew from material actions; thus children will only understand abstract information if their experiences are grounded in practical problem solving.

Vygotsky, the Russian psychologist, has also contributed greatly to thinking about learning. He attempted to understand the nature, evolution and transmission of human culture and how people 'come to act upon, construe and represent their world' (Wood, 1999, p.11). He also queried the notion of static ability and his 'zone of proximal development' refers to the gap between *actual* and *potential* developmental levels, as shown by a child's ability when supported by a more able adult or peer. The process of guidance and support (known as scaffolding) can be removed when the child is able to stand alone at a particular level of learning. The type and amount of instruction required is the link between the child's learning and the transmission of knowledge. Consequently the focus shifts to an interest in the child's *process* of learning and his or her potential for change. Such work provides opportunities to change the emphasis from limitations on a child's learning to how he/she learns about his or her world. Gipps (1994), in summing up the work of these theories, proposes that:

> ... learning is a process of knowledge construction; that learning is knowledge-dependent; and that learning is tuned to the situation in which it takes place. (pp.21–2)

She stresses the role of motivation in learning and emphasises that, as new knowledge is mapped on to an existing schema which is personal to the learner, such an action does not demand that the pupil merely passively absorbs facts. Learning becomes an active partnership between teacher and pupil, and both assessment procedures and the curriculum need to fit this pattern.

Consequently, in such a learning partnership there is a greater demand for a 'thinking curriculum': one which teaches skills of metacognition or 'thinking about thinking'. This shift in understanding about learning, and about the curriculum in general, has greatly influenced perceptions of a student's ability; in other words, the focus has changed from a model of limited potential or capacity (measured by IQ tests), to a consideration of what students need in order to be motivated and for their learning to be sustained. There is now a more fluid understanding of the learning process and greater emphasis must therefore be placed on the understanding of individual learning styles (qualitative assessment) rather than set categories of measurement against IQ figures (quantitative assessment).

One of the roles of the educational psychologist should now be concerned with challenging thinking about learning styles and how such styles relate to assessment, to the curriculum and to teaching. He or she should be in a good position to encourage those teachers and LEA staff currently involved with special needs to become part of the broader picture of education for all, and to take responsibility for pupils with different educational needs, rather than just those with 'special' ones. Such a view is supported by Read (1998) who emphasises that inclusive practices are not restricted to differentiation according to ability, but need to take account of how individual pupils learn most effectively. The role of the educational psychologist in assessment in this climate is placed within a specific context and related to classroom activities. As a consequence, the relationship between psychologist and teacher will change as the focus shifts from one 'expert' advising another, to one of collaboration and shared problem solving.

ADDITIONAL ROLES

Assessing the level of need or the degree of (dis)ability

Although the use of IQ tests is decreasing, standardised tests continue to serve administrative expediency. Many authorities, for example, continue to set criteria for admission to schools for pupils with moderate or severe learning difficulties largely based on the administration of a range of standardised tests carried out by educational psychologists. Psychologists who are employed by LEAs are inevitably influenced by the historical concepts of special education and can be 'forced' into a position of perpetuating segregation.

Changing the perception of need

Dessent, as far back as 1987, advocated that children need to be seen as lying on a continuum of learning need with an entitlement to the same educational opportunities. He stressed the importance of focusing on the *level* of need rather than the *degree* of (dis)ability. He maintained that one of the fundamental barriers to change was the belief that 'special' education remains the domain of 'somebody else', an 'arm' of an LEA or of a separate department of a school 'disembodied' from mainstream education. More recently, Farrell (2001) has argued that neither the 1981 Education Act nor the 1994 Code of Practice moved any further towards the 'abolition of categorical ways of conceptualising special needs' and he reminds us that even the new *Code of Practice* (DfES, 2001) encompasses children within four broad areas. He cogently summarises the arguments for the abolition of categories as they perpetuate the focus on 'within-child' learning difficulties and do not encourage the acceptance of a continuum of learning need. He does, however, accept that categories and labels are very much part of life in general and will continue to be used in the special needs field for some time. He stresses that they should be 'handled with care' and suggests that, with cautious management, labels and categories can be used positively to gain pictures or snapshots of children's learning which can inform research into specific areas of difficulty. It could be argued that until there is a more universal public understanding of *learning* (as opposed to *special*) need, it may be helpful for educational psychologists to continue to use labels and categories cautiously as a 'shorthand': a means of encouraging schools to appreciate fully the vast range of learning styles and learning needs which exist amongst pupils.

Monitoring the quality of resources

A whole authority approach to a continuum of learning demands the existence of an agreed policy which constitutes a framework for action (see the chapter by Fagg) by all professionals involved, including educational psychologists. In the development of such a policy an important focus, directly involving these professionals, will be a consideration of the different ways of resourcing children with 'special' educational needs, which does not depend on individual-based Statementing procedures. For example, new forms of allocating resources, which encourage all schools to take responsibility for all pupils, could be identified and, consequently, the role of the LEA psychologist might be to monitor the quality of the resources, and ensure that teachers are trained in using them appropriately, rather than identifying the recipients.

Casework

Beaver (1998) stresses the importance of educational psychologists supporting teachers by using their knowledge of case work to focus upon the successful learning which every child, despite his or her complex needs, has acquired. At this level, educational psychologists can encourage teachers and parents to redefine 'success' and to identify what learning needs children have, as well as celebrating differences. In a similar way, they have an important role to play in supporting teacher colleagues to work through attitude change, to confirm that they have the skills to be 'inclusive' and to encourage them to identify their own additional training needs in relation to the learning styles and teaching requirements of *all* pupils, including those with the most complex needs.

Consultancy

Such activities place the educational psychologist in the role of a 'consultant'. Many services, in the hope of consolidating a drive towards more inclusive education, are moving towards a model of consultation rather than retaining individual child-focused work carried out in isolation. Stratford (2000) sums up the skills offered by educational psychologists in whole-school work as:

- a psychological perspective, involving a holistic, interactional view of the pupil as part of the wider school context;
- a knowledge of organisational processes: systemic approaches to explanation, prevention and interaction;
- collaborative problem-solving skills;
- pupil-focused input skills which involve the promotion of metacognitive strategies,
- research skills: objectivity, data collection and evaluation.

In addition, Battle, Fredrickson and Sharp (2001) suggest that the unique knowledge gained by regular visits to the school can enable the educational psychologist to help to change ethos and to create positive social relationships. These authors also recognise the presentation of INSET as another important skill.

Arguments for the appropriateness of a consultation model in educational psychology practice, include the following, that it:

- challenges a 'medical model' view of service delivery which emphasises 'within pupil' problems;
- moves away from a traditional approach founded on individual testing, which has dubious validity, towards one where the full range of skills of the educational psychologist can be utilised;
- shifts the focus from a 'within pupil' problem to one examining context and environment;
- creates greater equality of status between educational psychologists and teachers and offers greater opportunities for multi-agency work;
- encourages schools to take 'ownership' of pupils' difficulties;
- allows the educational psychologist to influence the problem-solving strategies of a number of school staff;
- moves the focus of attention from assessment to action;
- makes more efficient use of educational psychologists' time, allowing them to be involved with more pupils and to scrutinise patterns of school-based difficulty;
- can encourage greater use of effective consultation when planning policies within the school.

It is the combination of these roles, particularly the final point, which may facilitate the role of the educational psychologist in helping to develop inclusive policies and practices.

EDUCATIONAL PSYCHOLOGISTS AND THE DEVELOPMENT OF POLICIES WITHIN SCHOOLS

Palmer, Redfern and Smith (1994) developed a model for policy development which was based on a consideration of, what they called, the 'Four Ps':

> *Philosophy* – where do we come from?
> *Principles* – what should we do?
> *Procedures* – how do we do it?
> *Performance* – is it happening?' (p.4)

Under the first heading, they emphasise that policies should begin with statements about beliefs which relate to the school's respect for the individual needs of its pupils. They propose that the declaration that all teachers are responsible for meeting pupils' individual needs is a sound starting point. Statements under the second heading will indicate how philosophy can be put into practice and may include examples of differentiation, the responsibilities of SENCos and ways in which parents might be involved in the teaching and learning process. 'Procedures' include the practical actions which all staff need to take to ensure that the agreed principles are adhered to. 'Performance' refers to how the policy's effectiveness might be recorded and measured. In the light of the discussion on the additional roles of the educational psychologist, he or she is in a good position to contribute to all areas identified by Palmer and his team.

Beaver (1998), in a consideration of the psychologist and case work, provides ideas on the prerequisites of a successful policy statement. By adapting his ideas the following could form useful basic guidance. The policy:

- is considered important and all staff should be committed to its contents;
- should be congruent with the beliefs of those involved;
- should be clear and specific and agreed by everybody in the school;
- includes actions which can be put into practice by everyone in the school including those writing it;
- will be positive in its wording; in other words, agreements made when drawing it up relate to what people will do, rather than to what they will not do;
- should be for a fixed time and dates should be set for reviews.

The key role of the psychologist might be in supporting staff in the formulation, implementation and evaluation of the policy. Activities such as making sure that all members of the team have had opportunities to contribute to the process, or to ask questions about broader issues, will be important. Such questions may involve discovering what various members of the school understand by terms such as 'inclusion', 'special educational needs', 'learning difficulties', 'emotional and behavioural difficulties', for example. It will be useful to explore how this is reflected in existing documentation or to which theory of learning individual teachers/senior management subscribe.

By supporting staff in the writing and development of policies, opportunities are naturally provided for the educational psychologist to reflect upon how the whole school is addressing the educational needs of all pupils in a number of key areas; to encourage staff to communicate and collaborate; to share their skills and expertise; and to further inclusive practices. Examples of key areas are: access to, and within, the building; the nature of in-class support for pupils; equal opportunities; differentiation at all levels, including learning styles, resources and teaching approaches; links with other policies such as those on bullying, conflict management and behaviour. A consideration of the strategies for assessment, recording and reporting within the school and an examination of partnership with parents are also possible 'spin-off' areas for research and exploration.

Not only can educational psychologists support discussion and debate on the views that members of staff hold on such matters, but they may be able to encourage a consideration of relevant literature and research and, through their knowledge of a range of schools, share information on good practice.

Many of the key areas identified above are reflected in Giangreco's (1997) list of school features which encourage inclusive practices:

- collaborative teamwork;
- a shared framework;
- family involvement;
- general educator ownership;
- clear role relationships among professionals;
- effective use of support staff;
- meaningful IEPs;
- procedures for evaluating effectiveness.

Florian (1998, p.22) takes this list further and identifies the following set of *conditions* which form the basis of inclusive education:

- a positive attitude about the learning abilities of all pupils;
- teacher knowledge about learning difficulties;
- skilled application of specific instructional methods;
- parent and teacher support;
- an opportunity for pupil participation in the decision-making process.

Although considering successful school factors in reducing *behaviour* difficulties, Watkins and Wagner (2000, p.133) identify the essential *processes* necessary for the formation of policies. They see these as :

- internal problem solving;
- teamwork as opposed to hierarchy;
- classroom focus as opposed to individual focus;
- multi-level, multi-causal thinking

This section, in particular, has considered the various models contributing to, the pre-requisites for, and the processes involved in the development of school policies linked to inclusion. The educational psychologist is in a good position to encourage people to recognise their unique skills and qualities; to reflect upon their own practices; to support the facilitation of team work; to link theories of child development to the real situations in the classroom; and to bring together a range of perspectives which will contribute to the development of inclusion policies.

CONCLUSIONS

Ainscow (1998) believes that schools will only foster the learning of all children if:

> ... teachers become more reflective and critical practitioners, capable of, and empowered to, investigate aspects of their practice with a view to making improvements. Only in this way can they overcome the limitations and dangers of deficit thinking; only in this way can we be sure that pupils who experience difficulties in learning can be treated with respect and viewed as potentially active and capable learners. (pp.12–13)

The process of fostering effective teaching and learning for all children including those with the most complex 'special needs' is dependent on all staff becoming more reflective of their own attitudes and practices. Stoker (2000) suggests that although an educational psychologist is part of the school system, she or he is also outside it. This can enable him or her to become more objective and apply psychology by reconstructing the dialogue using critical analysis and reflecting back key issues.

It perhaps is not enough to be critical of what is said but also to help others to be critical of what is done in practice!

The report of the DfEE (2000b) working party into the roles, the practices and the future of educational psychology services advises that educational psychologists should work at a whole-school level, using their knowledge of organisational psychology to support an overall approach to learning and development. Specific reference is given in the report to offering advice on policies and practices. Interestingly the document decries the lack of national clarity in the past on the precise role of educational psychologists, and indicates that it has been the responsibility of individual educational psychologists themselves, and the LEAs and the schools that they have worked with, to determine their own working methods, many of which have, unfortunately, been idiosyncratic. The report defines the aim of the educational psychology service as existing to:

> ... promote child development and learning through the application of psychology by working with individuals and groups of children, teachers and other adults in schools, families, other LEA officers, health and social services and other agencies.
>
> DfEE 2000b, p.5

Such an aim reinforces the need to define a broader role for educational psychologists who have traditionally been seen as assessors of the special needs of children who require access to specialist resources or additional funding. Now it is possible to encompass a role, which includes the making of a contribution to the teaching and learning of all children and to working with a range of agencies. As discussed in the first section of this chapter, central to the work is an opportunity to reclaim our position as purveyors of theory and practice in the areas of psychology and education. What educational psychologists have been trained to do, and what they are especially good at, is helping others to apply theory in practice, whether in terms of systems or individuals. Helping others, in this context, means supporting the formation of effective policies, which will inform and develop inclusive practices.

REFERENCES

Ainscow, M. (1998) 'Would it work in theory? Arguments for practitioner research and theorising in the special needs field', in C. Clark, A. Dyson and A. Millward (eds.) *Theorising Special Education*. London: Routledge.

Ainscow, M., Farrell, P., Tweddle, D. and Malki, G. (1999) 'The role of LEAs in developing inclusive policies and practices', *British Journal of Special Education*, 26 (3) 136–40.

Battle, S., Fredrickson, N. and Sharp, S. (2001) 'Supporting a school in special measures: implications for the potential contribution of the educational psychologist', *Educational Psychology in Practice*, 17 (1) 53–68.

Beaver, R. (1998) *Educational Psychology Casework. A Practical Guide*. London: Jessica Kingsley.

Dessent, T. (1987) *Making the Ordinary School Special*. London: Falmer Press.

DfEE (1994) *Code of Practice on the Identification and Assessment of Special Educational Needs*. London: DfEE.

DfEE (1997) *Excellence for All Children: Meeting Special Educational Needs*. London: DfEE.

DfEE (1998) *Meeting Special Educational Needs: A Programme for Action*. London: DfEE.

DfEE (2000a) *Draft Code of Practice on the Identification and Assessment of Pupils with Special Educational Needs and SEN Thresholds*. London: DfEE.

DfEE (2000b) *Educational Psychology Service (England): Current Role, Good Practice and Future Directions*. London: DfEE.

DfES (2001) *Special Educational Needs: Code of Practice*. London: DfES.

Eysenck, H.J. vs. Kamin, L. (1981) *Intelligence the Battle of the Mind*. London: Pan.

Farrell, P. (2001) 'Special education in the last twenty years: have things really got better?', *British Journal of Special Education*, 28 (1) 3–9.

Florian, L. (1998) 'Inclusive practices: what why and how?', in C. Tilstone, L. Florian and R. Rose (eds.) *Promoting Inclusive Practice*. London: Routledge.

Giangreco, M.F. (1997) 'Key lessons learned about inclusive education: summary of the 1996 Schonell Memorial Lecture', *Intellectual Journal of Disability, Development and Education*, 44 (3) 193–206.

Gipps, C.V. (1994) *Beyond Testing. Towards a Theory of Educational Assessment*. London: Falmer.

Kaufman, A.S. (1979) *Intelligent Testing with the WISC-R*. London: Wiley.

Lunt, I. (1993) 'The practice of assessment', in H. Daniels (ed.) *Charting the Agenda of Educational Activity After Vygotsky*. London: Routledge.

Lunt, I. and Farrell, P. (1994) 'Reconstructing educational psychology training in the UK', *The Psychologist*, 7 (6) 268–71.

Palmer, C., Redfern, R. and Smith, K. (1994) 'The Four Ps of Policy', *British Journal of Special Education*, 21 (1) 4–6.

Read, G. (1998) 'Promoting inclusion through learning styles', in C. Tilstone, L. Florian and R. Rose (eds.) *Promoting Inclusive Practice.* London: Routledge.

Stoker, R. (2000) 'The 6th discipline of the learning organisation – understanding the psychology of individual constructs and the organisation (or PICTO)', *Educational and Child Psychology,* 17 (1) 76–85.

Stratford, R. (2000) 'An analysis of the organisational constraints on educational psychologists working at whole-school levels; the opportunities for inclusion', *Educational and Child Psychology,* 17 (1) 86–97.

Watkins, C. and Wagner, P. (2000) *Improving School Behaviour.* London: Paul Chapman Publishing.

Wood, D. (1999) *How Children Think and Learn. The Social Contexts of Cognitive Development.* (2nd edition) Oxford: Blackwell.

Chapter 15

Professional development of staff
Steps towards developing policies

Christina Tilstone

Christina Tilstone considers the implications of some of the major changes in professional development and highlights the need for policies to include all staff. She outlines the principles underpinning the formulation of current policies and suggests steps towards their effective development.

SETTING THE SCENE

Throughout this book there has been reference, both implicit and explicit, to the professional development of all members of staff concerned with pupils with special educational needs and their inclusive education. Professional development, particularly for teachers, has been a topic of concern for successive governments, but little has been done to co-ordinate approaches or to ensure that a clear model has been devised. Even less has been achieved for the many other professionals, practitioners and administrators who are part of the staff of schools, and who all make a contribution to the teaching and learning of their pupils.

A comprehensive framework for the initial and continuing professional development of the teaching profession was drawn up in the James Report (DES, 1972) which identified three cycles of 'continuous learning' throughout a teacher's career underpinned by important principles including:

- broad attributes of intellectual competence;
- human understanding;
- desirable educational attitudes.

Such attributes went far beyond the emphasis on the mastery of basic teaching skills, which, in an attempt to raise standards of teaching and learning, appears to be the preoccupation of Government policy today. The report emphasised that initial teacher education and continuing professional education should be part of the same life-long process; a relationship which is particularly important in the teaching of pupils with special educational needs where the knowledge acquired (or not) in initial teacher education will have a bearing upon inclusive practices and, subsequently, upon the routes and approaches selected for each teacher's continuing development. Unfortunately, many of the ideas in the report were considered too radical or too expensive to implement, and the 'framework' and its sound principles were abandoned.

There was, however, a recognition that all teachers deserve, and need, a positive plan of professional development during their careers (Robson, Sebba, Mittler and Davies, 1988; Smith and Varma, 1996), but unfortunately the nature and consequence of teacher development has received inadequate disciplined research. The result has been 'bolt-on' or 'piecemeal' changes, made often in responses to the reorganisations that have taken place in the education system itself.

It is not our intention to provide a historical overview of teacher development in this chapter, and readers who require such information are recommended to consult the introductory chapters in Davis and Garner (1997) or in Smith and Varma (1996). It is important, however, to highlight some of the changes that have had a major impact on the professional development of teachers of pupils with special educational needs.

INITIAL TEACHER EDUCATION

Initial teacher education is crucially important in familiarising new entrants to the profession with the nature of special education, and in providing them with the relevant skills for teaching all such pupils with whom they come into contact. Formal undergraduate programmes with an award in teaching children with severe and profound and multiple learning difficulties were abandoned as a result of the recommendation of the Advisory Committee for the Supply and Education of Teachers (ACSET, 1984) on the grounds that all teachers should be teachers of children with special educational needs. A laudable ideal, but history has shown that teachers in mainstream schools are more reluctant to include pupils with complex needs in their classes for a variety of reasons which include feelings of inadequacy and the lack of appropriate skills (Tilstone and Upton, 1993; McLaughlin and Tilstone, 2000). Their undergraduate training has focused on academic subject teaching in the core and foundation subjects of the National Curriculum and any special needs matters usually 'permeate' each element of the course; this approach has been heavily criticised as an inadequate foundation for meeting the needs of a wide range of pupils with special educational needs. In addition, the introduction of the one-year PGCE courses has meant that any *attempt* at permeation has been shoehorned into an overcrowded curriculum (Robertson, 1999). Research indicates that many newly qualified teachers are entering the profession ill-equipped to teach these pupils (Garner, 1996, 2001).

In addition, the increased school-based element in initial training which Garner (2001) refers to as 'on the job training' does not often allow adequate consideration of approaches to the teaching and learning of a range of pupils with special educational needs. He emphasises that students have to rely on 'picking up messages from the prevailing culture and ethos of the school in which they are placed' (Garner, 2001, p.57). He goes on to argue that as the fostering of inclusive practices varies from school to school, it is likely that some students will learn little from their school-based experiences. Unfortunately, limited access to appropriate training has often resulted in the perpetuation of negative attitudes towards pupils with special educational needs.

CONTINUOUS PROFESSIONAL DEVELOPMENT

Changes in funding have inevitably had a dramatic effect on the ways in which the professional development of qualified teachers has been financed and delivered. The reduction in full-time secondments was hastened by Circular 3/83 (DES, 1983) and the arrival of GRIST (Grant Related In-Service Training; DES, 1986), with its emphasis on the need to provide short courses in designated areas, dealt a death blow. GRIST was quickly followed by an initiative which ensured that professional development was identified in accord with local need and was funded locally, which in turn was replaced by a scheme that provided government funding for some national and local priority areas such as the delivery of the National Curriculum. The latter move left LEAs with dwindling resources to fund other areas that they, and the schools, saw as important; their priority lists determined whether SEN was considered in detail. Now schools themselves are mainly responsible for funding in-service training, with the result that they have tended to use their precious resources for one-off 'quick-fix' training days. Continuing professional development courses in SEN do still exist, mainly on a part-time basis, and they cover a range of approaches including distance education and web-based learning. Although the ACSET Committee (1984) recommended that mandatory qualifications for teachers of pupils with visual and hearing impairments should be withdrawn, this proposal was dropped and mandatory qualifications for these teachers, including those who support pupils with multi-sensory impairments, have remained. In addition to changes in funding, two important committees and agencies, the Special Educational Needs Training Consortium and the Teacher Training Agency have had a crucial impact on professional development.

The SENTC Report

The Special Educational Needs Training Consortium (SENTC) was established in 1993 to consider current levels of effectiveness in both initial teacher training and the continuing professional development of teachers, and it set up 'monitoring groups' to record the number of newly qualified teachers (NQTs) entering the profession, in particular those teaching pupils with designated special educational needs. In addition, the 'groups' were concerned with evaluating the effectiveness of the quality of national special needs courses for more established teachers. Inevitably, all groups highlighted the shortage of teachers able to support pupils with special educational needs. Consequently the DfEE funded the establishment of a working party in 1995 with terms of reference to review the systems currently in place for the training of teachers with SEN, and to recommend how they could be improved. The working party made thirty-two wide-ranging recommendations (SENTC, 1996) that can be summarised as a need for a coherent approach to teacher education in special educational needs at every level. The report reinforced the views of previous writers (Robson, Sebba, Mittler and Davies, 1988; Smith and Varma, 1996) of the need for a systematic plan of teacher development in SEN for every teacher (from initial teacher education through a range of opportunities for their continuing professional development). It also called for the planning and funding of such opportunities at a variety of levels including the (then) DfEE, LEAs and individual schools (Miller and Garner, 1997).

The response from the Government was disappointing, but it was made clear that a newly appointed Teacher Training Agency (TTA) would be the key agency to take forward any of the recommendations it saw fit.

The Teacher Training Agency

The agency has a brief to raise standards in schools through the development of the teaching profession. The term 'development' can of course be interpreted in many different ways and, unfortunately at present, the agency has clearly failed to aid the 'development of the teaching profession' by encouraging new recruits. Despite ingenious advertising campaigns the perceived demands made on teachers for little financial gain (in comparison with similar professions) has not encouraged newcomers, neither has the exposure of established teachers to seemingly endless criticisms of their competence and of their motivation by successive governments. There is now a serious teacher supply crisis and Garner (2001), reporting on research into national surveys, estimates that there will be a general shortfall of approximately 50% of teachers by 2010, with inevitable consequences for pupils with special educational needs.

One of the ways in which the TTA has attempted to raise standards through teacher development is by the publication of sets of national standards. These are the demonstrations of 'the impact' of members of the teaching profession as a measure of their competence to carry out their jobs appropriately as they progress through their careers. There are now National Standards for Qualified Teacher Status (TTA, 1998a), National Standards for Subject Leaders (TTA,

1998b) and National Standards for Head Teachers (TTA, 1998c). The specific standards are regarded as the essential minimum and do not necessarily focus on issues of inclusive education and the teaching and learning of pupils with special educational needs. Indeed the standards for qualified teacher status have come under severe attack as the sheer numbers (several hundred) make it impossible to assess adequately every teacher training student and, despite the SENTC report, they make oblique reference only to teaching pupils with special educational needs, two examples of which are:

- understanding how pupils' learning in the subject is affected by their physical, intellectual, emotional and social development;
- setting appropriate and demanding expectations of pupils' learning, motivation and presentation of work.

The standards for subject leaders are equally problematical. They clearly need to take account of meeting the needs of all pupils (including those with special educational needs), but there is a lack of specificity on the practical application of meeting these needs and on the planning of inclusive practices. In line with this trend, the standards for head teachers make reference to equal opportunities, but do not embrace the management issues of promoting inclusive education.

National Standards for Special Educational Needs Co-ordinators (SENCOs) (TTA, 1998d) was introduced in 1998. Like the one for students in initial training, the list is large but centres on the *management* role of the co-ordinator and embraces leadership skills, decision-making and self-management as well as the co-ordination of special educational needs within the school. The last skill involves the organisation of teaching and learning, the management of staff, and the effective deployment of resources. Again criticism is levelled at the 'turn off' factor of the sheer numbers and the almost impossible task expected of SENCos. Mittler (2000) tersely comments that 'any job description resulting from the standards calls for a combination of Machiavelli and Mother Teresa; the latter not only for her saintliness but for her vow of poverty!' (p.141).

The last set of National Standards to be announced are specialist Standards for Special Educational Needs (TTA, 1999) comprising two sets: core and extension. The core standards are seen as representing the basic skills, knowledge and understanding that are common to all teachers engaged in the education of pupils with special educational needs. They are grouped under five headings which include the identification, assessment and planning of SEN; effective teaching; ensuring maximum access to the curriculum. Again, the list is long (some forty-three core standards) but they have been seen as a genuine attempt to ensure that teachers receive some training in SEN.

The extension standards are statements about the specific skills that teachers need in the education of pupils with more complex forms of SEN. Like the core standards they are grouped under headings, which represent aspects of disability or difficulty:

- communication and interaction;
- cognition and learning;
- behaviour, emotional and social development;
- sensory and physical development.

These have been less well received. They number sixty-three and additional ones are given for some areas of disability such as: autism spectrum disorder; multi-sensory impairments and sensory difficulties. At present, course providers are struggling to package the standards in ways which make sensible training programmes (Porter, 2001). There is also concern over the categorisation of children under the four headings. One strength of the extension standards is that the list provides a useful auditing tool for professional development.

One hopeful sign for professional development is the consultation paper, *Professional Development: Support for Teaching and Learning* (DfEE, 2000), that attempted to lay down a new financial framework for funding. Some of the positive ideas contained in the paper are being piloted as this book goes to press, including:

- career planning at regular points;
- the development of professional portfolios;
- teacher bursaries;
- support for teacher research in designated areas, including special educational needs.

The report indicates the importance of school-based professional development, but it does raise questions of where such training is to come from and how it will be planned and organised. Mittler (2000) emphasises the need for coherent training 'pathways' to be established and questions how these pathways will be decided upon and planned for, both for individual teachers and for groups of professionals within each school.

Such 'training pathways' are not the prerogative of the teaching profession alone, but must encompass a long list of people who make a contribution to the teaching and learning of the pupils within a school. Such a list will include learning support assistants, governors, lunchtime supervisors and transport escorts at the very least. Fortunately, the professional development of learning support assistants has been the focus of recent major reports (Mencap, 1999; Farrell, Balshaw and Polat, 1999) and it seems likely that the Government will give the needs of these undervalued professionals due consideration.

Griffin, however, as far back as 1987 highlighted a number of features that can be applied to the professional development of all school staff and contain important messages for the establishment of policies. Based on research reports his findings revealed that successful staff development is dependent on a number of factors, four of which are:

- context sensitive (connected to the context where teaching and learning is taking place);
- collaborative and encouraging participation;
- reflective and analytical;
- ongoing (not tied to one-off events).

THE FORMULATION OF POLICIES TO PROMOTE STAFF DEVELOPMENT: SOME CONSIDERATIONS

Context sensitive

All the ideas embedded in the previous chapters suggest that professional development should be school-focused and school-driven. The essence of school-focused work is that it is based on the realistic needs of the school as an organisation and that the 'work' must ultimately raise the standards of the teaching and learning of all children including those with complex needs. School-driven work implies a responsibility on the part of the school for the professional development of *all* members of its staff. Initially, each member of staff should be encouraged to identify his or her own portfolio of training needs based on his or her priorities (Brighouse and Woods, 1999, refer to these as 'personal learning plans'). In some cases these needs will be immediate; in others long-term, but, more often than not, a combination of both.

The immediate training needs of the lunchtime supervisor working with Ben in the chapter by Marie Howley and Sue Kime may well include the acquisition of some basic counselling skills and an understanding of fundamental behaviour management techniques. It is likely that members of the school, particularly the school's behaviour co-ordinator (see Ted Cole's chapter) could provide the necessary training. Her longer-term professional development needs may require work on raising the self-esteem of all pupils, including Ben, and encouraging positive pupil relationships in the informal settings in which she is working.

Cole's chapter on establishing proficient classroom behaviour management could involve many staff in drawing up an individual profile or personal plan, which includes immediate training in the use of environmental check lists, and longer-term training in in-depth behaviour assessment, together with classroom management strategies and specific methods for its evaluation. In addition, knowledge of highly developed observation skills may also be a requirement. Such a range of aspects of behaviour management may best be provided by a combination of school-based INSET, involvement in school-based research projects, and through accredited courses.

Once a portfolio of needs of every member of staff has been completed, Mittler's suggestion of 'pathways' to suitable training can be established, and agreed by all staff. Such a process leads into a consideration of the second feature on Griffin's list: collaboration.

Collaborative staff development and its place in policy making

Taking into account each member of staff's individual portfolio, it is important that whole-staff discussions take place on the identification of agreed priority needs for *whole-school* development. Such priorities will naturally be reflected in the school's development plan, and may centre upon such issues as multi-culture, gender and race, and, at the same time, be subject specific. In addition, agreement will need to be made on the individual needs of members of staff, which reflects their career progression (Tilstone and Upton, 1993). The importance of staff involvement in decision-making at all levels is recognised as a crucial feature of successful schools, and a prerequisite for effective collaborative practice (Hopkins, Ainscow and West, 1994; Brighouse and Woods, 1999). The individual ingredients of fruitful collaboration include respect, trust, and common understanding, which, when mixed, results in what Ted Cole refers to as 'talking schools'. The notion of staff collaborating by talking and learning from each other has been referred to in all the chapters of this book. In the case of the identification of the priorities for professional development, 'collaborators' need to acquire the skills that enable them to negotiate and to have ownership of the outcomes. As teaching has in the past often been an isolated experience, the acquisition of such skills should be given consideration within the document. The 'collaborators' become a *learning team'* but, as Penny Lacey stresses in her chapter on multi-agency work, the *strategies* to facilitate teamwork also need careful consideration and planning.

Reflective and analytical practices as part of professional development

All the chapters in this book emphasise the importance of evidenced-based practice and its direct relevance to professional development. Richard Byers and Linda Ferguson in their exploration of creating access to the Literacy Hour, for example, state that the research undertaken by all colleagues gave them the opportunity to reconsider established ways of working. Sue Sanderson's chapter stresses that staff need not feel isolated in their attempts to research into their own practice as other professionals (in her case, educational psychologists) can also lend support. But one-off isolated initiatives, whether they are supported by other enthusiastic colleagues or not, do not usually have the impact on the development of inclusive practices of other collectively agreed-upon and 'owned' staff initiatives.

Beveridge (2001) stresses that collectively researching into practice by embracing a range of exploratory and evaluative activities not only helps staff to extend their knowledge, skills and understanding at a classroom level, but encourages them to work in co-operation with colleagues 'to monitor and appraise practices across the whole-school' (p.258). Such a reflective and analytical stance will take on different resonances as the collective knowledge and understanding of staff deepen through the schools' own increased capacity to research into its own practices. Reflective and analytical practices, carefully considered through policy documents and adequate resources, are powerful instruments for the professional development of all school staff.

Increased opportunities for teachers to participate in classroom-based research is central to the encouragement of greater reflection upon practice. Government initiatives such as the introduction of 'Best Practice Research Grants' may also have a role to play, but will have an impact only so long as practitioner research is given a higher regard than has been previously seen within education (Grosvenor and Rose, 2001; Rose, 2002).

Ongoing professional development: implications for the development of policies

Acquiring knowledge skills and understanding is a continuous process, and it is important to recognise the fluid activity of teaching and learning undertaken by all staff and applied in the widest sense to the education of the pupils in the school. All staff, including school secretaries, administrators, caretakers, governors and teaching staff will have built up their personal theories about the pupils they come into contact with, which then become the basis of subsequent work. Such theories are rarely articulated and often remain unchallenged, and the professional development policy of any school must encourage the *implicit* theories of staff on what pupils can and cannot do to become *explicit*, based on evidence that is open to scrutiny and debate (Tilstone, 1998). The document should be drawn up in such a way that the preconceptions and prejudices of all staff are challenged in order to establish a positive knowledge base for the valuing of both the diversity and the dissimilarity of pupils. Ultimately the emphasis within the document must be on enabling staff at all levels to encourage the full participation of pupils with special educational needs in all aspects of the life of the school, of the community and, ultimately, of society.

REFERENCES

ACSET (Advisory Committee on the Supply and Education of Teachers) (1984) *Teacher Training and Special Educational Needs*. London: HMSO.

Beveridge, S. (2001) 'Teachers researching the curriculum', in B. Carpenter, R. Ashdown and K. Bovair (eds.) *Enabling Access* (2nd edition). London: David Fulton.

Brighouse, T. and Woods, D. (1999) *How to Improve Your School.* London: Routledge.

Davis, J.D. and Garner, P. (eds.) (1997) *At the Crossroads: Special Educational Needs and Teacher Education.* London: David Fulton.

Department for Education and Employment (2000) *Professional Development: Support for Teaching and Learning.* London: DfEE.

Department of Education and Science (1972) *Teacher Education and Training* (The James Report). London: HMSO.

Department of Education and Science (1983) *The In-Service Training Grants Scheme* (Circular 8/83). London: HMSO.

Department of Education and Science (1986) *Local Authority Grants Scheme: Financial Year 1987–88* (Circular 6/86). London: HMSO.

Farrell, P., Balshaw, M. and Polat, F. (1999) *The Management Role and Training of Learning Support Assistants* (Research Report RR 161). London: DfEE.

Garner, P. (1996) 'Students' views on special needs courses in Initial Teacher Education', *British Journal of Special Education*, 23 (4) 176–9.

Garner, P. (2001) 'Goodbye Mr Chips: Special needs, inclusive education and the deceit of initial teacher training', in T. O'Brien (ed.) *Enabling Inclusion: Blue Skies ... Dark Clouds?* Norwich: The Stationery Office.

Griffin, G.A. (1987) 'The school in society and social organization of the school: implications for staff development', in M. F. Wideen and I. Andrews (eds.) *Staff Development for School Improvement.* London: Falmer Press.

Grosvenor, I. and Rose, R. (2001) 'Educational research – influence or irrelevance', in R. Rose and I. Grosvenor (eds.) *Doing Research in Special Education.* London: David Fulton.

Hopkins, D., Ainscow, M. and West, R. (1994) *School Improvement in an Era of Change.* London: Cassell.

McLaughlin, M. and Tilstone, C. (2000) Standards and Curriculum: the core of educational reform', in M. McLaughlin and M. Rouse (eds.) *Special Education and School Reform in the United States and Britain.* London: Routledge.

Mencap (1999) *On a Wing and a Prayer: Inclusion and Children with Severe Learning Difficulties.* London: Mencap.

Miller, O. and Garner, M. (1997) 'Professional development to meet special needs: the role of the Special Educational Needs Training Consortium', in J. D. Davis and P. Garner (eds.) *At the Crossroads: Special Educational Needs and Teacher Education.* London: David Fulton.

Mittler, P. (2000) *Working Towards Inclusive Education: Social Contexts.* London: David Fulton.

Porter, J. (2001) 'Issues in teacher training and development', in B. Carpenter, R. Ashdown and K. Bovair (eds.) *Enabling Access* (2nd edition). London: David Fulton.

Robertson, C. (1999) 'Initial teacher education and inclusive schooling', *Support for Learning*, 14 (4) 169–73.

Robson, C., Sebba, J., Mittler, P. and Davies, G. (1988) *In-service Training and Special Educational Needs: Running Short, School Focused Courses.* Manchester: Manchester University Press.

Rose, R. (2002) 'Teaching as a "research based profession": encouraging practitioner research in special education', *British Journal of Special Education*, 29 (1) 44–8.

SENTC (1996) *Professional Development to Meet Special Educational Needs* (Report to the Department for Education and Employment). Stafford: Flash Ley Resort Centre.

Smith, C.J. and Varma, V. (eds.) (1996) *A Handbook of Teacher Development.* Aldershot: Arena.

TTA (Teacher Training Agency) (1998a) *National Standards for Qualified Teacher Status.* London: TTA.

TTA (Teacher Training Agency) (1998b) *National Standards for Subject Leaders.* London: TTA.

TTA (Teacher Training Agency) (1998c) *National Standards for Head Teachers.* London: TTA

TTA (Teacher Training Agency) (1998d) *National Standards for Special Educational Needs Co-ordinators.* London: TTA.

TTA (Teacher Training Agency) (1999) *National Special Educational Needs Specialist Standards.* London: TTA.

Tilstone, C. (1998) *Observing Teaching and Learning.* London: David Fulton.

Tilstone, C. and Upton, G. (1993) 'Enhancing the quality of provision', in J. Visser and G. Upton (eds.) *Special Education in Britain after Warnock.* London: David Fulton.

Author index

Subject index